BERENICE

By the same author

SOPHIE DOROTHEA
(1971)

Titus's Arch of Triumph in Rome,
depicting Jewish captives and some of the temple spoils

Ruth Jordan

BERENICE

BARNES & NOBLE
BOOKS
10 East 53d St., New York 10022
(a division of Harper & Row Publishers, Inc.)

Published in the U.S.A. 1974 by
HARPER & ROW PUBLISHERS INC.
BARNES & NOBLE IMPORT DIVISION
ISBN —06–493402–0

Contents

Contents

Illustrations

Acknowledgements

This book owes a debt of gratitude to all those scholars whose works are listed in the bibliography. I am also grateful to Professor A. Fuks for his interest and goodwill, to Rabbi Isaac Newman for clarifying some of the intricacies of Jewish laws and practices of the period, to Mr Benjamin Tammuz for suggestions for illustrations, and above all to Mr Stanley Mayes, who so generously put his classical scholarship at my disposal.

I would like to thank the following for permission to quote: the Cambridge and Oxford University Presses, for *The New English Bible*; Penguin Books, for Josephus, *The Jewish War*, translated by G. A. Williamson and for Suetonius, *The Twelve Caesars*, translated by Robert Graves; William Heinemann, Ltd, for Dio, *Roman History*, translated by E. Cary and for Quintilian, *Institutiones Oratoriae*, translated by H. E. Butler; and the Harvard University Press for *Corpus Papyrorum Judaicarum*, edited by V. Tcherikover and A. Fuks. Other translations quoted are my own free renderings of the original texts.

My thanks are also due to the following for permission to reproduce photographs: The Ashmolean Museum, Oxford, the Israel Department of Antiquities and Museums, the Israel Ministry of Tourism, the Reifenberg Collection, Jerusalem, the Beirut Museum, the British Museum, the Bibiothèque Nationale, Paris, the Staatliche Münzsammlung, Munich, the Museo Nazionale, Naples, the Museo Capitolino, Rome, the Uffizi Gallery, Florence and the Alinari-Mansell and Anderson-Mansell Collections.

Introduction

Berenice, like Jezebel of the Bible, seems to have attracted more defamatory adjectives to her name than most other queens of antiquity. She was called immoral and licentious, scheming and disloyal. In her own lifetime she was accused of incest and depravity. Among nineteenth-century scholars Emile Schürer branded her as 'a bigot as well as a wanton',[1] and Theodor Mommsen as a 'Cleopatra in miniature'.[2] Joseph Derenbourg saw her as the 'beautiful sinner'[3] while Adolf Hausrath called her 'the notorious mistress of Titus' who wielded 'undesirable power even over men of intellectual eminence'.[4] In our own time H. Lockyer firmly asserts that 'the story of Berenice reads like a horrible romance, or a page from the chronicles of the Borgias',[5] while C. J. Ellicot describes her as a 'a traitor' who profited by her sexual charms 'in the hour of her country's ruin'.[6]

What most of these moral judgements fail to bring out is that queen Berenice, daughter of the last king of Judaea and great grand-daughter of Herod the Great, was one of the most remarkable women of the first century of the Christian era. Descended from the royal house of the Hasmonaeans, she grew up against a background of political unrest and incessant intrigue. She belonged to an aristocratic family which regarded power and wealth as its birthright. At a time when the fanatic freedom lovers of Judaea were straining to throw off the Roman yoke she was a political realist. Like Cleopatra a century earlier she did not hesitate to use her charms to further political aims; but unlike Cleopatra she was never a queen in her own right. She was always an appendage. The only way she could make her influence felt was through the men around whom she had entwined herself: her father, Agrippa I, last king of Judaea; her three husbands, two of whom were kings; her brother, Agrippa II, king of territories across the Jordan and in Lebanon; and lastly Titus, conqueror of Jerusalem and emperor of Rome. She moved easily between

Judaism and Hellenism and was as much at home in the Court of Women in the temple of Jerusalem as later in the imperial palace on the Palatine hill in Rome.

Because her part in history was secondary to the men whose lives she shared, no independent account of her career ever appeared in the works of contemporary writers. There are brief references, some tantalizing hints, a few inscriptions. It is partly through cautious deductions based on the available data that the gaps in her life can be filled. A knowledge of the period helps towards an understanding of her motives and her behaviour, but a certain amount of conjecture is inevitable.

If, in spite of the scant material, her life story can still be sketched, her looks are bound to remain a mystery. Not a single statue of her has survived; her face appears on no coins; and there is not a single pen-portrait of her by a contemporary or near-contemporary writer. All that is known with certainty is that she was a woman of charm and beauty, and that in her middle age she was attractive enough to keep her hold over the much younger Titus. Whether she was tall, slim, dark or fair remains a matter for the imagination.

Fiction throughout the ages has tended to highlight one aspect of her life at the expense of another, sacrificing facts for the sake of drama. But it is only her life as a whole which can offer a balanced evaluation of her personality. Berenice was a child of her time and a product of her background. During her lifetime Christianity struck roots in many countries, the temple of Jerusalem was burnt down and Rome continued to reign supreme. It is only when seen against the larger canvas of the period that she may cease to be a butt for moral indignation and emerge as the Jewish princess whose heritage included the Hasmonaean tradition of patriotism as well as the Herodian flair for practical politics. I hope this biography may show that Berenice was neither the noble heroine of some seventeenth-century French tragedies, nor the calculating whore of some modern writings, but a woman who, like the rest of mankind, had her faults and her virtues.

THE IDUMAEAN HOUSE

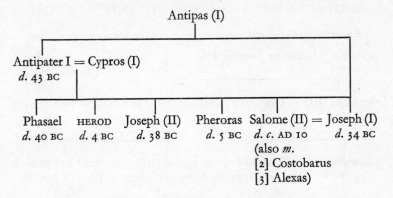

Antipas (I)

Antipater I = Cypros (I)
d. 43 BC

| Phasael | HEROD | Joseph (II) | Pheroras | Salome (II) = Joseph (I) |
| *d.* 40 BC | *d.* 4 BC | *d.* 38 BC | *d.* 5 BC | *d. c.* AD 10   *d.* 34 BC |

(also *m.*
[2] Costobarus
[3] Alexas)

THE CHILDREN OF HEROD

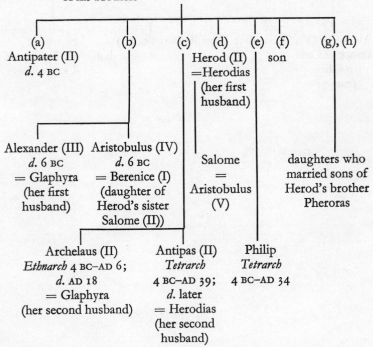

HEROD = a. Doris, b. Mariamme (I) *d.* 29 BC, c. Malthace *d.* 4 BC, d.
Mariamme (II), e. Cleopatra, f. Pallas, g. Phaedra, h. Elphis,
i. a daughter of his sister Salome (II), j. a daughter of one
of his brothers

| (a) | (b) | (c) | (d) | (e) | (f) | (g), (h) |
| Antipater (II) *d.* 4 BC | | | Herod (II) =Herodias (her first husband) | | son | |

Alexander (III)   Aristobulus (IV)
d. 6 BC   *d.* 6 BC
= Glaphyra   = Berenice (I)
(her first   (daughter of
husband)   Herod's sister
                      Salome (II))

Salome
=
Aristobulus
(V)

daughters who
married sons of
Herod's brother
Pheroras

Archelaus (II)   Antipas (II)   Philip
Ethnarch 4 BC–AD 6;   *Tetrarch*   *Tetrarch*
d. AD 18   4 BC–AD 39;   4 BC–AD 34
= Glaphyra   *d.* later
(her second   = Herodias
husband)   (her second
                      husband)

THE DESCENDANTS OF HEROD AND MARIAMME

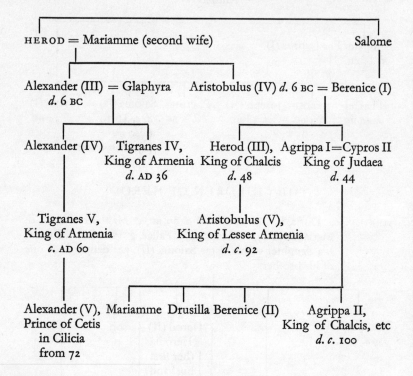

HEROD = Mariamme (second wife)   Salome

Alexander (III) = Glaphyra   Aristobulus (IV) *d.* 6 BC = Berenice (I)
d. 6 BC

Alexander (IV) Tigranes IV,   Herod (III), Agrippa I=Cypros II
                King of Armenia   King of Chalcis King of Judaea
                  d. AD 36   *d.* 48   *d.* 44

Tigranes V,   Aristobulus (V),
King of Armenia   King of Lesser Armenia
c. AD 60   *d. c.* 92

Alexander (V), Mariamme Drusilla Berenice (II)   Agrippa II,
Prince of Cetis   King of Chalcis, etc
in Cilicia   *d. c.* 100
from 72

Chronological Table

46	Queen Helena of Adiabene arrives in Jerusalem
46–48	Tiberius Julius Alexander procurator of Judaea
48	Death of Herod king of Chalcis
	Death of Messalina
48–52	Ventidius Cumanus procurator of Judaea
50	Agrippa II made king of Chalcis
52–60	Antonius Felix procurator of Judaea
53	Agrippa II receives Philip's tetrarchy, relinquishes Chalcis
	Marriage of Mariamme and Drusilla
53–54	Drusilla goes to Felix
c. 54	Berenice marries Polemo king of Cilicia
54	Nero succeeds Claudius, until AD 68
	Agrippa II sends auxiliaries to the Parthian campaigns
	Receives Tiberias etc. from Nero
	Berenice divorces Polemo
55	Death of queen Helena of Adiabene
57	Aristobulus, son of Herod of Chalcis and husband of Salome the dancer, becomes king of Lesser Armenia
58–60	Paul held in prison by Felix
60	Paul's trial in Caesarea
60–62	Festus procurator of Judaea
62–64	Albinus procurator of Judaea
63–66	Cestius Gallus governor of Syria
64	The fire of Rome
64–66	Florus procurator of Judaea
66	Outbreak of the Jewish war
67	Vespasian in Judaea
68	Nero's death
69	Galba's accession and death
	Otho's accession and death
	Vespasian proclaimed emperor until AD 79
	Vitellius's accession and death
70	Titus resumes war in Judaea
	Fall of Jerusalem and destruction of the temple
	Priscus makes speeches against Vespasian
71	Titus's return to Rome and triumphal procession

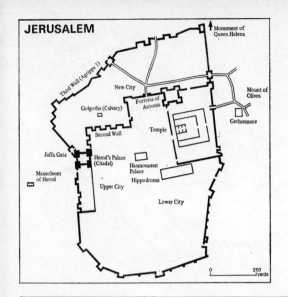

JERUSALEM

Third Wall (Agrippa I)

New City

Monument of Queen Helena

Golgotha (Calvary)

Fortress of Antonia

Mount of Olives

Second Wall

Temple

Gethsemane

Jaffa Gate

Herod's Palace (Citadel)

Hasmonaean Palace

Mausoleum of Herod

Hippodrome

Upper City

Lower City

0   250 yards

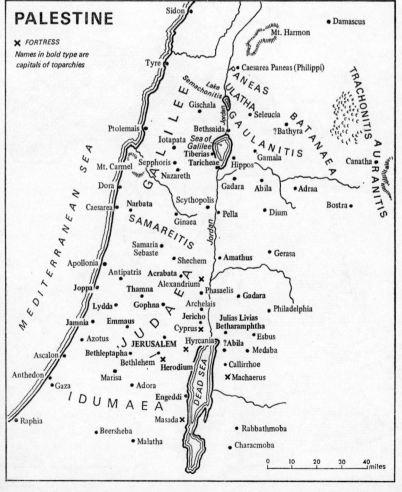

PALESTINE

✕ FORTRESS

Names in bold type are capitals of toparchies

Sidon

Damascus

Mt. Harmon

Tyre

Caesarea Paneas (Philippi)

PANEAS

Lake Semachonitis

ULATHA

TRACHONITIS AURANITIS

Gischala

Jordan

GAULANITIS

BATANAEA

Ptolemais

Seleucia

?Bathyra

Bethsaida

Iotapata

Sea of Galilee

G A L I L E E

Tiberias

Gamala

Canatha

Sepphoris

Taricheae

Hippos

Mt. Carmel

Nazareth

Gadara

Abila

Adraa

Dora

Bostra

Caesarea

Scythopolis

M E D I T E R R A N E A N   S E A

Narbata

SAMAREITIS

Ginaea

Pella

Dium

Samaria Sebaste

Shechem

Amathus

Gerasa

Apollonia

Antipatris

Acrabata

Joppa

Thamna

Alexandrium

Phasaelis

Gadara

Lydda

Gophna

Archelais

Philadelphia

Jamnia

Emmaus

J U D A E A

Jericho

Julias Livias

Azotus

Cyprus

Betharamphtha

Ascalon

Bethleptapha

JERUSALEM

Hyrcania

?Abila

Esbus

Bethlehem

Medaba

Anthedon

Marisa

Herodium

Callirrhoe

Gaza

Adora

Machaerus

I D U M A E A

Engeddi

DEAD SEA

Raphia

Masada

Beersheba

Rabbathmoba

Malatha

Characmoba

0   10   20   30   40 miles

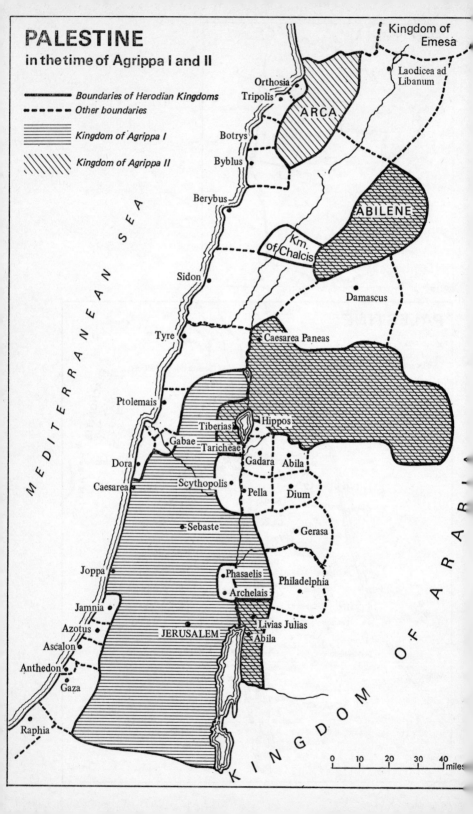

Chapter I

Violent deaths

I<small>N</small> the summer of AD 71 Titus Caesar, son of the emperor Vespasian and vanquisher of Jerusalem, returned to Rome to celebrate his victory over the small province of Judaea which for four years had defied the Roman legions. Some time after his return he was joined by his mistress Berenice, a Jewish princess and a descendant of Herod the Great, whom he installed in his palace.

Roman society viewed with alarm this latest importation from the east. A full century after their suicide, Rome still shuddered at the memory of Antony's enslavement to Cleopatra and her disastrous influence over him. Titus's attachment to another potentially dangerous queen from the east antagonized senators and scandalized their wives. When it was rumoured that, far from being content with the influence she exerted over Titus as his mistress, Berenice aspired to become his wife, alarm turned into open opposition. Strong political forces were set in motion against her.

Indeed Rome had every reason to fear her association with the man who would one day be emperor. Julia Berenice, daughter of the late king Agrippa of Judaea and sister of Agrippa II, had already proved herself one of the most resolute women of her time. Queen of Chalcis by her second marriage, queen of Cilicia by her third, she retained the royal style not as a reminder of past associations, but as a tribute to her own authority. Contemporary inscriptions called her *basilissa* or *regina* and described her as a great queen descended of great kings. Although she had no official arrangement with Rome, she made herself full partner of her brother Agrippa II, whom Claudius had appointed and his successors confirmed, as client-king of large territories across the Jordan. Through her own intelligence, drive, ambition and charm Berenice had raised her status from that of a dependent female to that of a virtual co-ruler. When in AD 69 Vespasian was making his bid for the empire and Agrippa II was away from the centre of events, Berenice took charge and offered her allegiance to the future emperor, carrying other client-kings of the east along with her. Yet it was precisely her acknowledged ability in the sphere of politics that brought about her eventual downfall. Rome had no use for politically minded queens.

But the Herodian princess who faced Roman society so proudly and tried to carry off its best prize was not prepared to let go without a struggle. Although in her middle age, she was still remarkably seductive and had a strong hold over the much younger Titus. She was a skilled manipulator who knew the value of wealth, ancestry, flattery and sexual attraction. At the same time she was too intelligent to underestimate the risks involved. Her experience, as well as that of her entire family, had taught her to temper ambition with caution. She had grown up against a background of political manoeuvring and treachery. She had seen relatives and friends fight and die for royal favour. If she had learnt anything from the past, it was to eschew pride and accept realities.

It is perhaps Berenice's intrigue-ridden family history that affords the first clues to her personality. It must have overshadowed her childhood and contributed to the moulding of her character. To understand it better one must go back to the very beginning of the house of Herod, the king whose spectacular reign was so punctuated by violent and arbitrary acts. Of the many tragic stories that came down to Berenice, none was perhaps so terrifying as that of her ancestress Mariamme who was put to death by her royal husband because he loved her not wisely, but too well.

Idumaea, where some of Berenice's ancestors came from, was a small territory round Hebron, about twenty miles south of Jerusalem. The Idumaeans were the descendants of the Old Testament Edomites, whom the Jews hated with particular ferocity. Towards the end of the second century BC they were conquered by the Hasmoneans, the Jewish kings of Judaea, and forcibly converted to Judaism. Although the Idumaeans practised Judaism without any serious deviation, the deep-rooted hatred of the Jews for the descendants of the Edomites died hard, and an Idumaean, circumcised and God fearing as he might be, was never considered one of the chosen people. For their part, many Idumaeans were not as particular as their co-religionists about marrying outside the faith. Thus Antipater, hereditary chief of Idumaea and loyal servant to the Hasmonaeans, married an Arab woman from the Nabatean kingdom across the Jordan, known as Arabia. The four sons and one daughter that Cypros bore him were therefore the product of a mixed marriage; and although the boys were duly circumcised and brought up in the Jewish religion, they could never blot out the blemish of their mixed parentage. When the second son of that marriage became king Herod of Judaea, he was contemptuously referred to by his Hasmonaean enemies as only a half-Jew.

Antipater distinguished himself as governor of Idumaea under the powerful Hasmonaean king, Alexander Jannaeus, and after his death, under his widow queen Alexandra. When she died, leaving two sons to dispute the succession, Antipater became the right-hand man of the eldest, Hyrcanus II, ranging himself against his brother Aristobulus II. Hyrcanus, who according to Hasmonaean tradition was both king and high priest, was a passive man, content to leave the management of his affairs to Antipater. Aristobulus on the other hand was ambitious and energetic, and felt that both kingship and high priesthood should be his by virtue of his natural abilities. There was a long-drawn-out war during which both brothers appealed to the Roman general Pompey, who in 63 BC was in Syria in connection with his struggle against Julius Caesar. Pompey decided to support Hyrcanus, defeated Aristobulus's army in Jerusalem and enraged every single Jew, irrespective of political sympathies, by entering the Holy of Holies, which was taboo to all except to the high priest on certain festive occasions.

Pompey re-established Hyrcanus as ruler, but demoted him from king to ethnarch, a national leader, at the same time allowing him to keep the dignity of a high priest. Antipater was confirmed as his minister and adviser. It was Antipater who, several years later when Pompey's luck had turned, advised Hyrcanus to send assistance to Julius Caesar in Egypt in his bid for power. Caesar showed his gratitude. He confirmed Hyrcanus as ethnarch and high priest and made Antipater a Roman citizen. Antipater's twenty-five-year-old son, Herod, was made governor of Jerusalem.

3

About that time Herod contracted the first of his ten marriages. His wife Doris was either Idumaean like himself or, according to another account, a native of Jerusalem. In either case she must have come of a good family, to suit the ambition of a rising young man. She bore Herod a son who was named Antipater after his grandfather.

In the meantime rebellion loomed ahead again. Although Aristobulus was dead, his son Antigonus was now grown up and able to take up the dynastic quarrel with the ineffectual Hyrcanus who maintained his rule with the help of the Romans. Hyrcanus reacted by leaning more heavily on his pro-Roman adviser Antipater and, when Antipater was poisoned by an enemy, on his son Herod. Herod, for his part, sought to strengthen his position even further by entering into matrimonial alliance with the royal house of the Hasmonaeans. The princess on whom his choice had fallen was Mariamme, Hyrcanus's grand-daughter by his daughter Alexandra and his late nephew Alexander. Mariamme was therefore Hasmonaean on both sides and thus doubly royal. An Idumaean officer born of an Arab mother could hardly have matched the hopes that the proud princess and her mother must have entertained. But Hyrcanus approved. With no male heir of his own, having killed various Hasmonaean pretenders to safeguard his own rule, he may have intended that a marriage between his grand-daughter and his ambitious military commander should set the royal seal on an unavoidable development. Herod made Hyrcanus's decision easier by undertaking to divorce Doris, although the Jewish custom of the day allowed polygamy. After five years of married life he was prepared to part with Doris without regret.

To avoid future complications Herod demanded that Doris should be banned from Jerusalem. It was a harsh sentence on a woman who had committed no offence and who, if she was indeed a native of Jerusalem, had no other home to go to. Nor was it one that could be easily enforced on a Jewish woman without infringing Mosaic law which required all Jews to make the pilgrimage to the holy city three times a year. Accordingly Doris demanded and was granted permission to perform the pilgrimages, no doubt hoping to use her brief returns to Jerusalem to bring herself back to the notice of her former husband. Years later, when the wheel of fortune had turned full circle, it was indeed an easy matter to trace her and bring her back into Herod's court and bed.

With the divorce through, the engagement of Herod and princess Mariamme was officially celebrated. No date for the wedding was fixed as Mariamme was still a child. She continued to live in Jerusalem with her widowed mother Alexandra, while Herod turned his attention to the rapidly deteriorating political and military situation.

The deterioration was caused by the arrival on the scene of the Parthians, the main power in the east, against whom Rome's entire defensive system along the Syrian frontier was directed. When in 40 BC the Parthians marched into Syria, Antigonus hastened to offer his allegiance and ask for help against Hyrcanus whom he rightly represented as a Roman puppet. With their support he entered Jerusalem and waged war on the combined forces of Herod, his brother Phasael and the Roman auxiliaries. After a series of indecisive battles the Parthians sent a messenger to suggest talks. Hyrcanus and Phasael went to the rendezvous and were immediately seized and put under arrest. Herod was left alone in Jerusalem, closely guarded by ten Parthian officers and two hundred men. Using cunning and possibly bribery, he gathered most of his womenfolk and together with ten thousand of his loyal soldiers slipped out of the city. This feat was carried out in absolute secrecy and it was some time before the Parthians woke up to his escape. They gave chase and caught up with him about seven miles south of Jerusalem. A desperate battle was waged, and Herod fought valiantly, sword in hand, until his men drove off the pursuers. Years later he built his fortress-palace Herodium on the same spot.

After the rout of the enemy a hurried council of war was held at which it was decided to disband the ten thousand men, keeping back only the manageable number of eight hundred. Herod's brother Joseph was instructed to march them off to Masada, by the Dead Sea, and there to install the womenfolk. Masada had been built by one of Mariamme's Hasmonaean ancestors and although it had not yet attained the magnitude and splendour that Herod was to give it in later years, it was already virtually impregnable and well stocked for a siege. It was there that Mariamme and the other women of the household, including her mother and Herod's, were to await his return.

Herod was thirty-three at the time, in the prime of his life. His mop of hair, which in his old age he took to dyeing, was still full and black. He was strongly built, fond of physical exertion and quite indefatigable. He was a keen hunter and in a single day was known to bring down as many as forty beasts; boars, wild asses, stags. He rode his horse well and was an accomplished fighter, marksman and javelin thrower. It was said that his performance in the field was matched by his personal charm. Mariamme, seeing him for the first time not as an imposed husband but as the heroic saver of her life, must have been moved.

But there was little time for tender feelings. The news that reached them was bad. Phasael, who could not bear the indignity of being a prisoner, committed suicide in his cell; while Hyrcanus, who was old and no more than a figurehead, had his ears cut off by Antigonus, to disqualify him for the high priesthood which by Jewish law could not be given to a maimed person. Leaving Mariamme in the safety of Masada, Herod hurried by devious ways to Egypt, persuaded Cleopatra to give him a ship, sailed to Rhodes, built a better ship, sailed to Brundisium (Brindisi) and proceeded to Rome. Antony and Octavian appreciated the help he could give them in rebuffing the Parthian encroachment into Syria and received him kindly. They proposed to the senate that the kingdom of Judaea, suspended for twenty-three years since the demotion of Hyrcanus by Pompey to the rank of ethnarch, should be revived in his favour. And thus, in the year 40 BC, Herod became king of Judaea.

Although his appointment seemed a deviation from the accepted Roman practice, which was to try to keep the traditional kings of dependent countries on their thrones, it was not altogether arbitrary. Hyrcanus was a prisoner; Antigonus had gone over to the Parthians; and Herod, besides being pro-Roman, was a near-Hasmonaean by virtue of his engagement to princess Mariamme. True, there was a young Hasmonaean heir in the offing, Mariamme's young brother Aristobulus, but he was only thirteen and could not be considered seriously.

As soon as the official celebrations of his new rank were over, Herod left Rome and hurried back to Judaea to start the long conquest of his kingdom. It was to take him the best part of three years. While he was gaining ground in Galilee, his brother Joseph was having a hard time in Masada. A long siege by Antigonus's men and a dry summer made his water supply run out. He was about to make a desperate dash out of the fortress in search of water when the rains mercifully came and saved the situation. Later Herod drove away the besiegers and had Mariamme and the rest of his womenfolk transferred to Samaria. Joseph was free to rejoin the war of conquest and became involved in a battle near Jericho, misunderstanding, or misinterpreting, his brother's instructions. He paid for his mistake with his life. Antigonus's men cut his head off, returning it to his family for burial only in return for a large ransom.

In the spring of 37 BC, about two and a half years after his return from Rome, Herod found himself outside the gates of Jerusalem, waiting for Roman reinforcement for the final assault on the city. The period of waiting gave him a chance to realize his matrimonial ambitions. He went to Samaria, where Mariamme and her mother, as well as his own mother and other members of his family had been waiting, and there the royal wedding took place according to Jewish tradition. The marriage at this juncture was a calculated political move. Mariamme belonged to the Hasmonaean family, the only one the Jews recognized as royal after the house of David. By marrying her, and naturally expecting to have sons by her, Herod could now claim to be the legitimate king of Judaea, while his enemy Antigonus could be represented as a Parthian puppet and a warmonger. Herod's calculations proved right, for the prospect of having a Hasmonaean princess for a queen won over many people who until then had been sitting on the fence.

But in Mariamme Herod got more than a political bargain. During the five years of their engagement the child had grown into womanhood and at the time of her wedding must have been in the full bloom of youth. She was a great beauty and bore herself like a queen. Herod succumbed at once. He fell deeply in love and was stirred by a depth of passion that he had not known before. Consummation only increased his desire and he became a willing slave to his wife's charms.

For a while domestic bliss and political success went hand in hand. Jerusalem fell, the Romans obligingly executed Antigonus the rebel, and Herod was able to install himself in the palace of the Hasmonaeans as the unchallenged king of Judaea, with Mariamme as his queen. Within a year she gave birth to a son who was named Alexander after her late father. There was only one thing wanting to crown her happiness and that was the return from exile of her grandfather Hyrcanus.

After the mutilation of his ears Hyrcanus had not fared too badly at the hands of the Parthians. They transferred him to Babylon and treated him with every mark of respect. The local Jewish community was particularly delighted to have a person of his rank in their midst, and with Parthian approval formed a court round him as befitted a former king and high priest. But Hyrcanus did not enjoy the life of an exile and yearned for home. When an invitation came from Herod to return to Jerusalem and share the royal honours he gladly accepted, disregarding the warnings of his Babylonian well-wishers. With the gracious permission of the king of Parthia he took his leave and returned home. Herod received him with open arms, called him father and gave him the seat of honour in royal councils and official banquets. Hyrcanus seemed content to step into the role of a venerable relative, showing no regret for the high priesthood he had lost through his mutilation, or for the rank of king that had proved too demanding for his unworldly personality.

Herod's reason for bringing Hyrcanus back was political rather than domestic. It was wiser to keep this aged deposed Hasmonaean under close supervision than to allow him to build up his popularity within the unfriendly Parthian empire. But to Mariamme he may have represented her grandfather's recall as an act of generosity aimed at pleasing a beloved wife. His next move however opened her eyes.

With the restoration of peace in Judaea it became necessary to sort out the question of the high priesthood. Traditionally a high priest should be a direct descendant of Aaron, brother of Moses; in default, descendants of the warrior-priest Mattathias the Hasmonaean were acceptable. According to early Hasmonaean practice the high priesthood and the kingship were vested in the same person, and both were hereditary. With Hyrcanus disqualified and Herod ineligible, the two offices had to be separated. A suitable candidate of Hasmonaean descent was near at hand, for the queen's young brother was growing up and it seemed only natural that he should fill the office that was his by birthright. But Herod thought otherwise. He turned a blind eye to Hasmonaean claims and, contrary to popular expectations, gave the vacancy to a priest from Babylon, a good and respectable man, but not of the blood.

A fierce storm broke over his head. Country and family alike voiced loud protests. Herod turned a deaf ear to criticism from the lower priesthood and took no notice of the mood of the country. But he had not reckoned with the bitter scenes at home. Mariamme harassed him with rebukes and would not let a day go by without pleading her brother's cause. Worse still was her mother Alexandra who, not content with seeing her daughter queen, wanted to see her son high priest, and possibly, in years to come, a substitute for the Idumaean usurper. Without wasting time she wrote to her powerful friend Cleopatra and asked her to intervene. Cleopatra had a word with Antony and Antony obliged by instructing Herod to send the young Aristobulus to Egypt, so that he could weigh the merits of his case at first hand.

Herod was unnerved. Antony was known to favour beautiful young boys and the chances were that he would fall for the attractive Aristobulus and grant him his request, punishing Herod for having unlawfully deprived him of his birthright. And so, much against his better judgement, Herod gave in. He dismissed his Babylonian choice and acknowledged his young brother-in-law as high priest in his place. Aristobulus was seventeen at the time, blessed with all the charm and beauty characteristic of his family. He was unusually tall, good looking, graceful, with most engaging ways. To all who saw him he seemed worthy of his office, the personification of that spiritual dignity which should mark a high priest of the temple. His appointment was immensely popular.

When the Feast of Tabernacles came round, Jerusalem was seething as usual with thousands of pilgrims from all over the country and beyond. For many it was their first glimpse of the new high priest, gravely officiating in the magnificent sacred robes handed down to him through the ages. As the handsome youth with his distinctive Hasmonaean features went up to the altar to sacrifice and perform the rites, a wave of patriotic pride swept through the crowd. There stood the epitome of all that was best in the Hasmonaean dynasty, a noble-looking young man, pure and unspoilt, serving God in his temple before his chosen people. At the end of the ceremony there was a tremendous burst of cheering.

Herod, as was the custom, was present at the temple during the ceremony, surrounded by his male friends and relatives, while his womenfolk sat in the special court reserved for women. He correctly interpreted Aristobulus's popularity as a sign of danger. The aristocratic young man might take it into his head to restore the old order of things, and the people would stand by him. It was necessary to strike at once, before he became too powerful.

After the eight-day feast the pilgrims left the city and the royal family drove down to Jericho for a rest. It was early autumn and, while in Jerusalem the days might have turned cold, Jericho, near the Dead Sea, was still pleasantly warm. Once his sacred robes were off Aristobulus became again the gay and carefree seventeen-year-old that he was. He ate and drank and walked and ran in the palace gardens until his party came to a halt before the royal swimming pools. He did not have to be persuaded to throw off his clothes and dive in. The day was hot and the water refreshing. He swam with the others and played pranks, with Herod benevolently looking on. The sun had set, but swimming in the growing darkness was still pleasant. Aristobulus and his companions splashed in the cool water, swam vigorously, and playfully ducked one another. But there was nothing playful about the ducking of Aristobulus. His head was firmly held under the water until he stopped resisting. When he was brought up it was too late to revive him. He was dead.

The news of his untimely death stunned the whole country. The people felt keenly the loss of the young high priest who had been their pride and their hope, and every household sat down in mourning as if it had suffered a personal misfortune. As for his family, they were deeply stricken. The bereaved mother nearly committed suicide and Mariamme was prostrate with grief. Herod, now that the danger was over, joined in the general manifestations of sorrow and gave his brother-in-law a splendid funeral. Mariamme found some consolation in the honour paid to her brother, but her mother vowed revenge. As soon as the funeral was over she communicated her suspicions of foul play to her friend Cleopatra and asked her to persuade Antony to charge

Herod with murder. Antony accordingly wrote to Herod commanding him to report to him in person and clarify the situation.

Fearing that his absence might be used by Alexandra and the Hasmonaean faction to undermine his position, Herod appointed his brother-in-law Joseph, his sister Salome's husband, to act as regent. He instructed him that should Antony indefinitely detain him or even execute him, he was to kill Mariamme. He explained that he could not bear the thought of his beloved wife marrying again after his death. Joseph promised obedience and secrecy.

The meeting in Laodicea (Lattakia, on the Syrian coast) was most successful. Antony heard the case and concluded that the business of the high priesthood was a purely domestic affair, to be resolved by the king of Judaea as he saw fit. To mark his goodwill he showered Herod with honours and sent him away well pleased with his achievement. No sooner had Herod arrived back in Jerusalem than his sister Salome whispered in his ear that during his absence his wife had been unfaithful to him with the regent Joseph, Salome's own husband.

Herod's jealousy was easily roused but he was sensible enough to ask Mariamme for her own version of the story. There was a scene of mutual recriminations at the end of which Herod was satisfied with his wife's innocence and tried to take her in his arms. But Mariamme was not pleased to be forgiven when no offence had been committed. She angrily told her husband that had he really loved her he would not have instructed Joseph to kill her.

Herod was flabbergasted. He felt certain that Joseph would not have betrayed his secret instruction had he not been Mariamme's lover. Unable to vent his rage on the woman he passionately desired, he took his revenge on Joseph. He had him put to death without even seeing him. That he was his own sister's husband mattered little. For good measure he had Mariamme's mother thrown into chains, as an accomplice to an imaginary plot.

Somehow he and Mariamme made it up, and when their second son was born they named him Aristobulus. It was a common enough name in the Hasmonaean family, but giving it to a son born so soon after the Jericho tragedy was a tacit tribute to the dead brother. During the next few years the queen presented her husband with a third son and two daughters. Herod was pleased. He designated his sons by Mariamme as royal and sent away his first-born Antipater, Doris's son, whom until then he had kept in the court. He brought them up as princes and made arrangements to send them to Rome to be educated as befitted potential heirs. Mariamme felt very secure. Knowing the tremendous hold she had over her husband she did not bother to hide her contempt for his sister and his Arab mother. She told them how inferior they were and flaunted her Hasmonaean descent on every possible occasion. The women fawned on her to her face and accused her of all manner of crimes behind her back. But Herod, deferential as he was to his mother and mindful of his sister's vested interest in his welfare, was too much under Mariamme's charms to take the accusations seriously. The women bided their time, waiting for a suitable opportunity to bring things to the boil.

Ten years after his accession to the throne of Judaea, Herod heard of Antony's defeat at Actium at the hands of Octavian. His whole future, as Antony's former friend and ally, was in jeopardy. It was essential to meet the victor, make little of his past association with his rival and convince him of his usefulness and future loyalty. Herod was by no means certain of the outcome of such a meeting and could foresee any number of reasons why Octavian should want to get rid of a former friend of Antony's and appoint somebody else instead. It was therefore a necessary precaution to eliminate any candidate whom Octavian might possibly consider as a replacement. Such a one was Hyrcanus.

Since his return from exile the old man had lived peacefully as a private individual. In his seventies he had put the vanities of the world behind him and was content to accept honour without power. All the same he was a Hasmonaean and in the new political situation may well have been considered by Octavian as a temporary substitute for a king of dubious loyalty. To anticipate any such consideration Hyrcanus had to be put out of the way.

An excuse was readily found. A king of Arabia had sent Hyrcanus a present of four horses and followed it up by an invitation to visit his country. Whether this was a preamble to a dark plot to overthrow him, Herod interpreted it as such. The old man was summarily tried and found guilty of high treason. As a public execution would have aroused a national outcry, Herod arranged for him to be strangled in secret.

To insure himself against any domestic upheaval during his absence, Herod split his family in two. His mother, his sister and Mariamme's children were sent to Masada, while Mariamme herself and her own mother were despatched to the formidable fortress of Alexandrium (Sartaba), built by a Hasmonaean king and fortified by Herod. A certain Sohaemus was put in charge of the queen and given the same instruction as the unfortunate Joseph a few years earlier on a similar occasion. Should Herod meet his death during his encounter with the Roman ruler, Mariamme was not to survive.

The meeting with Octavian took place in Rhodes and was a resounding success. Not only was Herod confirmed as king, but his territory was extended and his authority increased. As soon as he had acquitted himself of his duties towards his new ally, he hurried back to Alexandrium to share the great news with his wife. But Mariamme, having extracted from Sohaemus the secret death orders that her husband had left before his departure, received him with marked coolness. She expressed her disappointment at his safe return and rebuffed his advances. From then on she waged an open war on him. She never missed an opportunity to mention his lowly descent and publicly criticized his uncouth manners. Their quarrels became the talk of the palace and it was obvious that a showdown was inevitable.

A whole year passed in domestic strife, with Herod tormented by his passion, Mariamme contemptuously confident of her hold over him. One day, when Herod was relaxing alone on his bed and feeling his desire mount, he sent for her. The queen appeared as in duty bound but recoiled in horror when he tried to take her in his arms. The more he persisted the more she rebuffed him. As she could not push away a man who was far stronger than she was, she lashed out with her tongue. All the pent-up hatred and bitterness of the past years came out in a torrent. For the first time in her life she openly accused Herod of the murder of her brother and her grandfather. Herod was mad with rage and frustrated desire, and in his struggle to keep hold of her nearly caused her injury. Their voices were heard all over the palace and it was then that Salome knew that her chance had come.

Bursting in on them, accompanied by a cup-bearer who had been well rehearsed in advance, she pointed at Mariamme and accused her of having plotted to poison Herod on his return from Rhodes. The cup-bearer confirmed that the queen had indeed ordered him to prepare a love potion for the king, which could well have been poisonous. In his present mood Herod was prepared to believe the worst. He ordered an inquiry. Under torture Mariamme's faithful eunuch admitted that while at Alexandrium Sohaemus had revealed to the queen Herod's death orders. Convinced as before that such a confidential instruction could have been betrayed only in bed, Herod had Sohaemus executed forthwith on charge of adultery with the queen.

This time, egged on by Salome, he went further. He had Mariamme committed for trial. The indictment was not clear, confusing as it did an unproven attempt to poison with unsubstantiated adultery. But Herod was in a savage mood and the death of Sohaemus was not enough to cure him of his senseless jealousy. The court pronounced the death sentence. The tormented husband ordered a stay of execution and confined Mariamme to the Antonia fortress in Jerusalem, but Salome bolstered up his flagging resolution. Defeated at last by his own tortured imagination, he gave way.

Now that her end was near Mariamme rose to her full stature. Dignified and majestic she walked past the assembled court, neither begging for mercy nor showing any fear. Her terrified mother, reacting in self-defence, attacked her for her ingratitude to a kind husband and even pulled her hair to demonstrate her non-complicity in her daughter's plotting. The queen walked on in silence, revealing that greatness of soul that was part of her Hasmonaean heritage.

After her death Herod was more consumed with desire than ever. He refused to believe she was dead and kept sending his servants to fetch her, all but killing them when they failed to produce her. His passion and remorse worked havoc with his health. He became ill and went into the wilderness to give vent to his fits of rage and melancholy. Only suspicions of further plotting brought him back to his senses, and putting his mother-in-law to death helped him to regain his equilibrium. He survived Mariamme by twenty-five years, but although he had many more wives after her, not one of them ever became so completely the mistress of his body and soul as she had been.

The young Berenice must have heard the story of Mariamme more than once during her early childhood in Tiberias. Born fifty-seven years after the execution, she might have met as a child some elderly people who could still remember the dead queen and possibly remarked on the family resemblance. That she credited the story is certain, for so did her kinsman and contemporary the historian Josephus. By the same token she must have discounted a curious version that later found its way into the Talmud, the storehouse of rabbinical legends:

> Herod was a slave of the Hasmonaeans who set his eyes on a young Hasmonaean maiden. One day he heard a voice from heaven say: 'Now is the time for slaves to rise against their masters.' So he killed all his master's family sparing none but the young maiden. When she understood that he wanted to marry her she ran up to the roof of the palace and called out: 'Whoever claims to be a Hasmonaean is surely a slave, for I am the only survivor and I am going to jump down and die.' Then she jumped down and was killed. Herod preserved her body in honey for seven years. Some people claimed that he had her embalmed so that he could have intercourse with her body and thus gratify his desires. Others said that he did no such thing and only kept her to give the impression that he was married to a king's daughter.[1]

In her maturity Berenice was well able to understand the emotional obsession that had warped Herod's judgement and driven him to acts of folly. She was equally able to dismiss a legend that indirectly suggested that her descent was not Hasmonaean. She well knew that the king's daughter Herod had held in his arms was no maiden embalmed in honey but a woman of flesh and blood; for queen Mariamme, cut off in her twenties, was her own great-grandmother, and Berenice's younger sister was named after her.

Chapter II

Royal trials

O F the five young children that Mariamme left behind her, two were old enough to understand the circumstances of her death. Alexander was about seven when she died, Aristobulus about six. The memory of their mother's execution was to stay with them all their lives and affect their future behaviour.

For the first few years after her death the three boys and two girls were brought up in the palace, with their aunt Salome and there paternal grandmother Cypros never too far off. The two women who had rejoiced at the queen's downfall must have followed with anxiety the progress of her children. Herod still regarded them as royal, for they were born after he had become king. He intended the boys to be his heirs and when they reached their teens he took them to Rome and arranged for them to stay there for their education. One died young, but the other two flourished in their new environment. Alexander and Aristobulus were instructed in the arts and sciences, made useful contacts and were sometimes invited to stay in the palace of Augustus, formerly Octavian, their father's protector and friend.

Five years passed in this way. In 17 BC, when Alexander was about nineteen and Aristobulus about eighteen, their father came to Rome again on one of his political visits. The boys' education was considered finished, and when Herod concluded his business with Augustus he took them back home.

Both young men had inherited their mother's good looks and noble bearing. They were both tall, handsome, and unmistakably Hasmonaean in appearance. When Herod brought them back to Jerusalem he was dismayed to see how the crowds cheered them in recognition of their obvious parentage. Not at all liking this reminder of the past, he still proceeded with his plan to give them suitable wives. For his eldest, Alexander, he departed from his favoured policy of intermarriage within the family, and fetched him a royal bride from another country. Glaphyra was the daughter of Archaelaus Sisinnes king of Cappadocia, a large client state in eastern Asia Minor which played an important part in Rome's eastern frontier system. Aristobulus, the younger son, had to make do with a cousin. He married his aunt Salome's daughter Berenice, the first of the family to be called by that name. The princes and their wives were allowed to wear royal jewellery, ate at the king's table and kept their own servants.

Alexander and Glaphyra were temperamentally compatible and made a happy marriage. Both were proud of their royal descent and looked down upon anybody who did not have the good fortune to number kings and queens among their ancestors. Glaphyra never let anyone forget that she was descended on the one hand from Darius the son of Hystapes, on the other from the royal house of Macedon. Alexander, stressing his maternal genealogy, was equally boastful. Together they must have been the most insufferable snobs at court.

Aristobulus was less fortunate in his wife. Although he did not shun her bed and in due course gave her several children, he felt he owed her no respect for she was a commoner. Moreover, Berenice was the daughter of his mother's enemy. He had frequent rows with her and thus drove her back into Salome's camp. She soon developed the habit of reporting to Salome any chance remark of her husband's that could be interpreted as seditious and thus helped her mother prepare a case against the sons of Mariamme, whose power she had good reason to fear.

Unfortunately for the young princes they had inherited not only their mother's beauty, but also her arrogance. They were contemptuous of their low-born relatives, over-confident and inexperienced in the ways of the court. They let drop careless remarks about past injustices and the need to punish the real culprits. Their remarks were duly reported to Salome, either by her daughter or through paid agents, and she repeated them to Herod with a great many additions and embellishments. She represented the brothers as conspirators who, to avenge their mother, would not hesitate to kill their father and take over his kingdom. Herod had always had a morbidly suspicious nature. Under Salome's influence his unstable affection for his sons gave way to disenchantment and fear.

The crunch came as usual immediately after his return from one of his prolonged visits abroad.

For several years he had been cultivating the friendship of Marcus Agrippa, the second greatest man in the Roman world after Augustus. About the time that Alexander and Aristobulus returned to Jerusalem to get married, Marcus Agrippa was sent by Augustus to supervise Roman affairs in the east. During his tour of duty he visited Judaea, inspected Herod's new towns and fortresses, and finally arrived in Jerusalem. He was lodged in the new palace that bore his name and won the hearts of the people by sacrificing a hundred oxen in the temple. Next he went to the Aegean coast of Asia Minor where he was planning a punitive expedition against a refractory king. Herod hastened after him to offer reinforcements. The crisis proved to be a minor one, and when it was over Herod took the opportunity of touring the main Jewish communities of the area, promising to win them the goodwill of Marcus Agrippa. After several months' absence he returned to Jerusalem well pleased with his political achievement. He called a public meeting in the temple precincts, informed the people of his continued good standing with the Romans, and gave them real cause to rejoice when he remitted a quarter of their taxes for the past year.

But no sooner was he back in the bosom of his family than Salome confidentially reported on her recent findings. Alexander and Aristobulus were making inflammatory speeches. They were trying to involve the king of Cappadocia. They were planning to go to Rome to ask Augustus to re-examine the evidence brought up during Mariamme's trial.

Salome's accusations produced a curious effect. Not wishing to have an open confrontation with his sons, Herod decided to deflate their hopes by presenting them with a rival. After twenty years of exile, he recalled to court his first-born son Antipater.

Twenty years' fall from grace had made Antipater bitter and resentful. It had also taught him to fawn, dissimulate, make mischief and pretend innocence. As soon as he came to court he set out to undermine his brothers' position. Posing as their champion, he so artfully misrepresented their case to Herod that in a few months he did them more harm than Salome had done in several years. When Marcus Agrippa returned to Rome Herod arranged for Antipater to accompany him and be presented to Augustus as his potential heir. For the next two years, until Marcus Agrippa's death, Antipater worked to consolidate his favour in Rome, at the same time keeping the accusations going against his brothers at home with the help of a reliable côterie that included not only Salome, but also her brother Pheroras and his own mother Doris, who had been allowed to return to Jerusalem.

In the meantime Alexander and Aristobulus went on playing into their enemies' hands. When Herod distributed some of Mariamme's costly clothes among his wives, the young men were outraged. They protested that their mother had been a queen, whereas the other wives were commoners, married for their sexual attractions rather than for nobility of birth. They went about the palace saying that when they came to the throne they would strip the wives of their finery, make them wear sackcloth and force them to do rough weaving with the servant girls. About the sons of those wives, their half-brothers, they had even more scornful things to say. Contrasting their own princely education in Rome with the humble training given to the half-brothers in Jerusalem, Alexander and Aristobulus declared that once they were kings they would make them village clerks, for that was all they were fit to be.

With Antipater pressing from Rome and the young princes behaving foolishly at home, Herod was at last persuaded of their conspiratorial intentions. He dared not antagonize the people, for whom the princes constituted the last direct link with the popular house of the Hasmonaeans. The onus for any disciplinary action had to be thrust on somebody else. No arbiter could be more acceptable than Caesar himself. In 12 BC Herod took his sons to Italy and asked Augustus to sit in judgement on them.

It was not the policy of Roman emperors to interfere in the domestic affairs of their client-kings. To ask Augustus to judge between him and his sons was to admit that Herod was not master in his own house and therefore not deserving of continued Roman support. That Herod put aside such considerations and took his case to Augustus indicated the degree of his perplexity. He did not feel secure while his sons were around, yet he had not reached that state of morbid fear that would later make him overcome his feelings as a father and order their execution. It was perhaps with a subconscious hope of allowing them to prove their innocence that he took them to Aquileia, at the head of the Adriatic, to stand trial before an impartial judge.

It was a full court, with Caesar in the chair, Herod personally reading the indictment, and the accused standing apart. Antipater was in the audience, some of whose members he may have courted and bribed during his two-year stay in Rome, while others perhaps still retained kind memories of the young princes who had been brought up amongst them. After Herod had submitted his reasons for suspecting his sons of plotting against his life and throne, the young men were given permission to speak in their own defence.

Alexander was the more articulate of the two; it was mostly he who had been making public utterances and putting things in writing. The long sea voyage had given him enough time to prepare his defence and indeed he had it worked out very carefully. But the sight of the austere assembly unmanned him. He broke down in sobs. So did his brother.

In view of the splendid speech that followed, the sobbing may well have been no more than a gambit calculated to melt stony hearts. The assembly was visibly moved by the time Alexander began to speak, haltingly at first, then, as he gauged the mood of his audience, with growing confidence and eloquence. Profiting from the lessons in rhetoric he had received as a young man in Rome, he called both logic and sentiment to his aid, flattering Caesar on his love of justice, adroitly exonerating Herod of all suspicion of past murders. Addressing himself to his father but clearly speaking to Augustus, he gradually brought his speech to its climax:

No one will ever prove any disloyalty on our part, but how can we hope to refute the accusations against us if we are not given a hearing? Have we been too outspoken? If so, we did not speak against you, which would have been wrong, but against those who denounced us although we had said nothing wrong. Did we give offence by grieving for our mother? If so, it was not because she was put to death but because even in death she was slandered by unworthy people. Did we seem to covet our father's throne? What reason have we for doing so when we already have royal honours? Could we have expected to obtain the throne by putting you out of the way? The earth would not have been safe for us to walk nor the seas to sail. Could we have planned to kill you? Your devout subjects would not have tolerated a father's murderers as leaders of state and would have never allowed us to enter the most holy temple which you had built. And would we ever get away with murder while Caesar is alive and his punishment ready? No, your sons are neither undutiful nor foolish, only unfortunate.[1]

It was a masterly performance. The assembly was impressed by Alexander's passionate pleading, touched by Aristobulus's tragic silence. Augustus dismissed the case, at the same time giving the young men a paternal warning about the advisability of filial devotion. Turning to Herod he recommended a general reconciliation. It was an emotional occasion. The princes burst into tears and fell down on their knees to beg their father's forgiveness for past misunderstandings. Caesar made them get up and took each one of them separately in his arms to demonstrate his favour. Herod followed his example, no doubt relieved not to have to face the consequences of another domestic tragedy. Later he distributed large sums of money to the people of Rome to show his gratitude for imperial justice. The gesture was perhaps precipitated by the fact that Augustus had just conceded Herod half the revenues from the copper mines of Cyprus. As for Antipater, he pretended to rejoice at his brothers' proven innocence. The reconciled family left Rome together and on the way back home met king Archelaus who was delighted to see his daughter's husband restored to favour.

On his return to Jerusalem Herod called a public meeting, presented his three sons to the people and informed them that Augustus had conferred on him the unusual privilege of naming his own heirs:

Caesar made me lord of this kingdom and allowed me to determine the succession; this I am about to do in a manner beneficial to me and pleasing to him. I declare these my three sons kings, and I call first on God, then on you, to confirm my decision. The succession belongs to one son by priority of birth, to the

other two by their noble parentage. My kingdom is large
enough for more than three. I call on you to defend and protect
those whom Caesar has joined together and their father nominated. Honour them justly and equally, each according to his
birthright. . . . But I must insist that the officers of my army give
their loyalty to me alone. It is not the kingdom, but only the
honour due to kingship, that I am conferring on my sons. They
will enjoy the pleasures of power as if they were rulers, but the
burden of office, however heavy, shall be mine alone. . . . Whoever serves my sons in order to bring about my downfall shall
be punished for their sake as for mine. It is in their interest that
I should continue on the throne; it is in mine that they should
live in harmony.

As for you, my good children, turn your thoughts first to the
laws of nature, which instill affection even into wild beasts; then
to Caesar, who has brought about our reconciliation; and lastly
to me, who entreat when I might command, and at all times
continue as brothers.[2]

Herod's speech fell on deaf ears. The princes' supporters continued to resent Antipater's infiltration into power, while his own
faction was disappointed with the compromise. The designate
heirs were also far from pleased. Antipater was offended because
his father had conceded the princes' superior birth, while the
princes were piqued because he had recognized Antipater's primo-
geniture. All three accepted as of right their father's permission to
wear royal robes and maintain their own household and retinue.
Equally all three made use of the truce to fortify their positions
and get ready for the next round.

Alexander was the more clamorous of the two princes and
therefore the more open to attack. Partly because he was the elder,
partly because, thanks to his devoted Glaphyra, he had a powerful
ally in his father-in-law, he was more assertive than Aristobulus
who dared not speak his mind in his own house for fear of being
reported by his wife to his mother-in-law Salome. But even
Alexander learnt to be circumspect. Whenever he went hunting
with his ageing father he deliberately missed his shot to allow
Herod to make the kill. He also affected a drooping stance so as
not to make his father feel small against his own tall stature.

Unfortunately he spoilt his tactful efforts by bragging about them at home, little suspecting that many of his servants were in Antipater's pay.

In the meantime the Antipater côterie hatched up another plot.

Herod had always treated Glaphyra with a certain amount of kindness, due perhaps less to her charms than to her influence with her father. This kindness could be easily misrepresented. Pheroras, brother to Herod and Salome, took it upon himself to open Alexander's eyes and suggested that Herod's affection for Glaphyra was adulterous. Paradoxically, it was Alexander's impetuosity that saved him from disaster. He rushed off to his father and confronted him with the ugly accusation. Herod had Pheroras brought before him and asked him what he meant by spreading lies about his king and brother. Pheroras said it was Salome's idea. Salome tore her hair and beat her breasts and cried that everybody was against her. Herod dismissed them both with a severe warning.

The next plot met with more success. Herod had three handsome eunuchs who attended to his personal needs and wielded considerable influence in affairs of state. Alexander was accused of corrupting their minds against their master; and as the betrayal of state secrets could conceivably take place only in bed, it was suggested that he had had intercourse with them. The eunuchs were tortured until they confessed that Alexander had been saying his father was getting old and he would soon succeed him. Herod put the eunuchs to death and increased the number of agents spying on the princes. Soon a man was found who under torture admitted that Alexander and Aristobulus were planning to kill their father while hunting, then go to Rome to claim their kingdom. Herod immediately flung Alexander into prison. The torturing of frightened people went on until another man confessed that Alexander had planned to poison his father or implicate him in a Parthian plot against Rome.

When the news of this new accusation reached Alexander in his prison, he decided to take a chance. He sat down and wrote a long statement, stretching over four rolls of papyrus, in which he admitted partial guilt and gave the full list of his accomplices. It included Pheroras, Salome, and two of Herod's most trusted governors. The gamble paid off. Herod was completely unnerved

and did not know whom to believe. Now he mistrusted everybody and was in constant fear for his life. At times he imagined he
saw Alexander breaking out of prison and rushing at him sword
in hand.

He was still in this disordered state of mind when king Archelaus of Cappadocia arrived in Jerusalem in a last-minute attempt
to save his son-in-law's life. Correctly judging Herod's contrary
nature he used subterfuge. Instead of defending Alexander he
attacked him. He rebuked Herod for having been too lenient with
him and proposed to punish him further by forcing him to divorce
his wife Glaphyra.

The suggestion of a divorce had the expected effect, for Herod
was quick to appreciate how much he stood to lose from a break
with Cappadocia. His accusations against his son grew more
restrained. Then Archelaus decided to strike. He had already
studied Alexander's statement and extracted some names from it.
Those he now presented to Herod as the real culprits who had
used Alexander's name to further their own plot against the king.
Most prominent among them was Pheroras.

With Herod's mood changing from one extreme to the other
Pheroras knew that the game was up. He put on sackcloth and
ashes and threw himself at Archelaus's feet to beg for his life.
Archelaus forced him to go to Herod and repudiate in his presence all his former allegations against Alexander. Alexander was
immediately released and restored to his family. Tempering justice
with clemency, Archelaus then put in a good word for Pheroras
and obtained his pardon from the king.

Once the air was clear Herod arranged a series of banquets to
entertain his royal guest. No honour was too high for him. When
he left, Herod personally escorted him as far as Antioch (Antakya)
in Syria and gave him a parting present consisting of a generous
sum of money, a golden throne set with precious stones and, last
but not least, a beautiful concubine called Pannychia (All-Night-
Long).

The reconciliation brought about by Archelaus lasted even less
time than the one effected by Augustus a few years earlier. Oddly
enough, it was an utter stranger who precipitated the princes'
downfall. Eurycles of Sparta was an adventurer who made capital

out of other people's misfortunes. He arrived in Jerusalem in great state, sent lavish presents to the members of the royal house and ingratiated himself with one and all. It did not take him long to assess the undercurrents of hostility between the rival factions and calculate how best to use them to his own advantage. He won Glaphyra's trust by posing as an old friend of her father's, and Antipater's friendship by promising to work for him. He became a sort of double agent, receiving his pay from both sides while serving none so well as his own cause. In due course he came up with a new version of the old hunting plot. Herod was to be pushed off his horse and made to fall on his spear as if by accident. As the king had had some such accident a few years earlier, the plot seemed feasible. Both princes were put under arrest, with the lively Alexander being as usual the chief suspect. This time Herod himself conducted the enquiry. Alexander was brought before him in chains and interrogated at length. He denied any treasonable intent but admitted that he had planned to run away and seek refuge with Archelaus in Cappadocia, possibly continuing from there to Rome.

On Herod's orders Alexander was then dragged to his own house to be confronted with his wife, who was meant to break down and confess all. Glaphyra was indeed so shaken to see her husband in chains that she was prepared to say anything that might save his life. But Alexander, in the presence of his guards, warned her to say no more than the truth, after which she only admitted the plan to escape to Cappadocia. That was the last time she saw Alexander alive. His parting declaration that he loved her more than his life was to follow her to the grave.

While the two princes were languishing in their prison, Herod in his perplexity appealed again to Augustus to judge between him and his sons. Unfortunately Caesar was not in a conciliatory mood. Herod had recently displeased him by an unauthorized infiltration into Arabia, another client kingdom of Rome. By the time Augustus had smoothed over the political complications created by this action, he was not inclined to do Herod's dirty work for him. It was possibly then that he made the much-quoted remark, prompted by his knowledge of the king as a non-pork-eating Jew, that it was safer to be Herod's pig than Herod's son. However, he wrote a tactful letter authorizing him to start legal proceedings, suggesting that if the princes were found guilty of treason they might be severely punished, but if found guilty only of an attempt to run away a warning should be enough. Augustus instructed Herod to hold an open trial in Berytus (Beirut) and invite to the judges' bench not only the Roman officials of Syria, but also king Archelaus of Cappadocia.

In accordance with these written instructions Herod proceeded to Berytus and convened his court. The judges sat in three rows: first the Roman officials, including the governor of Syria and his three sons; then counsellors and gentlemen of the royal household, Herod himself, his sister Salome and his brother Pheroras; in the third row the dignitaries of the Syrian province. Altogether there were one hundred and fifty people on the judges' benches. One notable absentee was king Archelaus, whom Herod had taken the precaution not to invite.

The prisoners' bench was vacant. Herod had decided to have his sons accused *in absentia*. Alexander was a master of eloquence, and Herod had every reason to fear that, once the young man was given permission to speak, he would refute all charges and carry the day, as he had done five years earlier before Augustus. The accused were kept under guard in a village some distance away from Berytus, and their absence from court was left unexplained.

As before, Herod himself read the indictment. He hurried over the attempt to murder him, for which he had no proof, and dwelt heavily on the princes' other crimes such as criticism of his person, jokes at his expense, arrogance and lack of filial respect. He also mentioned the plan to run away to Cappadocia. The judges were not allowed to examine the evidence and were instructed to accept the king's word for it. Then they were told to pass sentence. The governor of Syria and his three sons recommended mercy, but the other judges took their cue from Herod's hysterical mood. The death sentence was passed by a majority of a hundred and forty-six to four.

As the execution could not very well take place in Syria, outside Herod's jurisdiction, the condemned were taken back to their own country and put in prison in Caesarea. There they awaited their father's pleasure, hoping he would use the royal prerogative to commute their sentence or grant them a free pardon. Herod was torn with indecision. His ambassador had just returned from

Rome with the information that Augustus clearly favoured a pardon. On the other hand he felt that his sons' lives meant his own death. He put off his decision from day to day.

In the meantime feeling in Judaea was running high. The princes were popular with the people not only for their Hasmonaean descent but also for their own personal charm. They had made friends in their father's army, and now a well-respected retired officer spoke up in their favour. Soon he had three hundred officers demonstrating with him against the savage sentence. The demonstration touched off Herod's contrariness. He allowed the three hundred officers to be lynched by an incited mob and gave the royal assent to the execution of his sons. They were quietly transferred to Samaria, where thirty years earlier their father had married their mother, and there they were strangled. Their bodies were carried by night to the fortress of Alexandrium and laid to rest among many of their Hasmonaean ancestors, near their uncle the young high priest who had suffered death by drowning. Like their mother, Alexander and Aristobulus were still in their twenties when they died.

After the death of the princes Herod found himself with two marriageable widows on his hands. In accordance with accepted policy they should have both been given to new husbands to cement new ties. Glaphyra however could not very well be used to further Herod's interests. With her father still seething under the insult of his son-in-law's execution, it was judged wiser not to do anything that might antagonize him further. Glaphyra was sent home and Herod paid back her dowry from his own purse to anticipate any possible cause for complaint. But the king of Cappadocia, like the king of Judaea, was not going to allow a marriageable daughter to go to waste. He married her off to Juba, king of Libya. The event must have taken place very shortly after Alexander's death and Glaphyra was unable to readjust. Her second marriage was a failure and a welcome divorce allowed her to resume her life at her father's court.

While Glaphyra was mourning her past, Herod was regretting his concessions to Antipater. Three years after the Berytus trial he ordered his murder. He himself died a few days later, leaving his kingdom to be divided between three of his remaining sons.

Archelaus, Herod's son by a Samaritan wife, became ruler of Judaea and Samaria.

It was probably on his return from Rome, where he had gone to have his rule confirmed by Augustus, that the young Archelaus called on his namesake, the king of Cappadocia, in order to revive the friendship between the two countries. He saw Glaphyra, still attractive and unattached, and fell in love with her. He was several years younger than her and already married, but to win her heart and her father's consent he divorced his wife. The old king probably welcomed a second chance to ally himself to Judaea, shrunken as it was after the division. As for Glaphyra, she may well have been tempted to return to the scene of her early domestic bliss now that most of her enemies were gone.

The marriage was unpopular in Jerusalem. According to Jewish law a man could, and in fact was duty bound, to marry his brother's widow if she was childless, in order to give her a son who would perpetuate the dead man's name. But if the widow had had issue by her first husband, the brother was forbidden to marry her. As Glaphyra had two sons by Alexander, she was forbidden to marry any brother or half-brother of her late husband. Both she and Archelaus were therefore guilty of religious transgression. The effect on Glaphyra of the antagonism the marriage aroused was unsettling. She felt she had betrayed her dead husband. She was consumed with remorse and her mental state affected her health. One night she dreamt that Alexander was standing before her, but when she joyfully rushed to embrace him he rebuffed her. Josephus later attributed to him the following speech:

You certainly confirm the saying that women are fickle, Glaphyra. Although you married me when a virgin and bore me children, you forgot my love in your desire to marry again. Not content with a second husband you had the temerity to take a third one to your bed, and in an indecent and shameless manner you again became a member of my family by marrying Archelaus, your own brother-in-law and my own brother. But I still love you and will clear you of all blame by making you mine as before.[3]

Glaphyra hardly survived the telling of her dream. Two days later she died. Her eldest son by Alexander grew up to become king of Armenia, while the younger became the father of another king of Armenia and the grandfather of a king of Cilicia, in Asia Minor. Long before that they had abandoned the Jewish religion and thus had no further place in the family history.

Disposing of Berenice, the widow of Aristobulus, was a simpler matter. In spite of the five children she had borne him she had no love for him. She dutifully married an old uncle of Antipater's, but was not allowed much time with him for Herod put him to death on a charge of treason. She then married a third time and went to live in Rome, where she became a respected figure in the imperial household.

By the time the young Berenice was born, the elder one had long been dead. Yet she was called after her, for the old lady was her grandmother, and the unfortunate Aristobulus her grandfather. Their history was another lesson in the family intrigue that formed part of the young girl's education and inevitably affected her outlook on life.

Chapter III

In search of a kingdom

ONE of Agrippa's earliest childhood memories was of his grandfather Herod picking him up in his arms and calling him a poor little orphan. At the age of six Aristobulus's son could have only dimly sensed the hypocrisy of the sentiment, expressed as it was by the very man who had ordered his father's death.

It was 6 BC, nearly a year after the trial in Berytus and the execution in Samaria. Herod had had time for second thoughts. Antipater was behaving as if he were already king and his father regretted having vested so much authority in him. The best way to bring him to heel was to show favour to the young orphans left by Alexander and Aristobulus, whose Hasmonaean blood was a constant source of worry to the heir-apparent.

There were eight of them at court, all still under ten. First there were two sons and one daughter of Alexander and Glaphyra. Their lot was the hardest, for having lost their father they also had to part with their mother when she was sent back to Cappadocia. Then there were the three sons and two daughters of Aristobulus and Berenice. They fared better than their cousins, for although their mother had married again she did her best to protect them from harm.

Herod kept his own counsel so as not to give Antipater a chance to forestall him. One day he summoned the whole court, complete with women and children, and announced what must have seemed a complete about-turn in view of recent events. Putting his hands on the heads of the little boys and girls, who were too frightened to make a sound, he proceeded to tell the court of the plans he had just made for them:

Some evil spirit has robbed me of these children's fathers; but natural love and pity for the orphans commend them to my care. I have been an unfortunate father; I will try to be a better grandfather. After my death I shall entrust the care of these children to those I hold most dear in the family. Your daughter, Pheroras, I give to the elder of Alexander's two boys, and so make you his natural guardian. To your son, Antipater, I give Aristobulus's daughter, so that you become father to the orphan girl. Her sister my own son Herod shall marry. . . . Let my wishes be carried out and let no friend of mine go against them. I pray God to bless these unions to the good of my kingdom and my descendants, and I ask Him to look at these little children more compassionately than He has looked at their fathers.[1]

As the court watched in stunned silence, Herod ceremoniously joined the hands of the newly engaged couples, then picked up all the children one by one and kissed them, his eyes streaming with tears. The only one who was not deceived for a moment by these histrionics was Antipater, who immediately set out to undo his father's plans. In due course he persuaded him to cancel the advantageous engagements he had arranged for the Hasmonaean orphans and to make new ones to suit his own schemes. But long before he got his way the watchful Berenice had packed her boys off to Rome, away from Antipater's machinations.

Berenice had three sons by Aristobulus. The eldest was called Herod after his grandfather. The youngest bore his father's name. The middle one was the first of the Herodian family to be called Agrippa. He was so named after his grandfather's friend Marcus Agrippa who was favourably remembered in Jerusalem as the Roman commander who had sacrificed a hundred oxen in the temple and who later reaffirmed the civil rights of some Jewish communities abroad.

Berenice made careful provision for her sons in Rome. She was on friendly terms with Antonia, wife of Drusus and sister-in-law to the future emperor Tiberius, and she recommended the boys to her care. As it happened they were not left long without maternal supervision. Berenice's second husband, like her first, was executed by Herod; and on marrying a third she settled down in Rome and took charge of her children. The friendships she helped them form at a tender age stood them in good stead all their lives.

When Herod died in 4 BC, having ordered from his deathbed the murder of his heir-apparent Antipater, he left his kingdom to be divided among three of his remaining sons. All three were in due course confirmed by Augustus, though none of them with the title of king. Eighteen-year-old Archelaus became ethnarch of Judaea and Samaria, with the promise of kingship should he prove worthy of it. Philip became tetrarch of Gaulanitis (Golan), Batanea and Trachonitis (in southern Syria); and Antipas became tetrarch of Galilee and Peraea (Trans-Jordan).

Archelaus's reign was the shortest. Far from proving himself worthy of promotion, he so angered his subjects by his mal-administration that Augustus decided to deprive him of what authority he had. Tiberius, later to become emperor and then at the beginning of his civil career, made a speech in Rome in his defence, but to no avail. Archelaus was banished to Gaul and there lived until his death. His banishment marked a turning-point in the history of Judaea. The country which had come under Roman influence through its own appeal to Pompey, which had not been at war with Rome and had not ceased to be autonomous, was now quietly annexed as a Roman province. For the first time since the Hasmonaeans' rise to power, nearly a century and a half before, there was no Jewish ruler in Jerusalem. Instead Augustus and his successors sent out procurators whose rule lasted for thirty-five years. One of them was Pontius Pilate, during whose term of office the crucifixion of Jesus took place.

Philip's reign as tetrarch was both successful and uneventful. He concentrated on the administration of his territories and dealt summary justice to his subjects from a portable throne he used to take with him on his frequent tours of his principality. His main claim to fame lay in his rebuilding and enlarging the small town of Caesarea Panias above one of the sources of the Jordan and re-naming it Caesarea Philippi. He died without issue after thirty-eight years and his tetrarchy was also annexed by Rome though only briefly. Within a few years it was to become the nucleus of another Jewish kingdom.

Antipas, the third brother, was the Herod described in the Gospel as 'that fox'. He certainly showed political cunning when he declined to shoulder responsibility for the misbehaviour of one of his subjects in Jerusalem and allowed Jesus of Nazareth to be caught and tried by the Roman procurator of Judaea, outside his own jurisdiction. One of his lasting achievements was the foundation of a new city on the western shore of the Sea of Galilee which he named Tiberias after the emperor Tiberius who had succeeded Augustus. But he is mostly remembered as the step-father of the young Salome who obtained from him the head of John the Baptist as a reward for her dancing.

Antipas's marital history followed a familiar pattern. Not content with the wife he had, he decided to divorce her in order to marry his niece Herodias who was already married to one of his half-brothers and had children by him. Such a marriage was forbidden by Jewish law and it was small wonder that John the Baptist rebuked him for his impious act. Herodias resented the open criticism even more than did her husband, and it was her daughter by her first marriage who brought about John's end.

While Antipas and Philip were ruling their tetrarchies and a Roman procurator governed Judaea, the emperor Augustus died in Rome, naming his adopted son Tiberius as his successor. Agrippa, Berenice's second son, lost no time in making himself agreeable to the new emperor, in the hope of winning himself a tetrarchy.

Agrippa's date of birth is usually given as about 10 BC, but he may well have been born two or three years earlier. Marcus Agrippa, after whom he was named, died in 12 BC. The whole flattery value of calling a grandson after an influential Roman would have been lost for Herod if the boy was born two years after Marcus Agrippa's death. Herod was no sentimentalist and, except in the case of his brother Phasael, who had committed suicide while in the hands of the Parthians, and his father Antipater, who died from poisoning, he named his buildings and his offspring only after the living. Thus he named a tower in his new citadel in Jerusalem after Mariamme when she was still his beloved wife; the Antonia fortress adjoining the temple after Antony in his heyday; and a village near Jericho after his mother in her lifetime. There was no political reason to commemorate the name of Marcus Agrippa after his death, particularly when his name had already been given to the new royal palace in Jerusalem and to one of the temple gates. It would be more in keeping with Herod's character to assume that he bestowed the name on his newly born grandson to flatter Marcus Agrippa while he was still alive and useful. In that case the young Agrippa would have been born not later than 12 BC, possibly even late 13 BC, when Marcus Agrippa was back in Rome, obliging Herod by biasing Augustus in favour of Antipater.

When Tiberius became emperor Agrippa was in his mid-twenties. He had been brought up in the best Roman society. By virtue of the hereditary honour conferred on his ancestor Antipater by Julius Caesar, he and his family were Roman citizens. They were members of Caesar's *gens*, or clan, and were entitled to use the Julian name. Indeed his full name was Marcus Julius Agrippa. Moreover, his mother Berenice's excellent connections opened many doors before him. He was roughly of the same age-group as Germanicus, Antonia's brilliant son; Claudius, her less favoured son who many years later became emperor; and Drusus, Tiberius's own son. Agrippa cultivated the friendships of these young men, hoping to rise with them. He was lively, handsome, and thoroughly at ease with the Roman way of life. Unfortunately he developed a taste for luxury and good living that was far above his means. As long as his mother was alive he had to curb his spending and try to live within his allowance, for Berenice tightly controlled the purse strings and was only free with her advice. Agrippa had to wait for her death before he could give rein to his extravagance. Then he began to entertain lavishly and showered bribes on every freedman he thought might be useful to him in his quest of a tetrarchy. But fate was against him. The two young men with whom he had grown up and on whom he had pinned his hopes died before they were in a position to do anything for him. Germanicus, heir-apparent to Tiberius, died in AD 18. Five years later Tiberius's son Drusus died. Tiberius himself was becoming unpredictable and refused to see any of his dead son's friends. Worst of all, Agrippa had squandered all his fortune and was at the mercy of creditors. There was nothing for it but to leave Rome and hide as far away as possible. And so, some time after the death of Drusus, he returned to Roman-dominated Judaea and took up residence in a small bleak fortress which he had inherited in Idumaea, near Beer-Sheba.

He arrived there with his newly married wife Cypros. Contrary to family tradition he married fairly late in life; but in accordance with it he married within the family. Cypros was, like himself, a grandchild of queen Mariamme the Hasmonaean. The marriage probably took place after his inglorious return from Rome, while knocking on rich relatives' doors in Jerusalem before proceeding to his unprepossessing retreat in Idumaea. Cypros turned out to be an excellent choice. She became a devoted wife and a most resourceful helpmate in the difficult times that followed.

The change from the gay and eventful life in Rome to the dreary existence in a desert fortress was more than Agrippa could bear. He became despondent and nothing would reconcile him to his lot. Not even the birth of a son named Agrippa after him, and a daughter, named Berenice after his late mother, could console him. He saw no future for himself and talked of committing suicide. It was entirely thanks to his wife's string-pulling that he was given a fresh start in life.

His sister Herodias was already living in Tiberias with her second husband Antipas the tetrarch. Nothing daunted by the irregularity of the marriage, Cypros wrote to her new sister-in-law and asked her to do something for her impoverished brother. Antipas was duly approached and in his dual capacity of uncle and brother-in-law was prevailed upon to help Agrippa out. He offered him the post of *agoranomos,* an inspector of markets, in his new capital. There was a reasonable salary attached, and so Agrippa and his family left their desolate fortress and went back to civilization where they settled down in greater comfort. In Tiberias Cypros gave birth to another daughter who was called Mariamme, after the common grandmother. While they were there Agrippa and his family must have learnt something of the new religious movement that was sweeping across the country. Jesus had been active in Galilee and John the Baptist had followers within Antipas's own household. It was during Agrippa's term of office in Tiberias that John was beheaded, and he may well have attended the banquet during which Salome's dancing led to the Baptist's death. He was still in Antipas's employ when Jesus was tried and crucified in Jerusalem.

The humble post of an inspector of markets did not satisfy Agrippa long. His salary seemed meagre and certainly insufficient to keep him in the state he desired for himself. His relations with his employer grew strained. During a public feast in Tyre, when both were in their cups, they told one another a few home truths. Agrippa provoked Antipas by criticizing his meanness, while Antipas shouted in front of everybody that his brother-in-law was living on charity. Drunken insults flew round the crowded tables until Agrippa lost his temper altogether and walked out.

Casting about what to do next, he remembered that the governor of Syria had been a good friend of his during his days in Rome. He already had a useful connection in the household in the person of his younger brother Aristobulus who was acting as the governor's political adviser. So to Antioch Agrippa went, taking his wife and children with him. Pomponius Flaccus received him cordially and appointed him too a political adviser.

Young Aristobulus was also married by then. He had deviated from the accepted custom of marrying within the family and had taken for a wife a foreign princess, the daughter of the king of Emesa (Homs), by whom he had a deaf daughter. This, however, was a calamity he could bear with more equanimity than the loss of his influence to his smooth-tongued brother. Family loyalty meant little to ambitious princes who had grown up against a background of Herodian intrigues. They tried to push each other out of the way and before long were crossing swords in earnest.

The people of Damascus had a border dispute with the people of Sidon and took their case to Flaccus. The Damascenes bribed Agrippa to put in a good word for them while the Sidonians probably approached Aristobulus in the same way. Agrippa, being the more persuasive of the two, induced Flaccus to give judgement in favour of the Damascenes. Aristobulus retaliated by informing on his brother. Without reversing his decision, the governor had no alternative but to dismiss his corrupt adviser. Once again Agrippa and his family found themselves on the move.

More than ten years had passed since he had left Rome. His old patroness Antonia was still living there while Tiberius had retired to Capri and was ruling the empire from a distance. Agrippa felt the time was ripe for a return to the centre of power. He took his wife and children to Ptolemais (Acre, Akko) and persuaded a freedman of his late mother to lend him seventeen thousand five hundred drachmas against an iou of twenty thousand, to cover previous loans. With this sum of money at their disposal the family went to a small landing-place at Anthedon, near Gaza, hoping to sail away without attracting attention. They had actually boarded a ship when fate struck again.

True to character, Agrippa had never tried to live within his means and had supplemented his income by borrowing large sums of money wherever he could. By the time he was about to leave the country his debts amounted to three hundred thousand drachmas, which through some unspecified transactions were owing not to private money-lenders but to the imperial treasury in Judaea. Just as he was about to sail, the imperial agent caught up with him and put him under arrest on board ship. Agrippa was nothing if not resourceful. He bribed the captain and when night fell they cut the mooring cables and gave the Roman the slip. The family dropped anchor in Alexandria where Agrippa, counting on the patriotic sentiments of the Jewish community, hoped to raise some more money.

The man on whom he particularly pinned his hopes was Tiberius Julius Alexander the elder, usually known as Alexander the *alabarch*, the inspector-in-chief of customs duties for the Romans on the eastern part of the Nile. Having been made a Roman citizen by Tiberius, the *alabarch* was like Agrippa a member of the Julian *gens*. He was also a devout Jew and had the nine gates of the temple in Jerusalem covered in gold and silver at his own expense. He was one of the richest men in Alexandria.

He was also one of the most cautious financiers of Alexandria, and would have turned down Agrippa's request for a loan but for Cypros, who conducted the negotiations with so much dedication that in the end he agreed to help. As he had more faith in her solvency than in her husband's, it was to her he handed fifty thousand drachmas in cash, with a draft on a hundred and fifty thousand more, which Agrippa was authorized to cash only after landing in Italy. At this juncture a change of plans took place. Either because Cypros was guarantor for the loan and was required to stay within legal reach, or because she may have been expecting another child, the family decided to split up. Agrippa sailed to Italy on his own while Cypros collected her brood and returned to Judaea to await the results of her husband's fortune-hunting.

Agrippa landed in Puteoli (Pozzuoli) in the north-east corner of the bay of Naples, and from there sent a deferential note to Capri to inform the emperor of his return. Tiberius invited him over and gave him audience, but the following day a letter arrived from the Roman agent in Judaea, asking for the arrest of the person who owed the imperial treasury so much money. Tiberius immediately forbade Agrippa the court until the debt was paid. Agrippa's resourcefulness never failed him. He went to see his old friend Antonia and got her to lend him three hundred thousand drachmas with which he promptly paid up his debt to the treasury. Tiberius became gracious and appointed him tutor to his grandson Tiberius, son of the dead Drusus who had been Agrippa's youthful companion. It was probably about that time that Cypros gave birth in Judaea to another son, and Agrippa instructed her to name him Drusus to flatter both emperor and heir-presumptive.

His sympathies, however, were with Tiberius's other heir-presumptive Gaius, son of Agrippa's youthful companion Germanicus and grandson to Antonia. To keep in their good books he borrowed from a freedman the enormous sum of one million drachmas, paid Antonia back and proceeded to spend the rest in his usual way, lavishing presents on men of influence. Twenty-four-year-old Gaius Caligula was the most frequent recipient of his hospitality.

Gaius had won his nickname Caligula, translatable as Little Boots, when as a small boy in his father's camp he used to wear a soldier's uniform including a small *caliga,* the military half-boot. Although he was popular with the people Tiberius had by no means made up his mind to make him his successor. He was undecided between him and his own grandson, and naturally each young man had his own hangers-on who hoped to reap a rich reward on the emperor's death.

In AD 36, when Agrippa returned to Italy, Tiberius was in his mid-seventies and far from well. Because he had enjoyed good health most of his life he rarely consulted a doctor, but during his last years he wasted away without being noticeably ill. He suffered from fainting fits and at times his body would become so rigid that he could be taken for dead; then, to everyone's consternation, he would come to and be as fit as ever.

It was possibly while discussing the emperor's disconcerting habit of all but dying that Agrippa expressed the hope that Tiberius would really die soon and make way for Caligula. The two friends were driving in Agrippa's chariot when the remark was made, within earshot of the freedman who was driving it. When some time later Agrippa accused his freedman of stealing his expensive clothes and had him arrested, Eutychus informed Tiberius that his master was guilty of treason. Tiberius, to give him his due, was well aware that both his heirs-presumptive had their followers and was not inclined to make a case of it. But Agrippa felt honour bound to clear his name and insisted on a hearing.

In the summer of that year Tiberius made one of his rare sorties out of Capri. He put up at Tusculum (near the modern Frascati), some thirteen miles south-east of Rome, where the Roman nobility came out to pay their respects. Tiberius had just had lunch and was taken in his litter round the hippodrome for what must have been his constitutional. Agrippa and Caligula walked ahead of him while Antonia walked by the side of the litter. She took the opportunity to repeat Agrippa's pressing request for a trial. Much against his will Tiberius gave in and had Eutychus fetched and interrogated in his presence. Eutychus repeated what he had heard in the chariot and possibly added some more. When he finished Tiberius instructed the commander of his guards to arrest the culprit, then beckoned to his litter-bearers to resume their walk round the hippodrome. The commander, like the rest of the nobles present, was not quite clear who the culprit was and waited for Tiberius to complete the circuit and come to a halt again in order to ask him whom exactly he should arrest. The emperor wearily pointed to Agrippa and when his meaning was still not grasped, mentioned him by name.

It was too late for Agrippa to protest his innocence and remind Tiberius of his past loyalty. He was arrested there and then, and in keeping with the security practice of the day was handcuffed to a soldier to prevent his escape. There he stood in the heat of the sun, still wearing his sumptuous crimson robe, thirsty after his heavy lunch and stunned by the sudden turn of events. Instinctively he beckoned to one of Caligula's slaves to get him a drink of water and had the presence of mind to thank him and promise to repay him for his kindness.

When the excitement died down a little he was taken to a prison camp nearer Rome. The camp commander kept him waiting in the courtyard with the other prisoners while arrangements were being made to distribute them to their prison quarters. The rest of the story is best told in Josephus's own words:

There he stood in chains in front of the fortress together with many other prisoners, leaning despondently against a tree. An old German prisoner noticed that a certain bird which the Romans call a *bubo* [owl] had alighted on the tree. He asked the soldier to whom he was handcuffed who the crimson-dressed prisoner was, and when he learnt that his name was Agrippa, that he was Jewish and one of the most distinguished men of Judaea, he asked permission to talk to him about Jewish customs. His request granted, he came up to Agrippa and said to him through an interpreter:

'Young man [Agrippa was in the middle or late forties], you must be in despair at the turn of events which has upset your fortune, and you may not believe me when I tell you that Providence has already ordained your release. I swear to you by my ancestral gods and the gods of this country that what I am about to tell you is based on the interpretation of a divine message, not on a desire to cheer you up by false hopes. Although I am exposing myself to danger when I speak to you in this way, I feel bound to clarify to you what the gods intend. You shall be released forthwith from these chains and elevated to the highest point of honour and power. You will be the envy of all those who now pity you, and you will be blessed with children to whom you will leave your wealth'.[2]

Into this astonishing piece of prophecy the German wove a request and a word of warning:

Remember, when you have this good fortune in your hands, help me also to gain release from this bitter fate which we now share.[3]

And remember, when you see this bird again, your death will follow within five days.[4]

It was all very well for the old man to prophesy future grandeur, but for the time being Agrippa found it more practical to put his trust in friends rather than in owls. Antonia was as reliable as ever and bribed the prison commander to grant his prisoner some concessions. Agrippa was allowed a daily visit to the baths, his favourite dishes, a bedding of smuggled clothes. He could receive friends and, most important of all, was daily handcuffed to guards who had been chosen for their relatively even temper. Six months passed in this way.

In the spring of the following year Tiberius again ventured out of Capri, intending to visit Rome. He never reached it. He died without ever returning to the city he had left eleven years earlier. When the news trickled out one of Agrippa's freedmen drove as fast as he could to the prison camp and met him just as he was leaving the baths, handcuffed as usual to an armed centurion. The freedman called out in Hebrew that the lion was dead. Agrippa had heard that one before. He guardedly expressed the hope that this time it was really true. An excited explanation poured out. The centurion did not like the sound of that exchange in a foreign language and demanded to be told what was going on. As soon as he learnt that Tiberius was dead he released the prisoner from his chains and ordered a celebration. While they were feasting another messenger arrived hot foot from town and said that the rumour was false, the emperor was very much alive. It was back to handcuffs for Agrippa with his guards doubled.

But this time Tiberius was really dead, having been helped along by the impatient Caligula who, according to one account, refused him refreshment when he recovered from a fainting fit or, according to another, had someone deal him the *coup de grâce* by smothering him under a pillow. At long last Gaius Caligula was emperor. Tiberus's hated reign was over and Rome looked to his successor with hope and enthusiasm.

One of Caligula's first actions was to have his old friend transferred from prison to his house in Rome, where he was still kept under guard although without the inconvenience of the handcuffs. A few days later he was summoned to the palace. Agrippa carefully resumed his mean clothes and unkempt appearance before presenting himself to the emperor for whose sake he had suffered imprisonment. Caligula had him shaved, washed and changed.

When he was presentable he hung on his neck a heavy chain of gold instead of the iron one from prison and informed him that he was bestowing on him his dead uncle Philip's tetrarchy. Then, with his own hands, he placed a diadem on his head. Agrippa was king.

The fortress of Herodium, built by Herod the Great

Herod's Tower of Phasael, now known as the Tower of David, scene of Berenice's barefoot appeal to Florus

The Banyas near Caesarea Philippi, capital of Agrippa II and Berenice

Tomb of Queen Helena

Chapter IV

A king's daughter

BERENICE was nine years old when her father became king. The girl who until then was no more than the offspring of a cadet branch of the Herodian-Hasmonaean house suddenly became a princess. After an insecure childhood, punctuated by frequent changes of scene to avoid unpleasantnesses, a glamorous future was opening up before her. The unknown daughter of a vagabond fortune-hunter was now the envy of the entire Herodian family, whose ramifications spread from Judaea through a large part of the Roman empire to include Syria, Lebanon, Armenia, Greece and Italy.

Her full name was Julia Berenice; Julia to denote her connection with the Julian house, Berenice after the grandmother she had never known. In naming his daughter after a mother he had no cause to remember with affection, Agrippa was simply acting in accordance with family tradition. The house of Herod was not adventurous in its quest for names. Some were used over and over again to the confusion of outsiders. Aristobulus was a popular one. Once borne by a Hasmonaean high priest, it was proudly bestowed on sons, cousins and distant descendants for generations to come. Alexander was another popular importation from the Greek. Other recurring names were Antipas, or Antipater, and Philip. Agrippa was a notable departure from tradition, but the name was immediately absorbed by the family and later given to more than one descendant.

It is interesting to reflect that the very family who led the Jewish revolt against hellenization during the reign of Antiochus IV in the second century BC and whose ancestral name—Hasmonaean—became a symbol of nationalism, was the first to succumb to foreign influence when it came to the naming of children. Hebrew names like Mattathias, Judas or Eleazar virtually disappeared; and even those Hasmonaean high priests and kings who boasted Hebrew names like John (Yochanan) or Jonathan for religious representation, had Greek ones for the rest of the world.

Girls' names followed the same pattern. Mariamme remained high on the list, and so did Salome; neither because they were Hebrew, but more likely because their original bearers were ladies of distinction in the house of Herod. Cypros was another favourite. Derived from the Greek form of the Semitic *kufra,* a sweet-smelling flower, it was first borne by Herod's Arab mother and then given to a number of descendants. Berenice, from the Macedonian *Pherenice,* meaning the Bearer of Victory, was a departure from tradition. Why the first Berenice was so called is difficult to establish; but once the name made its appearance it was fully accepted and put into circulation. Names, like marriages, were sought for preference within the family circle.

Agrippa was no innovator. His first son was called Julius Marcus Agrippa like himself; his first daughters Berenice and Mariamme. It was only when he was in Rome trying to win imperial favour that he departed from tradition and called a second son by the name of Drusus, to commemorate Tiberius's dead son. Agrippa's Drusus did not survive either and died in infancy.

Berenice was born about AD 28, probably in the desert fortress near Beer-Sheba, at the time when her father was going through the blackest period of his life. Shortly after her birth the family moved to Tiberias where she lived until she was about six. That was the longest single residence in one place she was to have for many years. Life in Tiberias must have left an impression. She would have met her relatives, Antipas the tetrarch and his wife Herodias; she would have known her cousin Salome; and although she would have been too young to understand much of the adult life about her, she would have absorbed some of it. As she grew older she might have overheard scornful whispers against her father and would have sensed the growing tension between him and the tetrarch's family. Equally she would have sensed the harmony between her parents and noted the fact that, unlike so many of her married relatives, her mother and father had affection for one another. Materially Berenice lacked little. Agrippa's extravagance provided his family with luxuries even when his revenue could not.

She was five when Jesus was crucified in Jerusalem, an event which must have been discussed by the tetrarch's family but which could not have been understood by her. She was six when her father's quarrel with Antipas brought to an end her relatively sheltered existence in Tiberias. She would well remember how one day, after a visit to the foreign city of Tyre, she was told that the family was not returning to what she must have considered home, but was going on to a big town in Syria called Antioch. There was a new house to get used to, new people and new ways. There was an uncle named Aristobulus who did not seem pleased to see them, and a young cousin who was deaf. The climate was much cooler than Tiberias, and clothes were different.

For reasons that Berenice would have been too young to understand, the stay in Antioch was brief. The family left it for the port of Ptolemais and from there travelled by road to a smaller port called Anthedon. Berenice knew that she was going on a long sea voyage, to the legendary place of her father's youth. Expecting so much from Rome, she must have been confused to see a Roman official come on board and arrest him; still more confused and quite likely frightened to be woken up in the dead of the night to the sound of strange activity, culminating in the cutting of cables and a stealthy sailing out to sea. Alexandria, the next port of call, would have been even more unsettling. There were many strange and unfriendly faces, and both parents were preoccupied with other people. At last Berenice saw her father board a ship to go alone to the promised land of Rome, leaving her behind with her mother, her elder brother Agrippa and her younger sister Mariamme.

In the midst of all these bewildering events Cypros must have been an island of security. Her unswerving devotion to her husband must have had a stabilizing effect on her children and helped them to accept the frequent changes in their circumstances. For the next year or two Berenice lived with her mother in Judaea, waiting for news from the father who had gone away to Rome. When it came it was full of contradictions. Agrippa was received at court. He was forbidden the court. The emperor held him in high esteem. The emperor put him in prison. Then came the most startling news of all. Agrippa had been made king. Her mother Cypros was queen, her brother was a prince and she and her sister were princesses. The royal family awaited with impatience the return of the king, in order to take up residence in their new kingdom.

They had to wait a long time. Either because it was discourteous to leave too soon after his elevation, or because he felt the need to consolidate his position, Agrippa stayed on in Rome for eighteen months. He was experienced enough to know that what had been so easily given could just as easily be withdrawn. Client-kings had no treaty with Rome. They held their office on grace and favour tenure and could be dethroned at any time at the whim of the emperor. The length of tenure depended on satisfaction given. Against the title conferred on them client-kings had to pay tribute. They were required to help when help was needed and to ensure the safety of their own frontiers. They were autonomous and more or less free to decide their internal policy, but they did not have the right to name their heirs. A native prince, thanks to his familiarity with local conditions, was often better qualified to govern than an official sent from Rome, but he was by no means indispensable. Thus Archelaus, son of Herod, who was not even a king but an ethnarch, was dismissed by Augustus; and Archelaus Sisinnes, king of Cappadocia and father of Glaphyra, was dismissed by Tiberius. Agrippa may well have felt it advisable to remain near the new emperor and make sure that no unexpected intrigue should deprive him of his kingship. For Caligula was distributing kingships left and right. In one session of the senate he gave Ituraea to Sohaemus; Pontus to Polemo; Lesser Armenia to Polemo's brother Cotys; and to Rhoemetacles a part of Thrace he had taken away from Cotys.

For the time being Caligula could not do enough for his old friend. Having made him king, he also got the senate to give him the rank of praetor. Together with Antiochus, whom Caligula had nominated king of Commagene (in south-east Turkey), they made an inseparable trio. They spent so much of their time together that jealous courtiers accused the two kings of being the emperor's evil spirits and alleged they were encouraging him to behave like a tyrant. Not that Caligula needed such encouragement. The golden promise of his first year as emperor was not fulfilled. It was not long before he manifested those traits of cruelty and megalomania for which his short reign became notorious. It required tact

46

and insight to retain his favour. Agrippa possessed both. Antiochus did not and was dethroned.

In the autumn of 38 Agrippa set out to take possession of his kingdom which, thanks to Caligula's generosity, included not only uncle Philip's tetrarchy but also Abilene (between Damascus and Anjar). In his retinue travelled a young freedman who, as a slave, had once offered him a drink of water. True to his promise Agrippa had bought his freedom from Caligula and made him steward of his estate, in which capacity he later served Berenice. There is no record of what happened to the old German who had prophesied grandeur to a fellow-prisoner. Perhaps he died before Agrippa was released.

On the way back he stopped in Alexandria. For the local Jewish community it was a great day. They revelled in the glory of the Jewish king who did them the honour of visiting them and he was escorted everywhere by a splendid bodyguard with shining armour of silver and gold. Alexander the *alabarch* congratulated himself on the foresight which had led him to lend money to the fugitive who was now king. But the jubilation of the Alexandrian Jewry was short lived. The Greek inhabitants of the city gave vent to their anti-Jewish feelings by demonstrating against the king. The demonstrations led to riots and bloodshed, openly encouraged by the Roman governor of Egypt. Agrippa, who all his life had been concerned only with personal ambition, now showed the other side of his nature. He took up the case of his co-religionists and sent a representation to Caligula. But no sooner had he left the city than the mob got out of hand. They put statues of Caligula in synagogues and demanded that the Jews should worship them like the rest of the empire. Meeting resistance, they set the synagogues on fire, looted stores, drove the Jews to one section of the city and killed many of them. In the meantime Agrippa's message had reached Rome and Caligula sent instructions to punish the Roman governor who favoured the rioters. Law and order were gradually restored and Jewish civil rights reaffirmed. But in the general turmoil the *alabarch*'s family suffered a loss. One of his sons, Tiberius Alexander, went over to paganism. Judaism was too much of a handicap in the military career he intended to follow.

The arrival of Agrippa in his new kingdom caused a stir all over the country. He would not have been true to himself had he let the occasion go without ostentation. In the capital Caesarea Philippi there were celebrations and receptions for congratulatory delegations. Uncle Philip had lived frugally. Agrippa, with a queen at his side and a family, proceeded to live in his usual style. His palace was full of freedmen, fawning courtiers, servants. The king's word was law, and members of the family benefited from his reflected glory. For young Berenice it was her first taste of power.

Agrippa's nearest relatives viewed his rise with a speculative eye. His younger brother Aristobulus was quick to apologize for the past and was invited to join the royal household as political adviser. But his sister Herodias was bitterly jealous. She could not forget that it was she who had given Agrippa his first chance to come back to the public eye as a paid servant in her husband's employ, nor could she forgive the insults he had flung on Antipas before walking out on him. It was galling to think that this man was now king while her husband was only a tetrarch. She nagged him to go to Rome, accuse Agrippa of some treachery and claim as a reward the title of king. Antipas was old and not as ambitious as his wife, but in the end he succumbed and set out with her for Italy.

Agrippa got wind of the plot and sent a trusted freedman to represent him before Caligula, preferring to stay away while the outcome was in doubt. When he heard that the emperor had given judgement in his favour and decided to punish Antipas by banishment, he followed his freedman to Italy. He found Caligula more generous than ever and received from him Antipas's tetrarchy. In AD 39 he was king of Gaulanitis, Batanea, Trachonitis, Abilene, Galilee and Peraea. To mark his gratitude he called the daughter born to him that year Drusilla, after Caligula's dead sister and mistress. As for his own sister Herodias, although she was offered the choice of staying behind, she preferred to follow Antipas to his place of banishment near the border between Spain and Gaul, where they ended their days in obscurity.

On his return from Rome, Agrippa moved his seat from Caesarea Philippi to Tiberias which was the more civilized of his two capitals. The palace that Antipas had built in the Graeco-Roman style and decorated, pagan-like, with animal carvings became his new home. Berenice however was not allowed to stay long in any one place. Sometime during her father's commuting between his kingdom and Italy, the family was moved to Rome and installed in a sumptuous house fit to entertain an emperor. Berenice's education was given its finishing touches. Like her parents she spoke Aramaic, which was the popular language of the Jews in her time, and Hebrew, which was the language of the scholars and the learned. She was also familiar with Greek, through the infiltration of Hellenistic culture and expressions into everyday life. In Rome she perfected her knowledge and became quite proficient. There she also learnt some Latin, while her mother watched over her religious education. To these accomplishments she added natural charm and beauty. She was reputed to be as beautiful as her ancestress Mariamme the Hasmonaean. Romantic writers have described her through the ages as red-haired, auburn, or even fair. In the absence of any authentic description or representation, and taking into account the laws of heredity, one would imagine she was most likely dark and Semitic in type, like the Idumaeans and Hasmonaeans from whom she was descended.

In the meantime the eastern part of the empire was becoming a scene of recurring trouble. Caligula had conceived the notion that he was a god and demanded to be worshipped like one. All over the empire his statues were being erected in temples, and in the course of things they had to be put up in synagogues. For Jews it was out of the question to allow an idol in their place of worship. When the order was forced on them bloody riots burst out, first in Alexandria, then in Jamnia (Yavne) which had once belonged to the elder Salome and was now imperial property. The Jews were prepared to die for their faith. Many did. The survivors were deprived of their civil rights. After much bloodshed the Jewish community in Alexandria decided to send a deputation to Rome to plead with the emperor for the restoration of their rights and the revocation of the order to place statues in synagogues. The deputation was headed by two brothers. One was Alexander the *alabarch*, high official in the service of the Romans, and a personal friend of Antonia's; the other was Philo the philosopher, the most prominent Jewish thinker of his time, who had striven to reconcile Greek philosophy with traditional Jewish thought. Together the two brothers represented the temporal and the spiritual, with Philo acting as the head of the delegation. The mission was a complete failure. The deputation was dismissed in disgrace and the *alabarch* put in prison for good measure.

In the spring of 40, barely six months after he had taken over Antipas's tetrarchy, Agrippa returned to Rome leaving his youngest brother Aristobulus in charge. Their eldest brother Herod, a widower, was already there with a son who was also called Aristobulus. There were two reasons for Agrippa's early return. For one thing it was politic to be near Caligula to make sure of his continued goodwill; for another, having collected the revenue from his enlarged kingdom, he was at last in a position to live in style in the exciting capital of the empire. He little imagined that immediately on his arrival he would be faced with one of the most difficult moral conflicts of his life.

Caligula had not only rejected the pleas of the Alexandrian deputation, but had instructed Petronius, the governor of Syria, to teach the Jews a lesson they would never forget. Petronius was to proceed to Jerusalem and place a statue in the Holy of Holies. Reluctantly he started for Judaea. In Ptolemais he was met by a mass demonstration, followed by another in Tiberias, led by Agrippa's brother, the regent Aristobulus. Petronius correctly deduced that the erection of a statue in the temple would result in a horrible bloodbath for both Jews and Romans. He over-reached his authority, postponed the execution of the order, and wrote to Caligula to explain his deviation from discipline. Then he settled down to await retribution.

Agrippa had left his kingdom before Petronius started for Judaea. It was only after his arrival in Rome that he heard of the failure of Philo's mission and of Caligula's recent order about the temple in Jerusalem. The two extant accounts of how he heard of the order and the courageous stand he took against it vary in detail, but basically they are the same. They both testify to his complete identification with Judaism and his readiness to risk his position and indeed his life to stand by his people.

According to Josephus, Agrippa learnt of the order on his arrival in Rome and proceeded to work against it in a truly oriental fashion by inviting Caligula to a sumptuous feast in his house. Already one of the most lavish hosts in Rome, he now surpassed

himself and offered Caligula such a regal banquet that even the
luxury-satiated emperor was impressed. With the wine Agrippa
adroitly mingled some reminders of his past suffering under the
hands of Tiberius because of his devotion to Caligula. The
emperor became sentimental and told Agrippa he had not rewarded him enough for his loyalty. Agrippa replied that he wanted
nothing. Caligula drunkenly pressed him. Agrippa demurred.
Caligula pressed again. Then Agrippa asked for the revocation of
the order. Caligula, says Josephus, was too embarrassed in front
of all the guests to go back on his word, an emperor's word,
and agreed.

Against this account, which is highly reminiscent of the scriptural story of queen Esther and the Persian king Ahasuerus,
there is Philo's, which on the whole strikes a more realistic note.
Allowing for some dramatic exaggeration, which apparently even
Philo could not resist in retrospect, it is also more in character.

According to Philo, Agrippa hastened to pay his respects to
Caligula and was dismayed at the sour looks he was given. Soon
the truth came out. Caligula told his friend he had no quarrel with
him, only with his co-religionists who were refusing to honour
him as a god. Agrippa was well aware of the emperor's obsession
and did not shrink from paying him lip-service like the rest of the
courtiers. But he was horrified when he heard of his determination
to put an idol in the temple. For once his wits deserted him and
his mind went blank. Philo narrates that Agrippa fainted and had
to be carried away to his house, where he remained unconscious
for the best part of two days. It is more in keeping with Agrippa's
character to assume that after the initial shock he only pretended
faintness in order to make an honourable exit; and that once in
the safety of his house he continued the pretence in order to gain
time to think. He had to work out his attitude to the situation. In
spite of his easy ways in Rome he was a firm believer in the
Jewish idea of an incorporeal god. To allow an idol in the temple
would have betrayed his own conscience; to live up to his faith
would have meant risking his life. Agrippa probably came fairly
quickly to the conclusion that he must obey his conscience and
use his position to avert what would surely result in a general
catastrophe. He employed his solitude to draft in his mind a letter
to Caligula. By the middle of the second day he was ready.

Evidently keeping up the pretence, he weakly called for his freed-men and servants, asked them where he was and was prevailed upon to take a little food. The play-acting must have been part of of his plan, for he knew that the news of his poorly condition would reach Caligula and might help to soften his heart. Having had a meal washed down with nothing but water, Agrippa sent for a tablet and without any rough copy wrote to the emperor. As Philo recorded it, it was a well-thought-out letter, embodying the subtle reasoning of the experienced courtier with the desperate courage of a God-fearing Jew. Agrippa wrote:

Emperor,
Torn between fear and reverence, afraid to bring upon myself the wrath of your sacred person, I have presumed to lay down my petition in writing rather than by word of mouth.

It is accepted that all human beings have a natural affection for the country of their birth and the laws they have been brought up in; you yourself have proved this by your patriotic love for your country and its traditions. It is equally natural for all human beings to regard the customs of their country as excellent, whether this is the case or not, because their judge-ment is swayed by sentiment rather than reason.

As you know I am a Jew born in Jerusalem, the seat of the holy temple dedicated to the most high God. Some of my ances-tors were kings, others high priests; but all regarded priesthood as the greater dignity, for just as God is greater than man, so a high priest is greater than a king. Since this is my heritage, may I implore you on behalf of my nation, my city and my temple to show us your favour.[1]

Reminding the emperor how loyal to Rome the Jews had always been, Agrippa went on to describe the importance of Jerusalem not only as a capital of Judaea, but as a centre of world Jewry, incidentally revealing the extent of the Jewish dispersion in the Graeco-Roman world:

Jerusalem, the place of my birth, is not only the capital of Judaea, but of many other countries as well, because Jewish settlers have gone out to other lands like Egypt, Phoenicia,

Upper and Lower Syria, the distant countries of Pamphylia, Cilicia, most of Asia as far as Bithynia and the remote corners of Pontus; and in Europe to places like Thessaly, Boeotia, Macedonia, Aetolia, Attica, Argos, Corinth and the better part of the Peloponnese. It is not only the continents which are full of Jews but also the best-known islands like Euboea, Cyprus, Crete and the regions beyond the Euphrates. With the exception of a small section of Babylon, there is hardly a habitable region or city in the world without its share of Jewish settlers. When I appeal to you I do so not only on behalf of my country alone, but on behalf of Asia, Europe and Africa; for by showing kindness to one city you will be showing kindness to countless cities, as befits the dignity of Caesar; then every part of the world will resound with your praises and generosity.[2]

Agrippa reminded Caligula that Jerusalem was the first city in the empire to proclaim him emperor, then proceeded to the difficult task of convincing a pagan of the uncompromising nature of abstract monotheism:

The temple of Jerusalem is the house of God and has never admitted any man-made images into its boundaries. Painters and sculptors represent gods as they see them, but the true God is invisible and any attempt to represent his image is blasphemy.[3]

Agrippa went on to quote some praiseworthy precedents from the history of Caligula's own family. He reminded him how his grandfather Marcus Agrippa had paid several visits to the temple during his stay in Jerusalem, how he had sacrificed there on every occasion and how he had so won the affection of the people by his respectful behaviour that they spread flowers all along his route. Then he mentioned that even the wicked Tiberius had shown respect for the Jewish religion. When the Roman procurator Pontius Pilate hung some golden shields in the Antonia, Tiberius ordered them down so as not to offend the susceptibilities of the Jews, even though shields were not statues and a fortress adjoining the temple was not sacred ground. As for Augustus, he had gone out of his way to honour the Jewish religion. Not only had he allowed Jewish communities abroad to send their contributions to the temple funds—disregarding the common accusation that they were diverting the wealth of the empire to Jerusalem—but had ordered a daily sacrifice in the temple of a bull and two lambs. Augustus's wife Julia followed his noble example. She enriched the temple with costly vessels of silver and gold to show her respect for the cult.

Begging Caligula to follow in the footsteps of his illustrious ancestors, Agrippa began to harp on a personal note, dwelling with due gratitude on all the imperial favours he had received: his life, his liberty, his kingdom. He ended his long letter with the most courageous declaration of faith a client-king had ever made before a Roman emperor:

> I am indebted to you for the dignity of a crown and the gift of further territories in Trachonitis and Galilee. But having bestowed on me such extraordinary kindness, do not deprive me, I beg of you, of the most important thing of all. I am prepared to return to my former humble position and give up everything in exchange for one favour, the permission to preserve our native traditions. How will I ever be able to raise my head if the laws of my country are not protected and maintained? My people will regard me as a traitor, while others will consider me as unworthy of your friendship, and what can be worse than that? If you continue to call me a friend I should be taken for a coward who refused to call on your friendship to save the temple from disaster. If however you take your favour away from me, do not put me in chains as Tiberius did, but kill me at once. For what use would life be to your Agrippa if he loses your friendship, the only hope and comfort he ever had in the whole world?[4]

Unpredictably Caligula saw the good sense of Agrippa's plea and gave way, although with ill grace. He instructed Petronius to leave things as they were; if the statue had already been put in the temple he was not to dislodge it; if it had not, he was not to do anything more about it. His letter crossed Petronius's, in which the governor informed him of his decision to postpone the execution of the imperial order on his own initiative. That was a breach of discipline that Caligula was not going to overlook. He wrote again instructing Petronius to punish himself by committing suicide, presumably by cutting his veins, a method of self-disposal which although somewhat messy was considered both efficient and dignified. Fortunately for Petronius the suicide order was delayed en route and reached him only after the emperor's death, when it was no longer valid.

Berenice was twelve when she witnessed her father's brave stand against Caligula and mature enough to grasp the full implication of the situation. She had been brought up to believe in the most fundamental of Jewish principles, and her father's example may well have spurred her on when years later she herself felt called upon to use her high position to plead with a Roman procurator. This time she could only share in the general suspense that preceded Caligula's retreat. Like her father, she must have prayed fervently for good sense to prevail, and like him she must have been thankful for the happy outcome that meant a reprieve for her countrymen and continued imperial favour for her own family. For Agrippa's moral victory over Caligula did not lose him his friendship. He remained his companion and intimate for the remainder of the emperor's short life, until his assassination the following year. Even then Agrippa behaved with his usual tact and sense of propriety, paying his respects to the dead before going to salute his successor.

Chapter V

The go-between

WRITING many years after Caligula's murder, Josephus left a vivid description of the man who had been responsible for Agrippa's rise to power.

He was a first-rate orator in both Greek and Latin. His improvised speeches were more brilliant than other people's carefully prepared ones, and he could carry his audience with him on any topic he chose to discuss. He had a natural aptitude and took great care to develop it ... but the advantages of education could not put a stop to the corruption that set in with his rise to power.[1]

Even before he succeeded to office he was corrupt and perverse. He was a slave to pleasure, a lover of slander, a coward and a murderer. If he was afraid of anybody he had him put out of the way. He was greedy and obtained his wealth through miscarriage of justice. He considered himself above the law. When he tried to be generous he lavished his generosity on people who least deserved it. He was susceptible to flattery but indifferent even to his closest friends in their hour of need. He could not tolerate opposition to any of his whims and inflicted severe punishments at the slightest provocation.[2]

It speaks a great deal for Agrippa's political agility that he maintained the goodwill of such a person without having to give way to him on every single point. On the other hand he could not have done so without condoning his general behaviour and possibly even encouraging him in his mode of life. In the process he made himself a number of enemies who envied his success and resented his influence. Caligula's sudden death posed a dilemma.

To seek justice against the murderers was unrealistic; to declare himself at one with them would have been unconvincing.

As usual Agrippa's luck and his unerring instinct for self-preservation pointed out the right course of action. While the palace was thrown into confusion by the news of the murder, he approached the dead body, laid it upon a bed, covered it and gave it a reverential embrace. This allowed him time to glean enough information to help him calculate his next move.

Caligula's assassination in January 41 was the culmination of three years of hatred and fear. As soon as the news of the murder was confirmed, the senate was convened to consider what was to be done. Some favoured a return to republican rule; others wanted to continue the principate but could not agree on a candidate. While the senators were debating their views, the praetorian guard acted. Some soldiers running wild in the palace came upon Claudius, Antonia's son and Caligula's uncle, crouching in terror in an alcove behind a curtain. Half in jest they hauled him out, dragged him to their barracks and declared him emperor.

By the time Agrippa had finished paying his respects to the dead Caligula, he had made up his mind what to do. He had grown up with Claudius during his early Rome days and continued to cultivate his friendship well into their middle age. His course was clear. He pushed his way through the clamouring soldiers until he reached the barracks and was the first person of consequence to congratulate the reluctant emperor and offer his support. As a praetor his goodwill counted; as a man of proved shrewdness his services were of value. His offer was gratefully accepted.

Having come to an understanding with Claudius, Agrippa made his way back to his house as discreetly as possible. He quickly changed into indoor clothes to give the impression he had not been out and sprinkled his hair with a scent he was apparently known to use only when at home. The summons to join the senators in their deliberations found him having an intimate meal with his wife. He rushed out as he was and was most surprised to learn that the soldiers had made Claudius emperor. He agreed it was a bad business and that Rome needed a republic; but he was forced to point out that in case of a conflict, the soldiers would far outnumber the forces at the senate's disposal. Having thus dampened the senators' ardour, he offered a possible solution. As an old friend of Claudius, he would personally undertake the dangerous mission of going to the barracks and pleading with him to renounce of his own free will the power that had been thrust on him. The senate agreed.

Agrippa proceeded to the barracks slowly enough to allow a trusted messenger to get there before him and suggest to Claudius what answer to make to the proposal. When he actually delivered his message, Claudius told him to inform the senate that he had decided to keep the power the soldiers had vested in him, but assure them that he was not going to abuse it. By that time many of the senators had decided to play safe and had left Rome for their country houses. The hundred or so who remained were so divided and dispirited that when they heard Claudius's answer, as repeated by Agrippa, they decided not to offer any resistance. Claudius, who all his life had been considered stupid and a figure of fun, was proclaimed emperor. He proved to be a man of intelligence in spite of his unprepossessing ways:

He was in his fifties [at the time of his accession]. In mental ability he was by no means inferior, as his faculties had been in constant training; in fact he had actually written some historical treatises. But he was sickly in body, so that his head and his hands shook slightly. Because of this his voice was also faltering and he did not himself read all the measures that he introduced before the senate, but would give them to the quaestor to read, though at first at least he was generally present. Whatever he did read himself, he usually delivered sitting down.[3]

It was difficult to gauge how a man like Claudius, who all his life had been at the mercy of his imperious family, would react to power. Agrippa must have had some anxious moments while the new emperor was asserting his authority. One of Claudius's first orders was to destroy a collection of assorted poisons he had found in Caligula's house. Then he ruled that no one was to approach him without being thoroughly searched first. Having assured himself of his personal safety, he proceeded to show his gratitude. He confirmed Agrippa as king of all the territories that had been given to him by Caligula and added to them the greatest prize of all, the kingdom of Judaea.

For thirty-five years, ever since Archelaus the son of Herod had been banished to Gaul, Judaea had been governed by Roman procurators. Their reign had not been smooth, and the fifth of them, Pontius Pilate, had been recalled to Rome a few years after the crucifixion of Jesus Christ to answer charges of maladministration, after which he too was banished to Gaul. The sixth lasted only a year, and the seventh was in his fourth year of office when Claudius became emperor and decided to end the rule of procurators as arbitrarily as it had begun. He confirmed his arrangement with Agrippa by having it engraved on bronze tablets which were then displayed in the Capitol, and by taking the appropriate oaths in the senate. At Agrippa's request, he made his eldest brother Herod king of Chalcis (Hanjar, in Lebanon). At the same time Agrippa was made senator and Herod praetor. Together the two brothers went to the senate and made a speech of thanks in Greek.

Claudius's other acts of kindness included reinstating Agrippa's old friend Antiochus of Commagene, and confirming another friend, Polemo, as king of Pontus. Of less political importance, but of greater personal consequence, was the releasing from prison of Alexander the *alabarch*, whose son Marcus was engaged to Berenice. But matrimonial plans had to be put aside while urgent political matters needed to be settled.

Ever since the destruction of Jerusalem by Nebuchadnezzar in the sixth century BC, there had been a Jewish dispersion outside Palestine, which the passage of time increased rather than decreased. In the Graeco-Roman world nearly every city had its Jewish community; and although its members were loyal to Rome, their separateness made them suspect and hated. Sometimes the hatred stemmed from ignorance of their religious laws; often it was due to the Jewish custom of sending regular contributions to the temple funds in Jerusalem, when they might have spent them on the welfare of their host-cities. Troubles between Jews and pagans were not infrequent. The traditional Roman policy however was to protect the Jewish communities and allow them to practise their cult unmolested; so much so that sometimes

Jews were exempt from military service which would have required them to fail in their observance of the Sabbath.

Contemporary evidence suggests that during Claudius's time the number of Jews living in the empire amounted to seven or eight millions, which was about a tenth of its general population. The two chief centres were Rome and Alexandria. In Rome they had a considerable share of the import trade. They had their own communal organizations, their own synagogues and their own underground cemeteries, the forerunners of the Christian catacombs. Julius Caesar had been kind to them, Tiberius banished them. Still they thrived and many of them had wealth and position.

The Jewish community in Alexandria was even larger. It started when Alexander the Great attracted the Jews by offering them the same rights as the Greeks. They had thrived to such an extent that their numbers reached one-fifth of the city's total population, or even, according to some accounts, two-fifths. Their wealth and their separateness were a constant source of irritation to the Greek inhabitants, who had demonstrated their feelings during the riots that followed Agrippa's royal visit to Alexandria. After the failure of Philo's mission to Caligula, Alexandrian Jewry was in a worse state than ever. Those who survived the riots were deprived of their civil rights and continually harassed by the Greeks with the connivance of Roman officials. The news of Caligula's murder galvanized the Jews into action. They armed themselves and fought back for their lives and property. There were attacks and counter-attacks, plunder and more bloodshed. Alexandria was not a safe place for anybody to live in.

Apart from his usual concern for the welfare of his co-religionists even in territories outside his jurisdiction, Agrippa now had an added reason to desire the restoration of normal conditions in Alexandria. Berenice, after her marriage to the son of the *alabarch*, was likely to settle down in Alexandria, or at least live there part of the time. Neither she, nor her future husband and in-laws, could be expected to return to a city torn by civil strife and expose themselves to a hostile mob. Nor could it be visualized that in the event of Berenice having issue, the grandchildren of the great king Agrippa would be at the mercy of Roman officials or Greek rioters. With his personal concern enhancing his instinctive solidarity with his fellow-Jews, Agrippa urged Claudius to review the situation. So did his brother Herod, now also a king and a person of consequence in imperial circles. Claudius issued an edict confirming the right of the Alexandrian Jews to live according to their religion without being molested. On Agrippa's and Herod's requests he then issued a second one, somewhat differently worded, in favour of the Jews in the rest of the empire.

As could have been foreseen, the Jews of Alexandria were jubilant, the Greeks roused to further acts of hostility. They demanded justice against the Jews who had started the riots after Caligula's murder. The Jews sent another delegation to Rome to reinforce Philo's. After a brief enquiry Claudius made his final decision known in a letter he sent to the Alexandrians, a copy of which was found in the Fayum in Egypt. It reached Egypt towards the end of 41 and was conspicuously displayed for the customary period of thirty days.

The text of the letter suggests that Claudius was more strict with the Jews than Agrippa may have wished him to be, or Josephus made him out to be. While the Alexandrians were ordered to refrain from any acts of violence, the Jews were firmly told not to provoke them. Furthermore, they were to give up their ambition to benefit from Greek gymnastic education, which was the key to civil dignities; to stop encouraging Jewish immigration to Alexandria, and never again to importune an emperor with two delegations when one—presumably Philo's—should have done. In the course of his long letter Claudius wrote:

I conjure the Alexandrians to behave gently and kindly towards the Jews who have inhabited the same city for many years, and not to dishonour any of their customs in their worship of their god, but to allow them to keep their own ways, as they did in the time of the divine Augustus and as I too, having heard both sides, have confirmed.

The Jews, on the other hand, I order not to aim to more than they have previously had and not in future to send two embassies as if they lived in two cities, a thing which had never been done before, and not to intrude themselves into the games presided over by the *gymnasiarchoi* [men at the head of the education institutions of a Greek city] since they enjoy what is their own, and in a city which is not theirs they possess an abundance of all good things. Nor are they to bring in or invite Jews from Syria or Egypt, or I shall be forced to conceive graver suspicions. If they disobey, I shall proceed against them in every way as fomenting a common plague on the whole world.[4]

By the time Claudius's letter was displayed in Egypt, Agrippa had already left Rome. There was no question of his staying on and leading a life of pleasure away from his duties. Claudius was the first to urge him to leave and take charge of his new kingdom which, with the addition of Samaria, was as large as that of Herod the Great. Early in 41 Agrippa took his leave and returned to Judaea, little suspecting that he was never again to see his beloved Rome. With him went his wife and daughters, including the newly married Berenice and her husband, Marcus Julius Alexander.

Chapter VI

Life in Jerusalem

IT was an accepted practice in the house of Herod to arrange marriages for young princes and princesses at a very tender age in order to strengthen family ties and foster political alliances. Sometimes an arrangement made for a girl when she was three or four failed to materialize when she reached marriageable age, but the usefulness of the practice was never in doubt.

No early engagement could however be contemplated for Berenice. When she was three or four her father was a man of no consequence and no one was in a hurry to offer him the bride-price that a prospective bridegroom was expected to pay the bride's father. She reached the age of nine without any bids having been made for her hand. Then the dramatic change in her fortune took place. Her father became king and she a royal match. Still money was of great importance. Agrippa chose as a bridegroom the son of Alexander the *alabarch,* one of the richest Jews in the Graeco-Roman world.

The *alabarch* had two sons. The elder, called Tiberius Julius Alexander like himself, had military and political ambitions. The younger, Marcus Julius Alexander, was making a promising career in the world of finance and commerce. The same year that Agrippa was made king by Caligula, Marcus was already the head of a large commercial agency which exported goods to India and Arabia.

The idea of a match between the rising young merchant and the eldest daughter of the newly appointed king must have occurred to both fathers during Agrippa's short sojourn in Alexandria in AD 38 on his way back from Rome. The *alabarch,* who was his host on that occasion, was too realistic to expect the return of the two hundred thousand drachmas he had lent him a couple of years earlier. But if regarded as bride-price, it was not too large a

63

sum to pay for the privilege of being allied to a reigning Hasmonaean king. For Agrippa it was an honourable way of cancelling a debt he knew he would never be able to repay. It was a happy arrangement all round.

Berenice probably did not meet her intended husband for some time, but it was as a young woman already engaged that she went to Rome to put the finishing touches to her education. A date for the wedding had not been fixed. Although there was no specific ruling, custom favoured twelve and half as the earliest age for marriage. While Berenice was approaching that age in her parents' house in Rome, her betrothed continued his business transactions in the east.

Marcus's business agency was working for a large trading company owned by a certain Nicanor. The eastern trade of the Roman empire reached one of its highest peaks during that period. Merchandise destined for the Indian and Arab markets included wheat, wine from Italy, Greece and Asia Minor, anise, garments, leather goods, linden-wood products, hemp, silver bullion, oil. Such extensive trade required a large network of commercial agencies. Nicanor's transport service employed some twenty such agencies along the trading route, of which Marcus's was probably one of the largest.

Marcus worked to a set routine. The merchandise was assembled in Egypt from wherever it had been ordered, then sent up the Nile to Coptos. From Coptos his men took it along the caravan-route to the busy Red Sea ports of Berenice or Myos Hormos (Mussel Harbour), where it would be loaded on to ships. The Coptos-Myos Hormos caravan took six or seven days; the Coptos-Berenice caravan up to twelve. Both ports were equally busy and it was estimated that well over a hundred ships went through each of them every year.

The transports left their assembly points in Upper Egypt regularly throughout the year, and Marcus must have been a very busy man. He did not necessarily accompany them, for he had his subagents all along the route, but he would have visited the Red Sea ports from time to time to inspect shipments and keep in touch with Nicanor's company. Rome was not on his route, but he may have visited it occasionally to maintain contact with his future in-laws.

Still no date for the wedding was fixed. There were political difficulties. Alexandria, where Berenice would be expected to live, was torn by riots; moreover, her future father-in-law, the *alabarch*, had been put in prison by Caligula after the failure of Philo's mission. Agrippa was not the man to marry his daughter to the son of a state prisoner. Both families waited for better times.

The year 41 brought several welcome developments. Caligula was dead, the *alabarch* was released, Claudius reaffirmed the rights of Alexandrian Jewry, and Berenice was in her thirteenth year. The time was propitious for marriage. Any regrets that Agrippa may have felt, now that his kingdom was as great as Herod's, at having promised his daughter to a commoner, must have been soothed by the thought that as in-laws he was gaining not only the rich Alexander, but also Philo the philosopher.

The wedding ceremony was solemnized according to the Jewish religion, but the feast must have been more Roman than traditional. All Agrippa's influential acquaintances would have been there; senators, praetorian guard officers, freedmen. Some companions from Caligula's days, just reinstated or confirmed by Claudius, would also have attended; Antiochus king of Commagene, Polemo king of Pontus, perhaps his brother Cotys of Lesser Armenia, certainly Herod of Chalcis. Old Antonia was dead, but Claudius may well have wished to honour Agrippa with his presence. Berenice must have been in a whirl of excitement. Never before had a Herodian princess had so many crowned heads at her wedding.

At the end of the celebrations the royal family set out for Judaea. The triumphant entry into Jerusalem was an occasion that no member of the household could possibly miss.

For the people of Judaea, who for thirty-five years had been under Roman procurators, the accession of Agrippa was a boon beyond their wildest dreams. Whatever they might have felt about him in the days of his fortune-hunting was forgotten in the tremendous relief of having a Jewish king again. Agrippa made his return an occasion for a great show of religious devotion. All Jerusalem must have crowded into the temple courts on the day that the king had scheduled for his personal thanksgiving ceremony. He offered no less than a thousand sacrifices and presented the temple with the heavy golden chain once given to him by Caligula, ceremoniously hanging it up in its allotted place, probably over the horn-shaped treasure chests in the forecourt. Like his grandfather Herod he gave his subjects further cause to rejoice when he remitted their taxes for that year. He then took up his official residence in Jerusalem, moving between the old Hasmonaean palace near the temple and Herod's magnificent palace-fortress in the upper city, a part of which is still preserved in what is now known as the Tower of David near the Jaffa Gate.

Rabbinical tradition maintained that he who had not seen Jerusalem in its heyday had never seen a beautiful city. Making allowances for patriotic pride, it must still have been a beautiful place, not much different from the Old City of today. On the outside it was surrounded by a strong wall fortified by many towers of uneven height. Within, the splendid Herodian palaces and public buildings rose over clusters of small houses and dazzled the eyes with their white roofs and colonnades. Viewed from the height of the surrounding hills, it presented a striking array of noble buildings. The most magnificent of all was the temple, Herod's superb gift to the people of Judaea, with its gilded pinnacles soaring towards the ever-blue sky.

The town itself was a maze of narrow streets, lanes and alleys, with overlapping houses where some hundred thousand people lived, or even a hundred and fifty thousand. It was the largest city in the country, as befitted the capital. The lower town was densely built up with mean, mud-coloured houses roofed with reeds and beaten earth. The upper town, where the rich lived, had houses covered with tiles. There were scarcely any wide avenues or open spaces within the city walls. One exception was a paved square surrounded by colonnades and bounded on one side by the cube-shaped Antonia fortress. Smaller squares were called after the trades that flourished round them; the Butchers' Square, the Wool-Weavers' Square, the Fishmongers', the Fullers'. There were hardly any gardens and only a few trees grew in the inner courtyards of houses.

Some streets were paved and cut into steps to facilitate the passage of men and beasts in a city that was full of inclines. They were so narrow that two asses with side-baskets could hardly pass and even people on foot would jostle one another. The traders' stalls lined the streets in a permanent open-air market and robbed them of further precious space. There were no carriages driving over the stepped streets, only rich men's litters. The ways were mostly cluttered up with herds of sheep and cattle driven to the temple for the daily sacrifice. Their bleating and lowing mingled with the shouts of the tradesmen trying to attract custom, the cries of the water-bearers carrying their skins on their heads, the calls of the public criers ordering silence for an official announcement. Four times a day the triple blast of the seven silver trumpets of the temple would be heard over the general din, imposing a comparative silence during which the pious prostrated themselves.

This was the character of the city on ordinary days. Just before feast days its activity increased enormously. Three times a year it filled with a prodigious number of pilgrims. Rabbinical tradition claimed that nobody ever complained of overcrowding in Jerusalem; it had a miraculous capacity of expanding. In fact, the pilgrims slept outside the walls in the new suburbs or on the surrounding hills, in tents or huts made of branches or just under the open sky. Except for the Feast of Tabernacles that sometimes coincided with the first rains of the autumn, the other main feasts fell in the spring and summer. Pilgrims poured in from all over the Dispersion, and Josephus estimated their number at a million every year.

The Festival of the First Fruits was celebrated with much pomp in the summer of 41, the first year of Agrippa's reign over Judaea. Berenice had stayed in Jerusalem, where her husband was bound to return periodically to conform with the pleasant duty of celebrating the main religious festivals in the holy city. He may well have joined her on this occasion, although the Festival of the First Fruits was not a strictly religious one and may not have involved him directly. It mainly concerned people who had some land, a garden, or even a single fruit-bearing tree. Their first fruits had to be offered to the temple. The common people usually put their offering in wicker baskets, while the rich carried theirs in silver and gold baskets, which they placed on the altar as a gift to the priests. The feast fell in early summer and was an occasion for much ritual and sacred music. Philo the philosopher, Marcus's uncle, was particularly impressed with the sweet singing of the two temple choirs in a part-song which recalled the history of the nation and its deliverance from oppressors.

Agrippa took an active part in the celebration and shouldered his golden fruit-filled basket like one of the people. Berenice, probably dressed in the customary white, watched, perhaps for the first time in her life, the celebration of a feast that constituted one of the most beautiful rituals of an agricultural society. The Talmud preserved a detailed description of the occasion:

Those who lived near Jerusalem brought fresh figs and grapes, those who had a long way to come brought dried figs and raisins. An ox wearing a garland of olive branches over its gilded horns led the way, followed by a band of pipe-players. When the celebrants came within sight of the city, they stopped to arrange their *bikkurim* [first fruits] in pretty baskets, while messengers went ahead to herald their approach. Usually the governors of the temple, as well as the chiefs and the treasurers, came out to meet the celebrants, depending on their rank and status. On their entry into the city they were met by the local artisans who greeted them with the traditional formula: 'Brethren, men of such and such a place, you are welcome.' The procession marched on to the sound of reed-pipes until it reached the temple mount. At this point even king Agrippa picked up his basket and carried it on his shoulder all the way to the temple court.[1]

The white that Berenice and other young women were wearing was not mandatory, but a courteous concession to a Pharisee injunction. Ostentation in dress had become so common among the women of Jerusalem that during the various festivals girls and matrons tried to outshine one another in the splendour of their clothes. Things came to such a pitch that poor unmarried maidens felt unable to take part in the communal service for want of a suitable apparel. The religious leaders of the community then issued a directive commanding women, particularly young girls, to attend the festivals dressed in borrowed white linen; white for simplicity, and borrowed to pre-empt any embarrassment on the part of those who really needed to borrow. It became customary for the daughters of Jerusalem to celebrate in borrowed white

linen, and Berenice, married and fond of splendid clothes as she
was, may well have taken her cue from her father when it came
to courting the goodwill of the people.

Like her parents and her in-laws she was alert to political events
which affected her co-religionists abroad, and she must have followed with concern a development remarkably reminiscent of a
scene she had so recently witnessed in Rome.

News reached the palace that some hot-headed youngsters in
the small city of Dora (Dor), north of Caesarea, had put a statue of
Claudius in the local synagogue. The outraged Jewish inhabitants
were helpless against the mob, but Agrippa stepped in. He reported the case to Petronius, who was still the governor of Syria,
and asked him to put the matter to rights as Dora was under his
jurisdiction. Petronius sent a severe letter to the magistrates,
council and people of Dora, reminding them of Claudius's edict
and demanding the surrender of the culprits. His letter produced
the desired effect and Agrippa's intervention won many hearts.
But in the general chorus of adulation there were a few dissenting
voices.

In spite of his fundamental adherence to the principles of
Judaism, and in spite of his outward devotion, Agrippa was
entirely hellenized in his outlook and behaviour. He took pleasure
in foreign forms of entertainment like the circus, the theatre, the
gladiatorial games; and although he was careful to indulge his
tastes only in pagan cities, his mode of life was frowned upon by
Jewish traditionalists. True enough, hellenization had made in-
roads into the population in general; many devout Jews would
take their meals reclining like Greeks rather than sitting up like
their forefathers, and even the temple choir had adopted some
Greek musical instruments for its use. But it was all a question of
degree. Agrippa seemed to have pushed his identification with
hellenistic culture too far for some people's liking. His ways
invited criticism and his detractors were quick to ascribe his pre-
dilection for pagan pleasures to his foreign ancestry. After his
family had been practising Judaism for four generations nobody
could legitimately call him a non-Jew; but the general disapproval
of his hellenized ways found expression in one condemnatory
word which symbolized the whole attitude of the conservative
elements in the country. He was an Idumaean, an alien.

At the head of the faction that set itself against him was a certain scholar known as Simon the Pharisee. As long as the king and his family were in the capital and were seen to perform their religious duties without fail, Simon could say little. But as soon as Agrippa and the royal household went to Caesarea to enjoy some foreign spectacle, Simon took action. He called a public meeting and made an impassioned speech against the king, accusing him of unholy living and demanding that he should be barred from entry into the inner courts of the temple, like a gentile.

That was seditious talk. Simon was arrested and taken to Caesarea to stand trial before the king. Agrippa was most urbane. He invited the Pharisee to join him in the theatre, seated him in the middle of the royal entourage and made him watch the spectacle. When it was over he courteously asked Simon which particular part of the show contravened the laws of Judaism. Simon lacked the courage of his convictions; or he may have realized, having for the first time actually seen what he had hitherto condemned only on hearsay, that there was nothing offensive to Judaism in the entertainment. In the event he threw himself at the king's feet and begged for mercy. Agrippa was magnanimous. He granted him a free pardon and encumbered him with a parting present. The result proved the wisdom of his tactics. Simon had lost countenance and was never again heard to speak against the king. Agrippa had won a moral victory.

But there was still a section of the population that had to be won over if he was to reign in peace. His grandfather Herod, when encountering criticism, silenced it with blood; Agrippa had the gift of diplomacy. As usual, he thought out every detail in his plan of campaign and, like the skilled actor that he was, chose the setting to suit his performance.

The opportunity to put his popularity to the test occurred during the Feast of Tabernacles, in the autumn of his second year as king of Judaea. The temple ceremony was to follow the traditional pattern. The milling crowds were to stand in their apportioned courts, while the king was allowed to sit on a specially built wooden dais. Custom prescribed that the holy scroll of the law should be hoisted in full view of the people and carefully passed to the king to read out aloud. The attendant of the assembly would hand it to the president; the president to the high priest's deputy; the deputy to the high priest; and the high priest to the king. The king, who had been sitting on his dais, would stand up to receive the holy scroll, then sit down again to read out the prescribed passages.

Agrippa followed the custom of standing up to receive the holy scroll; but instead of using his privilege of resuming his seat, he remained standing throughout the reading. It was no mean feat. He had to read out quite a long extract from the Book of Deuteronomy, which was not a narrative text but a recitation of some of the laws that Moses had given the Children of Israel in the wilderness. The king's gesture warmed the hearts of the devout, but it also served to make his every move more discernible to the masses in the courts below. They could see him standing up to his full height and enjoy his fluent and articulate reading. He must have taken the trouble to study the text in advance, for he knew exactly when to introduce the dramatic element. He had begun on the law concerning the appointment of kings when suddenly his voice faltered and his face contorted with pain. The crowd strained their ears to hear him stumble over the painful verse: *You shall appoint over you a man of your own race; you must not appoint a foreigner.*[2] He was so affected that he had to stop reading, and the people nearest to the dais could clearly see that his eyes were filled with tears. His dilemma was apparent to all. Agrippa the pious, the God-fearing, the devout, suddenly realized that according to Mosaic law he was not fit to be king because of his racially mixed ancestry. His obvious concern for the law, his grief, his humility, touched all hearts. The masses surged forwards and cried in sympathy: 'Have no fear, Agrippa. You are our brother. You are our brother.'[3] It was only after the reassurance of the people that the king found his voice again and was able to continue with his reading. By the time he reached the verse: *You shall not regard an Edomite as an abomination for he is your own kin,*[4] he was fully vindicated.

From her stand in the Court of Women Berenice watched her father's performance with keen interest. Although young and impressionable, she was by no means naive. Her father's tears could not have deceived her; but far from despising him for his play-acting, she must have admired his technique. Many years later, when facing the masses with her brother, she copied her father's tactics and all but obtained the same results. Charm, persuasion and tears became her favourite weapons.

Not that she had any need to use them during those short peaceful years. Her position and her husband's wealth enabled her to enjoy life in Jerusalem. She associated with the aristocratic Sadducee families who supplied her father with candidates for his frequent changes of high priests, and must have become familiar with the lower priestly hierarchy as a matter of course.

It was a carefully defined hierarchy. One priest was responsible for the sacred seal; another was in charge of drink-offerings and another over offerings of birds. A coveted post was that of the priest in charge of the lots, by which the various tasks connected with the service of the altar were distributed. A less enviable post, but an essential one, was that of dealing with the sickness of the bowels; apparently priests were prone to it. Another priest was responsible for the digging and maintenance of ditches that supplied water to the pilgrims. An important post was that of the master of the keys, who had to see that the nine gates of the temple were locked last thing at night and unlocked first thing ing the morning. An exacting one was that of being in charge of the temple choir. Then there were the menial posts which were the backbone of the hierarchy. Someone was responsible for the making of wicks for the temple oil lamps, and a whole priestly family was in charge of baking the shewbread. Another made frankincense, and yet another was responsible for the making and maintenance of the priests' vestments. There were treasurers and superintendents, and there were the Levites to assist the priests. Altogether the temple hierarchy numbered about twenty thousand, all from the priestly tribe of Levi. Some remained obscure, others achieved a measure of celebrity; but none was so constantly in the public eye as the temple crier.

His duty was to summon the priests and the Levites to their holy duties very early in the morning; and as they lived all over the town and had to be woken up simultaneously, he was chosen for the carrying power of his voice. The further it carried the more respected the crier. His performance and his merits were discussed by Jerusalemite families in the same way that Roman or Greek families might discuss the merits of a public orator. The royal household was no exception. Once Agrippa and his family happened to drive out of the city at the crack of dawn, possibly to spend some time in Caesarea. They were well on their way when above the din of the carriages and the horses' hooves the voice of the crier reached them, summoning the priests to their holy work. The royal family was impressed. When they returned to Jerusalem Agrippa sent the crier a present to show his appreciation of a priest whose voice could be heard at a distance of three *parasangs* [about eleven miles].

There was always something happening in the royal household. There were the comings and goings in the two palaces, the intrigues round the dismissals and appointments of high priests, the holy festivals which marked the seasons of the year. There was Caesarea with its gaiety and its spectacles, and there were the costly presents that Marcus must have brought his wife from the east. It was a peaceful life, but by no means unexciting.

Chapter VII

Walking a tightrope

ONE of Agrippa's most striking achievements was his winning and maintaining the favour of the Pharisees, interpreters of Mosaic law and defenders of the faith.

There were two main parties that the Hasmonaeans and their successors had to reckon with: the Pharisees, who derived their name from a Hebrew word meaning 'apartness' for the sake of purity; and the Zadokites, or Sadducees, the priestly families, called after Zadok the priest who officiated during king David's reign many centuries earlier. Although primarily religious, both parties wielded considerable political influence over rulers and subjects, as religion and national politics were bound up together by the very nature of Judaism. The Sadducees were the natural spiritual leaders of the people by virtue of their ancestry; but as the high priesthood gradually lost its sacred aura, the Pharisees stepped in with their exemplary life of virtue and piety. By the time Agrippa became king of Judaea they had established their ascendancy over the Sadducees to such an extent that they could openly declare that a scholarly bastard was worthier than an ignorant high priest. While the Sadducees were the aristocracy of the blood, the Pharisees constituted the new aristocracy of the learned.

Basically the Pharisees were no more than interpreters of the law, but because Mosaic law embraced every aspect of human life, their influence infiltrated everywhere. They established synagogues and schools and instructed the masses in the sacred text of the *Torah,* the Pentateuch. They preferred precedent to the letter of the law and introduced rules more in keeping with contemporary needs. They were the first to reject the literal reading of *an eye for an eye* and interpreted it as meaning financial compensation for loss of limb. They were sober people, simple in their way of life,

74

Recent excavations of Agrippa's Wall, Jerusalem, known as The Third Wall

A tablet in the Court of Gentiles in Herod's Temple warning non-Jews against entering the inner courts on pain of death

Caligula

Claudius

austere in their attitude to luxury. They were everything that Agrippa was not.

By nature and upbringing the king had more affinity with the aristocractic and wealthy Sadducees than with the humble scholars. But the Sadducees were a dwindling party while the Pharisees were increasingly on the ascendance. Herod had been at loggerheads with them; Agrippa decided to win them over and rule through them. He observed their religious rulings, neglected no rites of purification and did not let a day go by without offering the prescribed sacrifice in the temple. With his inborn tact and sense of propriety he sometimes made such apparently spontaneous gestures of piety that even the unemotional scholars could not fail to be impressed.

He was being carried in his litter through the city one day, with the queen and Berenice probably following behind in theirs, when they came face to face with another litter. A young bride was being taken to the house of her bridegroom for the wedding ceremony, with all her relatives and friends walking on either side of her, singing the traditional wedding songs. It was in one of those narrow streets where it was impossible to make way. One party obviously had to retreat. Agrippa made a royal gesture. He signalled to his own litter-bearers to step into a side lane so as to allow the bride to proceed without delay to the place of the wedding. No king within living memory had shown so much courtesy to a woman of the people. When the story reached the Pharisees they were full of admiration. They quoted Agrippa's noble example in their learned discussions and suggested that the precedence shown by a king to a bride should be taken into account when other cases of precedence were debated.

Berenice could not have been surprised at her father's gesture, even if momentarily inconvenienced. Agrippa's household was geared to piety as other royal households were geared to protocol. It was deliberate policy, directed at winning public approval. What the palace did or did not was the talk of the town. Everybody in Jerusalem knew what kind of meat the royal family had for dinner, and what time of day they took it. The palace was particularly careful over ritual practices. The queen often sought advice from the Pharisee scholars on matters of daily routine, and it was through her that Berenice learned the complexities of everyday life that depended so much on the correct interpretation of the law concerning the smallest details of food, dress and social behaviour. It was Berenice's duty to familiarize herself with such things. She was in the public eye much more than the other royal children. Her brother Agrippa was mostly away in Rome for his education, while her sisters Mariamme and Drusilla were no more than little girls. As the eldest princess, and a married one at that, she had to sustain her part in the show of conformity. A further opportunity to do so occurred when the ever-present friction between the Pharisees and the Christians came to a head.

When Jesus was crucified about the year 33, his followers all over the country did not amount to more than a few hundreds. During the next ten years they so increased in number and influence that the Pharisees were alarmed again, never having ceased to regard them as dangerous dissenters from the faith of their fathers. Although the Pharisees believed in the messianic idea, they strongly disapproved of any section of the population that claimed to have found a short-cut to redemption. Jesus's followers were such a section. They put their own interpretation on the law, they deviated from tradition, they disseminated new ideas. Two men in particular were actively seeking new adherents and causing confusion among the people. Although they were not well educated, and in their native Galilee had been no more than fishermen, they had the gift of making rousing speeches. The people of Jerusalem, far from mocking their regional accent which was in sharp contrast to the clear incisive speech of the learned Pharisees, flocked to listen to them. One was James the son of Zebedee; the other was Simon, commonly known as Cephas or Peter.

Agrippa was no stranger to the activities and ideas of the Nazarenes, as the early Christians were called. Having lived in Judaea and Galilee during the last years of Jesus's career, he could not have failed to become as familiar with his preachings as any person who had little feeling for religion. Deep down Agrippa was quite indifferent to spiritual matters. He was a conformist rather than a believer. A man who had not hesitated to pay lip-service to Caligula's divinity and offered sacrifices in Rome to celebrate his own accession to kingship could not have been shocked by religious dissent. It was only when spiritual ideas threatened his political safety—as in the case of Simon the

Pharisee—that he felt obliged to crush them. James and Peter had overstepped the world of the spirit. They were making public speeches, they were preaching new ideas, they were upsetting the loyal Pharisees. Like a true Herodian, Agrippa was suspicious of people who could draw the crowds and give them reason to question the accepted order of things. He might have preferred to deal with them in the same lenient way that he had dealt with Simon in Caesarea a couple of years earlier. But Simon was no more than an over-zealous purist, while James and Peter had the uncompromising quality of the ancient prophets. There was nothing for it but to bring the full pressure of the law against them.

James was the first victim of Agrippa's policy of expediency. He was arrested and put to death. It was no Herodian strangling in the secrecy of a distant fortress. It was a legal affair, with all the trimmings of a public trial. He died in the full glare of the limelight. The execution by the sword, the only political execution recorded in Agrippa's reign, must have caused considerable stir. It pleased the Pharisees, but failed to discourage the Nazarenes. It was necessary to make another public example. Peter was arrested. Agrippa's plan was to have him tried soon after the Passover, when the crowds of pilgrims would have dispersed; then, as the outcome was a foregone conclusion, to have him tortured and executed. In the meantime the prisoner was closely guarded by four squads of four men each, with chains on both his wrists. The king who had once been a prisoner himself saw no irony in the situation. Miraculously Peter escaped before the trial and could not be found. After a while Agrippa abandoned the search and contented himself with the execution of the guards. Herodian by birth and Roman by upbringing, he saw the punishment as no more than disciplinary justice for failure in duty. Soon afterwards he went to Caesarea for the games.

Caesarea Maritima, so called to distinguish it from Caesarea Philippi or Panias in Trachonitis, was marvellously suited to give pleasure to a person of Agrippa's tastes. It boasted a theatre and amphitheatre, a hippodrome, beautiful palaces and, above all, a pagan tradition that allowed a king of Judaea to shed the restrictions of Pharisee discipline and enjoy himself like any hellenized prince of the Roman empire.

Herod had built Caesarea on the site of a small decaying coastal town to satisfy his need for a modern Mediterranean port. Before this there had not been one reliable harbour along the whole of Judaea's strip of coast. Ships had to use the inferior ports of Gaza and Ascalon to the south, or Dora to the north, where they lay off in the open sea, exposed to violent south winds which buffeted them against the rocks. Herod's harbour turned out to be one of the most brilliant technical achievements of his reign. When it was finished it was said to surpass in size and amenities even the Piraeus. No ship was too large to anchor in it.

The new harbour was twenty fathoms deep and protected by a stone mole two hundred feet long. Half of its length formed a breakwater, while the other half supported a sea wall which encircled the harbour. As a vessel sailed in, ten towers came into view, then six colossal statues. The statues on the left stood on top of a tower; those on the right rested on two gigantic rocks which had been sunk into the bottom of the sea. The sea wall round the wharf buildings was fitted with a series of vaulted recesses which served as sailors' quarters. There was also a modern system of underground sewerage, and the sea water was used to flush the city lanes and carry the rubbish through the sewers back into the depths of the Mediterranean.

The city proper was built on an equally grand scale. On a natural elevation a temple was erected in honour of Rome and Augustus; it was so placed that it could easily be seen by distant ships like a lighthouse. Herod also built a theatre and an amphitheatre, a number of palaces and public buildings including a market place, all of imported white stone. The work took twelve years to complete, and the new city was named Caesarea after Augustus Caesar. The dedication, coinciding with the one hundred and ninety-second Olympiad, was celebrated about 10 BC with true Herodian splendour. There were feasts and music, contests between naked gladiators and fights between gladiators and wild animals. The games became a quadrennial festival.

Caesarea's growth was rapid. By Agrippa's time the population had increased to between forty and fifty thousand. The numbers were fairly equally divided between Jews and Greeks, or Syrian Greeks, but the spirit of the place was predominantly hellenistic. It was said that when the games were held not a soul stayed at work, whether Jew or Gentile. During the rule of the procurators Caesarea was the centre of the Roman administration in preference to restriction-ridden Jerusalem. Agrippa, although he made Jerusalem his capital and his official place of residence, treated Caesarea as his favourite holiday resort. Only there could he indulge his love of luxury and ostentation without being hampered by his Pharisee watchdogs, and only there could he entertain the foreign dignitaries who called at the port in the style they were accustomed to.

The queen probably did not frequent Caesarea as much as the king; its laxity ran counter to her inborn sobriety. But the princesses took to it with enthusiasm. Gone were the customary consultations about dietary problems, the dignified decorum of the palace, the dresses of plain white linen for feast days. In Caesarea Berenice could wear muslins from India and transparent silks from western Asia. She could fling on an attractive woollen shawl from Miletus for the fashionable walk round the harbour in the cool of the evening, then reappear in gold-woven cloth for a reception or a feast. She could adorn herself with pearls from India and the Persian Gulf, emeralds from Ethiopia, amethysts from Egypt, sapphires, opals, beryls. She could use for her toilet articles made of tortoiseshell from India, set in gold by Alexandrian craftsmen. She could try any hairstyle freshly introduced from Rome. Dressed, perfumed and made up with all the art of the east, she could attend the games, admire the gladiators and turn her thumb down like any Roman lady.

It was in Caesarea that Agrippa allowed Berenice to enjoy the forbidden pleasure of seeing her own statue erected and publicly displayed. Nowhere else could the Mosaic injunction against the 'graven image', the artistic representation of humans or animals, be defied without rousing fierce national opposition. In Caesarea the royal palace was embellished with statues of Berenice and her two younger sisters, causing no comment beyond perhaps an artistic evaluation of the work. Unfortunately none of them survived the riots that broke out after Agrippa's death.

It was in Caesarea that Agrippa was able to indulge another of his non-Jewish cravings. By arrangement with Rome, client-kings were allowed to mint their own coins; mostly bronze, very rarely silver. The Hasmonaean rulers of Judaea, and even Herod the Great, put permissible Jewish symbols on their coins: ears of barley, a horn of plenty, an anchor. Agrippa too adhered to tradition, but only in Jerusalem. The royal mints at Caesarea and Caesarea Philippi issued a variety of bronze coins with human likenesses: Caligula, Claudius, Tyche the city goddess and Nike the goddess of victory. Agrippa had his own head minted on some of his coins, and even his young son's, although not his wife's and daughters'. The representational coins minted in Caesarea were introduced under the thin pretext that they were intended for use only in predominantly pagan territories. Philip the tetrarch had done the same years earlier. If such coins found their way into Jerusalem, they were tacitly accepted.

That Agrippa got away with what only a generation earlier would have been considered a flagrant violation of the sacred law was due no doubt to the growing acceptance of the hellenistic way of life. Greek customs, words and thinking had infiltrated so deeply into Jewish life that a resolute ruler could deviate from tradition as long as he did not flaunt his unorthodox practices in the wrong places. No criticism was voiced against another seemingly outrageous coin which depicted the Jewish king offering sacrifices to a Roman deity in celebration of his accession to the throne of Judaea. As long as Agrippa was a pious king in Jerusalem, he could be a Roman elsewhere. He was a Great King, as the legend on some of his coins described him, and a Friend of Caesar. Agrippa's Jewish subjects basked in his glory, alien as it must have been to them in spirit.

What must have helped to reconcile the Pharisees to the king's religious irregularities outside Jerusalem was his patriotic foreign policy; or so it seemed to be. A firm believer in Rome's supremacy, Agrippa could not have entertained any thoughts of national independence. But he was an ambitious man and soon set about establishing himself as one of the most powerful client-kings in the eastern part of the empire. He invited several of his fellow-kings to visit him in Tiberias. Whether he intended to form an alliance against Rome or just to display his grandeur before some other potentates will never be certain. What is certain however is that the congress did not end as Agrippa had intended.

The participants were mostly friends from earlier days in Rome, or relatives. There were Antiochus of Commagene, Cotys of

Lesser Armenia and his brother Julius Polemo of Pontus, all of whom owed their rise to power, like Agrippa, first to Caligula then to Claudius. There was also Sampsigeramus of Emesa, whose daughter was married to Agrippa's younger brother Aristobulus; and Herod of Chalcis. They arrived with their freedmen and advisers, were entertained in Agrippa's beautiful palace overlooking the lake of Tiberias, and given every opportunity to talk political gossip that would have pleased no loyal servant of Rome.

Such a one was Vibius Marsus, who in AD 42 had succeeded the well-disposed Petronius as governor of Syria. Marsus believed that a meeting of minds among so many client-kings was prejudicial to Roman interests. He hurried to Tiberias to see things for himself. Agrippa, who had neither sent him an invitation nor asked for his official blessing, went out to meet him. The five kings drove out with him, anxious to placate a representative of Rome who had the ear of Claudius. They never had a chance to say a word. Before they could so much as alight from their carriages, they were confronted by messengers from Marsus who instructed them, each one separately, to leave without ceremony and return to their respective countries. The intimidated kings departed there and then, leaving their host to sort things out with the governor. The six-kings-meeting that had been meant to show off Agrippa's power and high standing with Rome ended in a complete débâcle. It was a humiliation he never forgot.

Marsus went on keeping a close watch over developments in Judaea, and in due course was able to report to Claudius that his old friend Agrippa was behaving in a manner most suspicious in a client-king of Rome. He was building a formidable wall round the north end of Jerusalem, which, if completed, would render the city virtually impregnable.

Why Agrippa started building the wall, which to this day bears his name, has been the subject of some speculation. Pharisee tradition had it that his aim was to fortify Jerusalem and put it beyond an enemy's reach. Another explanation is that he had the Herodian urge to engage in public works on a grand scale. Whatever the reason, it filled the Judaeans with pride and gave them full employment.

The official excuse for continuing the old city wall was deceptively innocent. Jerusalem had expanded so much that an entirely new suburb had come into being north of the city, just beyond the Antonia. With its metal-workers' shops and market stalls it should have merged quite naturally into the rest of the town. But by Pharisee tradition it could not be considered part of the holy city as long as it was not encircled by the same wall. So a wall had to be built to preserve the integrity of Jerusalem. It was no more than a pretext; to give it weight Agrippa sent large bribes to Claudius's freedmen in Rome, who turned a blind eye to his activities.

When the wall reached a certain height, the new suburb could be dedicated and declared part of the city. The consecration was performed as required by tradition. The king and the high priest, together with the seventy-one members of the *Sanhedrin*, the supreme court, walked solemnly along the new wall, while the people of Jerusalem followed them in two orderly processions. After the dedication there was a festive gathering in the temple, with the choir singing the appropriate psalm. It was a moment of great national joy.

The joy was short lived. Marsus eventually succeeded in counteracting the effects of Agrippa's bribes and obtained an imperial order instructing him to cease work immediately. According to another version Agrippa did not wait to be told, but gave the order himself as soon as he felt which way the wind was blowing. According to yet another version the building work stopped only with his death. Whichever way it was, the wall was left unfinished.

In the midst of the political tension created by the Tiberias débâcle and the difficulty of fortifying a city in plain peace, an unexpected personal event occurred that started the royal house pleasantly speculating. Marcus Julius Alexander, Berenice's husband, suddenly died. No tears were shed at his death. The young widow could hardly feel the loss of a husband who even when he was alive was away more often than not. In practical terms his death meant the opening up of new matrimonial prospects. Berenice was fifteen, attractive, rich and unhampered by children. Her father was a great king and a friend of Caesar. This time she could expect to be married into royalty.

Chapter VIII

Diadem for a bride

THE house of Herod had always been most scrupulous in its observance of the law forbidding intermarriage. A candidate for the hand of a Herodian princess could well be a commoner, but he could not be a pagan. He had to be Jewish, either by birth or through circumcision before marriage. That was a law no political or sentimental considerations could ever waive. It was fundamental.

Herod, on whom history later bestowed the title of Great, had set the example, even though it was at the expense of his own sister Salome. During a time when his relations with the king of Arabia were strained, the Arab minister Syllaeus came to Judaea on an official visit, ostensibly to try to smooth things out, but more likely to do some political snooping. Syllaeus was young, handsome and shrewd. He looked around for an ally and soon found one in Salome, the king's influential sister. She was a grandmother several times over, but a widow and in obvious need of male consolation. She fell an easy victim to the gallantries of the young man and became his mistress and his informant. She also became the laughing-stock of the palace womenfolk. When the affair was reported to Herod Syllaeus took fright and departed. Three months later, probably acting on favourable information from the languishing Salome, he returned to Judaea and formally asked for her hand, pointing out the political advantages to Herod of a marriage between his sister and the man who was in virtual control of Arabia. Herod agreed to the match but demanded that the pagan bridegroom should be circumcised. Syllaeus cooled off. He explained that his Arab subjects would revolt if he went over to Judaism. Herod was adamant. So was Syllaeus. The negotiations were broken off and the marriage never materialized. Later Salome had to accept a Jewish husband of Herod's choosing.

Under Pharisee influence Agrippa was just as scrupulous as his grandfather; and like him he regarded marriageable female relatives as baits for potential allies. After he had married his eldest daughter to the son of the richest Jew in Alexandria, he betrothed his second daughter Mariamme to the son of his Jewish commander-in-chief Helcias, thus hoping to assure himself of the loyalty of the army. His third and youngest daughter Drusilla, who from early childhood showed signs of becoming a great beauty, was promised to the son of his old friend king Antiochus of Commagene, for which privilege the prospective bridegroom undertook to accept circumcision.

Berenice's return to the bridal market caused no consternation in the palace. Quite the contrary. Apart from relieving Agrippa of any feelings of regret at having married his eldest daughter to a mere merchant, Marcus's timely death enabled him to make better use of Berenice's marriageability. Mariamme and Drusilla, though profitably betrothed, were still under age and too young to be married. Berenice was the only one whose value could be put to immediate use.

By default of royal candidates who would be prepared to pay the price of circumcision, or possibly through calculated preference, Agrippa's choice fell on his widowed brother Herod, king of Chalcis and Berenice's uncle. That the bridegroom was nearly forty years older than the bride was no obstacle.

Herod had been born in Jerusalem and, like Agrippa and their youngest brother Aristobulus, was sent to Rome at a very tender age to escape the attentions of his grandfather Herod. Being the eldest of the three he was better able to recall the occasion when that redoubtable king tearfully kissed the orphans whose fathers he had so recently condemned to death. Later the brothers were joined by their mother Berenice, who settled down in Rome and looked after their education and their interests. Thanks to her, Herod had as many connections in the imperial household as Agrippa. Like him he spoke Latin and Greek, unlike him he had the ability of living within his means. He made an early marriage with a relative called Mariamme and had a son by her. After her death he continued to live quietly in Rome, never distinguishing himself in any capacity. It was only after Agrippa had won Caligula's favour that he too came into the limelight. But he lacked his younger brother's single-mindedness and drive and was content to follow his lead rather than make his own way. It was Agrippa who obtained for him the kingdom of Chalcis from Claudius.

His own qualities were of a different order. He was sober, loyal and not devoid of courage in times of crisis. He could turn out a glib political speech and was no stranger to the power-game. If he was not as brilliant as Agrippa, he made up for it by his solidity. He was dependable, if unadventurous.

To judge from his bust on a coin struck during his reign over Chalcis, he was still an attractive man when he was about to marry his fifteen-year-old niece. Although in his mid-fifties and a little older than the bride's father, he was better preserved. The coin shows a handsome and noble-looking profile, with a well-shaped nose and sensitive lips. Certainly Herod could not be faulted on his looks.

But his best asset was of course his royal diadem. That was Agrippa's first consideration, and that must have been Berenice's consolation, if indeed she needed any. Whatever reservations she may have had about the vast age difference must have vanished at the thought of becoming a queen. It could not have been much fun being a merchant's wife, while one of her sisters was engaged to a general's son and the other to a prince. To be queen, even of a tiny country, was to achieve the height of ambition. Now for the first time in her life she could rise over palace bickerings and jealousies. She could command, punish, dictate or be generous. She could have her own court and put into practice everything she had seen and learnt in Jerusalem. She could be gracious like her mother; but above all she could be grand like her father, for she had inherited his temperament and the need to shine in society, in good deeds, in piety.

The marriage could take place fairly soon after Marcus's death without giving offence to anybody. Jewish custom did not prescribe a long waiting period for a widow who wished to remarry. A girl's betrothal might last a year, but a widow's needed to last only a month. The contract fixing the bride-price would have been signed on a Tuesday, which was considered a propitious day for a widow, and the marriage was solemnized early in 44, before Berenice reached her sixteenth birthday. The wedding feast held in

85

Jerusalem was very different from the one held in Rome three years earlier. It was a traditional affair, accompanied by love hymns from the Song of Songs, with the cream of Sadducee and Pharisee society paying homage to the new queen of Chalcis. The title was like music to Berenice's ears. She kept it to the end of her life, long after she had ceased to have any connection with that country.

Herod was in no hurry to introduce his bride to her new kingdom. After the wedding they stayed on in Jerusalem to attend the Passover festivities, which that year must have been celebrated with more sense of occasion than usual, now that two kings and two queens were taking part. After the eight-day festival, marred as it was by the successful escape from prison of Peter the apostle, the entire royal family went to Caesarea Maritima for the games. It was to be one of Agrippa's finest displays. It turned out to be his last.

The games in Caesarea had been arranged to celebrate Claudius's return to Rome from his campaign in Britain. They were attended by vast crowds from neighbouring towns, and there were many distinguished visitors from the Roman province of Syria, all anxious to put on record their loyalty to Caesar through their attendance at the games celebrating his victory. Most notable among them was a joint delegation from Tyre and Sidon, who took the opportunity to try to smooth out a political misunderstanding with the powerful king who had embargoed the export of provisions from his country to theirs.

The opening day passed satisfactorily, promising more delights to come. On the second day the royal party arrived early in the morning and took their seats. The theatre was already full. That day Agrippa had put on a sumptuous costume made of silver cloth which reflected the bright morning sun and shone like a pillar of fire. The crowds had never seen anything so resplendent. The whisper went round that the aura encircling the king's person was a sign of divinity. It was taken up by fawning courtiers, including the Sidonians who were determined to have the embargo lifted. They assured the king that he looked like a god; in fact he was a god, and would he forgive them for not having realized it before and failed to worship him as one? Agrippa must have accepted the fulsome adoration with the same insincerity with which it was offered, but tradition has it otherwise.

If it is to be credited, Agrippa had hardly finished acknowledging the popular acclamations when his eyes caught sight of an owl perched on one of the awning ropes. For an owl to turn up in broad daylight in the midst of a noisy theatre, brave the crowds and find its way to the royal presence was surely a sign from God. Agrippa remembered the prophecy made by his old German fellow-prisoner a few years earlier and realized his end had come. God was punishing him for having presumed to accept an honour that was none but His. Immediately he was seized with severe pains in the stomach. He was carried back to the palace and installed in a room in an upper storey, from which he could see what was happening in the forecourt below.

Even on his deathbed his sense of the theatrical did not forsake him. Before making his final exit he took a gracious farewell of his friends, melting their hearts with his pious resignation:

I, whom you have called a god, am now commanded to depart this life, and fate disproves the divine status you have attributed to me. I, whom you have called immortal, am now about to die. I am resigned to God's will, for I have by no means fared badly, but have lived a splendid and happy life.[1]

He did not die immediately. His agony lasted five days and five nights and he was conscious almost to the last. From his lofty room in the palace he could see the multitudes anxiously waiting for news down below. They had gathered in their thousands, with their wives and children, the Jews wearing sackcloth and ashes, the Greeks a mournful expression, all praying to their gods to spare their beloved king. At the sight of so much devotion Agrippa broke down and wept with the people. But his condition was beyond hope. He died on the fifth day, having reigned for seven years, three under Caligula and four under Claudius. He was in his fifties, struck down at the height of his career.

The cause of his death has never been ascertained. One theory is that he suffered from intestinal worms, an abdominal condition not unusual at that time. A more modern diagnosis suggests that he died of acute peritonitis; but the latest suggestion, and one that is more in keeping with the practices of the period, is that he died of slow poisoning, probably by arsenic. Who should have wished his death is a matter of conjecture only. It may have been Marsus, the governor of Syria, who had every reason to suspect Agrippa's loyalty to Rome after the congress in Tiberias and the building of the wall in Jerusalem. On the other hand it may have been the act of a faction of disgruntled Caesarean Greeks who resented being the subjects of a Jewish king. Certainly their behaviour after his death showed they had no love for him.

Agrippa was the last Jewish king of Judaea. His brief reign gave his people their last taste of peace and freedom. Later opinion was divided as to whether his reign was in fact the golden age some enthusiasts claimed it to be. A new generation of Pharisees went as far as to declare that the temple was destroyed by Titus only because their hypocritical predecessors had hailed a descendant of the Idumaeans as a brother. Yet there was little of the Idumaean about Agrippa. His extravagance, his occasional callousness, his calculated friendships and his selfishness were traits common to many a politician, whatever his descent; while his generosity, his genuine affection for his family, his sophistication, his capacity to enjoy life to the full and finally his irresistible charm were personal characteristics. His vices were those of his time; his virtues all his own.

One person who was not entirely deceived by the multitude's show of devotion during Agrippa's last hours was his brother Herod. He had good reason to fear a military uprising and as soon as his brother breathed his last he took matters into his own hands.

The unrest in the army had started some time ago, when Agrippa had fallen out with his commander-in-chief Silas and had given his post to Helcias, whose son was engaged to the young princess Mariamme. Silas went about telling anybody who was willing to listen how ungrateful the king was towards an old friend who had been with him through thick and thin. As he was popular with the rank and file the only way to silence him was to put him in prison. After a while Agrippa repented of his harshness and offered to release him, but the proud old soldier preferred to stay in prison rather than accept reconciliation without rehabilitation.

Herod feared that the news of Agrippa's death might spur the army to release Silas by force and reinstate him. Acting on his own initiative and relying on Helcias's complicity, he sent a trusted soldier to the prison with instructions to execute Silas, making out that it was the king's order. Nobody suspected foul play. Only when he was assured that Silas was safely out of the way did Herod tell the court that Agrippa was dead.

Unfortunately he had misread the signs. The soldiers serving in the Caesarea cohort were mostly Greek natives of Samaria and Caesarea who had enlisted in the king's army not for the love of him but for the pay. Many of them must have seen service under the Roman procurators who preceded Agrippa. To them it mattered little whether their commander-in-chief was Silas or Helcias. What did matter was that they were both Jews, as was the king who had been imposed on them. As soon as the Greek population heard that Agrippa was dead, their mood changed. From prayers and grief they switched over to a riotous display of joy. They ran wild in the streets yelling out the good news, calling for a celebration. The soldiers joined in. They hurled insults at the dead man and drank ribald toasts to his passing. Women plied them with wine and hung garlands on their heads. When they had drunk themselves into violence they surged forwards towards the palace and tried to force their way in. They found doors and windows bolted and the palace guard ready to meet them. To console themselves for their rebuff they carried off the statues of the king's three daughters which adorned the palace precincts. They dragged them to the best-known brothel in town, heaved them on to the roof, and in full view of the frenzied mob below assaulted them as if they were live women, then smashed them to pieces.

When telling the story of the Caesarea orgy Josephus tactfully suggested that the insults inflicted on the statues were too indecent to describe. His reticence was understandable, for he was writing during the lifetime of the princesses, certainly of their brother Agrippa II who was his friend and patron. Yet his coyness begs the question. Taking revenge on a hated person's statue was by no means unusual. When Caligula was murdered the Roman mob pulled down his statues from their pedestals and destroyed them to express their hatred and relief. It was hardly surprising that the Greeks of Samaria and Caesarea should express their feelings in the same way. It was odd however that they should single out for revenge the statues of the three princesses who had little to do with them, and pass over the statue of the king who was the real object of their fury.

The anomaly must have struck Photius, the learned ninth-century bibliophile of Constantinople, who in his *Library* gave a different account of the happenings of that day. According to him the demented mob stormed the palace and carried off not the three statues but the three princesses, whom they dragged to the city brothel and exposed to the crowds below. Indeed it would be difficult to imagine that in their destructive mood the attackers would discriminate between the various royal statues which embellished the palace and pick up only those of the girls. It is more likely that they vented their fury on whatever came their way, destroying statues of any kind, smashing and looting, killing whoever offered resistance. The women's quarters would have been less well protected than the main part of the palace, where Herod and Helcias must have surrounded themselves with their loyal guards in anticipation of a military upheaval. Concentrating their defence on the main entrance, they would have had little thought from a distant part of the building. Only the voluntary withdrawal of the tumultuous crowds would have alerted them to what must have taken place. How soon Helcias's men succeeded in rescuing the princesses from a fate worse than death Photius did not mention. Of the three girls only Berenice had reached woman-hood. Mariamme was ten and Drusilla still under six.

At long last the riots were quelled. There was no question of a state funeral but of a quick and quiet exit from a hostile area. Herod, as the new head of the stricken family, took his women-folk back to the safety of Jerusalem. Although the news of Agrippa's death would have been reported to Claudius by Marsus, the governor of Syria, Herod sent in his own report. He demanded a severe punishment for the soldiers who had led the riots and suggested that seventeen-year-old Agrippa junior, who was being educated in Rome in Claudius's own household, should be sent back home to succeed his father. Relying on Claudius's proven friendship, he then settled down with Berenice in the old Hasmonaean palace to await the results of his suggestions.

They were not what he had been expecting. Claudius was indeed fond of his young charge and not averse to Agrippa's succeeding his father, but his freedmen had been studying Marsus's reports and felt that Judaea was getting out of hand. They convinced Claudius that a boy of seventeen was hardly the right person to control a notoriously difficult people and that the interests of Rome would be better served by a return to the rule of procurators. They proposed that Judaea and Samaria should become a province as in the days of Augustus, Tiberius and Caligula; and that it should be enlarged to include the late king's territories across the Jordan which had never before been under procuratorial rule. Claudius gave his consent.

One blow followed another. Soon after he heard that his brother's kingdom was to revert to Rome, Herod of Chalcis learnt that his request to punish the rioting soldiers had been shelved. True enough, Claudius had at first taken a serious view of the offence and intended to have the whole cohort transferred to Pontus. It was a severe punishment, for the soldiers were natives of Samaria and Caesarea, and the transfer would have meant exile from homes and families. The severity of the intended punishment may well be another indication that the offence was more than just a coarse practical joke played on statues. However, an officers' delegation went to Rome to plead and through the usual channels of bribed freedmen succeeded in getting Claudius to change his mind. The soldiers were allowed to stay and continued to serve in the army which was now taken over by Cuspius Fadus, the newly appointed Roman procurator. The princesses' honour remained unavenged.

Berenice must have been mortified, but private indignation had to give way to a more serious concern. The people of Judaea and their procurator were about to have their first fundamental clash. It was a situation in which Berenice found herself entirely on the side of her people.

Chapter IX

Queen of Chalcis

Cuspius Fadus arrived in his new province a very short time after his appointment. He reinstated Caesarea as the administrative capital and proceeded to put down the civil strife which had flared up across the Jordan. He also purged Idumaea of brigands. Having restored law and order, he went to Jerusalem and summoned the priests and the Pharisee leaders before him. To their unspeakable horror he ordered them to hand over the sacred robes of the high priest and deposit them in the Antonia, which had been taken over by a Roman garrison. Complying with the order was tantamount to a total surrender of religious freedom. It was something that no Judaean could accept without a struggle.

The precedent of keeping the sacred robes away from the priesthood had been set by Herod the Great when he realized that possession of the vestments gave him power over the spiritual leaders of the community. His Hasmonaean predecessors, who were kings as well as high priests, used to keep them in their own hands. With the separation of high priesthood from monarchy, Herod seized the robes and kept them in his newly built Antonia fortress. His act was bitterly resented, but he was too powerful to be opposed. The priesthood consoled itself with the thought that he was after all a practising Jew.

His son Archelaus, ethnarch of Judaea, continued the practice until he was banished to Gaul. The Roman procurators who followed him took the Antonia as well as its sacred deposit. That was the first time the vestments went entirely out of Jewish hands.

A humiliating routine was established. The high priest had to wear the holy robes four times a year; on the Feasts of Passover, Pentecost and Tabernacles, and on the Day of Atonement. On the eve of each such occasion the treasurers of the temple would present themselves to the Roman captain in the Antonia and receive the robes from him. Immediately after use they would return them to him, allow him to check that nothing was missing and then seal them in his presence with their own seal and that of the high priest. There were always fears of hitches and delays. The captain had it in his power to withhold the release of the sacred robes, knowing full well that even the slightest delay could upset the smooth running of the complex religious ceremony, which had to be observed down to the minutest detail. To all intents and purposes the ritual performance of a whole nation depended on the whim of a Roman soldier.

The robes were fabulously costly, but their intrinsic value was in their symbolism. Their design had been laid down by Moses and, although they had undergone some modifications through the ages, their basic components remained the same. They included a tunic with a sash, a surplice, a breast-piece, a mantle and a turban. They were made of fine linen, adorned with gold, violet, purple and scarlet yarn and studded with precious stones. They were handed over from one appointed high priest to the next.

The humiliating routine had been going on for nearly thirty years when the long-awaited chance to break it came to hand. It was towards the end of Tiberius's reign. Vitellius, the governor of Syria, paid a visit to Jerusalem and showed so much benevolent interest in the temple procedure that a deputation ventured to ask him to return the sacred robes to the priesthood. Vitellius was favourably impressed with what he saw and persuaded Tiberius to grant the request. The robes were returned to the hierarchy of the temple. A few years later, when Agrippa became king of Judaea, he took charge of them as his royal prerogative. That was acceptable, if not exactly palatable to the priesthood.

Philo of Alexandria, who saw the high priest wearing them during the Feast of the First Fruits that he attended during Agrippa's reign, declared that their beauty and craftsmanship surpassed anything that had ever been made by human hand. His enthusiastic description of the robes was unfortunately marred by his keenness to find allegorical meanings of Greek philosophy in each item of clothing. A description left by the author of *Ecclesiasticus* is far more vivid and poetic. Although he pre-dated Philo and Agrippa by several generations, the robes had not undergone any changes, except some of maintenance. They were the same robes that Cuspius Fadus was now proposing to remove from Agrippa's

palace and place under the custody of a pagan officer of guards:

He [God] honoured him [the high priest] with splendid
   ornaments
and clothed him in gorgeous vestments.
He robed him in perfect splendour
and armed him with the emblems of power,
the breeches, the mantle and the tunic.
Round his robe he placed pomegranates
and a circle of many golden bells,
to make music as he walked,
ringing aloud throughout the temple
as a reminder to his people.
He gave him the sacred vestment adorned by an embroiderer
with gold and violet and purple;
the oracle of judgement with the token of truth;
the scarlet thread spun with a craftsman's art;
the precious stones engraved like seals,
and placed by the jeweller in a gold setting,
with inscriptions to serve as reminders,
one for each of the tribes of Israel;
the gold crown upon his turban,
engraved like a seal with 'Holy to the Lord'.
What rich adornments to feast the eyes!
What a miracle of art! What a proud honour![1]

Although as queen of Chalcis Berenice had no legitimate grounds
to interfere in a quarrel between the subjects of a Roman province
and their procurator, her religious convictions could hardly allow
her to stand idly by. Like her father, indeed like her husband, she
could light-heartedly shed an inconvenient restriction imposed by
religion and behave at times with the freedom of a Greek or a
Roman. But like her father and her husband she was a firm believer
in the fundamentals of Judaism. Any attempt to interfere with the
freedom of worship was as outrageous to her as it was to her co-
religionists. As a young girl in Rome she had seen her father risk
his life to have an unacceptable ruling of Caligula's waived. As a
princess newly arrived in Jerusalem she saw him use his influence
with a governor of Syria to vindicate the freedom of worship of

the people of Dora, who were outside his territory. The present difficulty was not basically different. An ill-used community needed protection from an arbitrary ruler. It was up to highly placed personages like herself and her husband to do what they could for the people they belonged to.

In Herod Berenice found a person of a like mind. There was compatibility of interests and views between husband and wife. Herod had already shown his mettle a few years earlier, when together with Agrippa he persuaded Claudius to issue an edict confirming the civil rights of the Jews of Alexandria, and later of the entire Roman empire. Now, although he would not wish to jeopardize his position as king of Chalcis, he too felt that the exalted station to which providence had seen fit to call him made it incumbent upon him to act for his people.

While Berenice was a novice at the game, Herod was an old hand who knew how to go about such things. The Jerusalemites had elected a delegation which was to go to Rome to argue the case out before Claudius. Each delegate was forced to leave a son as a hostage in the hands of the Roman garrison before he was allowed to proceed on his journey. But Herod knew from past experience that a Jewish delegation had little chance of gaining the ear of the emperor. There was the impregnable wall of prejudiced freedmen between him and his supplicants. The groundwork had to start from within. Fortunately there were in Rome two favoured people who shared Herod's sense of duty. One was young Agrippa, whom Claudius treated as a son; the other was Aristobulus, Herod's son by his first marriage, who was living in Rome and maintaining a foothold in the right circles. Herod got in touch with them to co-ordinate their approach, then joined them in Rome, arriving at about the same time as the Jerusalemite delegation.

The three Herodians gave Claudius their own views on the vexed question of the sacred robes. The emperor agreed that to allow a Roman captain to exercise control over the high priest's ceremonial vestments was asking for trouble. He consented to revoke the order, basing his action on the precedent set by Vitellius during Tiberius's reign. But unlike Tiberius he was not prepared to return the robes to the custody of the priests. A third party had to be entrusted with them. Herod was the obvious choice. As a Jew he was acceptable to the priesthood, while as a client-king of Rome and a friend of Caesar's he had to be accepted by imperial advisers and procurators.

When the delegation was allowed to see the emperor the case had already been decided. Claudius paid tribute to the efforts made by Herod, young Agrippa and Aristobulus on their compatriots' behalf, and informed the assembly of Herod's new dignity. The compromise was accepted. Once the main point was settled, Herod asked for some further concessions. He was granted the right to administer the temple and its treasury and, most important of all, to nominate high priests as the late king Agrippa had done. At the same time he obtained permission to transfer the old Hasmonaean palace in Jerusalem to his own use, for as imperial custodian of the sacred robes he expected to be there four times a year. The larger and more fortified of the two royal residences was reserved for the use of the procurator during his visits to the capital.

The brief Roman visit marked another stage in Berenice's career. Claudius and court society remembered her as a small girl and a young bride. Now she was reintroduced to them as a queen. Her own family set the tone. The young sisters would look to her for favours, and even her mother, the dowager queen, would ask her mediation before Herod. Having lost her husband, Cypros also lost her foothold in Jerusalem. Her two royal residences had been disposed of, one to Herod and the other to the Roman procurator. There could be no pleasure in a life in Jerusalem shorn of status, if not of wealth. One alternative was to follow her daughter and son-in-law to Chalcis; another was to settle in Rome, like so many of her Herodian relatives. With her son already established there it was tempting to do the same and give her two young daughters the benefit of a Roman education. All these propositions needed to be discussed with Herod in his capacity of king and head of the family, and of course with Berenice, who was his wife and his queen.

When everything in Rome had been satisfactorily settled, the king and queen of Chalcis returned to Jerusalem, where Herod asserted his authority by dismissing one high priest and appointing another. Attending to the temple administration did not require his constant presence. Having made all the necessary arrangements for his return on the occasion of the next major religious feast, he departed for Chalcis. At long last Berenice was going to be queen in her own kingdom.

It was not much of a kingdom. Chalcis was a small mountainous territory beneath the mountain range of Lebanon, which had sometimes been ruled by client-kings, sometimes by Roman administrators. Because of its high altitude Strabo described it as the acropolis of the area. The native inhabitants, the Ituraeans, were Arabs who excelled in archery and made their living by brigandage. Indeed the terrain was ideally suited for such an occupation. The surrounding mountains were quite impassable, particularly after the winter snow, and the many deep caves could comfortably hide as many as four thousand men at a time. The victims of the robberies were mostly peasants from the plains, who used to come to Chalcis to trade their wool for corn and wood. Occasionally the brigands were more daring and ventured as far out as Berytus and Damascus. Pompey was the first who tried to mop them up. After the establishment of a regular Roman garrison in coastal Syria the brigands were driven back, but not eradicated. From their strongholds in the mountains they continued to molest the rich merchants travelling through the plain.

When Herod came to Chalcis he found the tradition of brigandage still alive. A fortress in the plain served as the main bulwark against infiltrations from the mountains, and regular punitive expeditions had to be kept up. Even those inhabitants converted to peaceful occupations were still unruly. They preserved their primitive customs, and to sophisticated people like Herod and Berenice they were barbarians. Herod set out to hellenize them, as he was bound to do under the terms of his kingship. He built them a temple and struck coins to commemorate his reign.

The dour fortress of Chalcis was very different from the royal residences Berenice had known in Jerusalem, the two Caesareas or Tiberias. Yet Chalcis had the advantage of being close to centres of Greek civilization. Berytus, grateful to her late father for some of its beautiful public buildings, was within easy reach. Antioch, the seat of the governor of Syria, was not too far off. Further to the north was the kingdom of Emesa with whom relations were particularly cordial, as the king's daughter was married to Herod's younger brother. There must have been a constant flow of visitors, and a certain amount of travel. A queen also had other duties. During the next two or three years Berenice presented her husband with two sons. The eldest was called Berenicianus, in honour of the young mother; the second Hyrcanus, after the parents' Hasmonaean ancestor.

Life in the semi-barbarian kingdom under Lebanon was brightened by the four annual pilgrimages to Jerusalem, when Herod would take up residence in the Hasmonaean palace and preside over the release and subsequent return of the high priest's vestments. Berenice accompanied her husband whenever she could, unless prevented by advanced pregnancy or childbirth. She took part in the temple ceremonies and occupied a seat in the Court of Women as of old. In Jerusalem she was in a unique position. She was more than the visiting queen of Chalcis. To the people who remembered her father's reign as the last golden age before the total Roman subjugation she represented a link with the past. In a nostalgic way she was the spiritual queen of Judaea.

But she was not the only royal lady who graced the Court of Women with her pious attendance. Another queen often came to pray there. She was the dowager queen Helena of Adiabene, who had embraced the Jewish religion and in her old age had come to live in Jerusalem.

Adiabene, in northern Mesopotamia, was a client-kingdom of Parthia, Rome's great rival in the east. It lay in the path of merchants from Judaea, who had the entry of the palace. The king was well disposed towards them and did not mind when they converted all his wives to Judaism, including his favourite one and his queen, who was also his sister. Helena was so impressed with her new religion that she allowed her sons to be instructed in it too, only drawing the line on circumcision. The prudent queen explained to them, particularly to the heir apparent, that the people of Adiabene would not tolerate the rule of a Jew over them. The sons refused to accept half measures and took the irrevocable step. When Helena found out what they had done, she went to the king and told him that his sons had grown ulcers which had to be removed by operation.

After her husband's death, her favourite son succeeded to the throne and ruled for many years. The elderly Helena decided it was time to accomplish a lifelong dream and go to Jerusalem to worship in the temple. Her arrival coincided with the great famine of AD 46. The generous queen sent her attendants to buy grain from Alexandria and dried figs from Cyprus and distributed them to the hungry and the needy. That Herod of Chalcis did not do the same for the people of Judaea was due perhaps to the fact that the famine ravaged his own country too, and his resources had to be used to help his peasants and rescue them from hungry brigands. Helena's generosity earned her the everlasting gratitude of the Jews. She added to it by offering work to the unemployed, engaging them to build her a palace in town and a royal tomb outside the city wall. Most archaeologists identify the Tombs of the Kings near the Damascus Gate in Jerusalem as the triple tomb she built for herself and her two eldest sons.

She also had a residence in Lydda. During the Feast of Tabernacles she had a booth built there, as prescribed, and entertained seven other sons of hers, all learned in Judaism. Her piety spurred her on to further generosity. She gave the temple a golden candlestick which was placed over the door of the sanctuary and a golden tablet inscribed with the Mosaic law concerning the married woman who goes astray. Nobody commented on the incongruity of a Jewish proselyte, once incestuously married, putting on record the laws about adulterous wives. The royal family of Adiabene was above criticism.

The year 46, which saw queen Helena's arrival in Jerusalem, was also the year when the procurator Cuspius Fadus was succeeded after a two-year term by Tiberius Julius Alexander.

The new procurator was well known to Berenice, although she may not have met him more than once or twice in the past. He was the eldest son of the rich *alabarch* of Alexandria, brother to her first husband Marcus. Although after the anti-Jewish riots of 37 Tiberius Alexander went over to paganism, he showed no hatred for the religion he had abandoned and did not interfere with the religious freedom of his province. On the other hand he showed much zeal in crushing any attempt to undermine the Roman rule. He crucified two leaders of the Zealots, the Jewish patriots who were forming themselves into a dangerous resistance movement against the Romans.

His relations with Berenice must have been doubly cordial. Not only had she been his sister-in-law, but she was now the wife of the king of Chalcis, who had an official position in Jerusalem as the imperial custodian of the sacred robes. Tiberius must have met them both officially and socially, and although he would not have consulted them on his campaign against the Zealots, they would have approved of his policy. As Roman dependants, Herod and Berenice would condemn any attempt to stir rebellion against Rome. Being in a privileged position, they little realized how fiercely the fire of freedom burnt in the hearts of the common people of Judaea.

Four years of busy married life passed quickly. Then, one day in 48, Herod died, leaving Berenice a widow for the second time. She was just twenty.

This time her widowhood was a blow. She was entirely on her own, with two small children on her hands, in a virtually foreign country, with no roots and no family connections. Tiberius Alexander had left Judaea, while her mother, brothers and sisters were in Rome, some fifteen hundred miles away. At one stroke her husband's death robbed her of her royal position in Chalcis and her status in Jerusalem. A client-king's widow had no claim to a state that even her late husband held only on a grace and favour tenure. There was nothing Berenice could do for the moment, except sit tight and wait to hear what Rome would decide to do with the kingdom that for the past four years had acknowledged her as queen.

Chapter X

Brother and sister

THERE were two strong candidates for the vacant throne of
Chalcis. One was Aristobulus, son of the late king Herod of
Chalcis by his first wife. The other was young Agrippa, son of the
late king Agrippa of Judaea.

On the face of it Aristobulus's case was much the stronger.
Although client-kingdoms were not hereditary, a suitable son had
a better claim to a father's territory than a mere stranger. Aristobulus was a man of mature judgement and proven diplomatic
ability. He possessed the Herodian flair for administration and was
well thought of by Claudius. By all accounts he was a serious
candidate, and he must have pressed his claim with as much skill
as his young cousin.

Agrippa however, although young and inexperienced, had the
stronger moral claim. When he was seventeen he was not allowed
to succeed his own father through no fault of his. Claudius then
let it be understood that the young man would be given another
chance to rule as soon as a suitable vacancy occurred. Herod's
death provided just such a vacancy. Claudius may well have felt
he owed young Agrippa a moral debt. Certainly Agrippa would
have used all his cunning to persuade the emperor that this indeed
was the case. Even so it took Claudius the best part of two years
to make up his mind, but in the end he decided in favour of his
old friend's son. At twenty-three Agrippa II became king of
Chalcis. With the title also went the right to appoint high priests,
keep the sacred vestments and use the Hasmonaean palace during
his visits to Jerusalem.

The news from Rome could not have relieved Berenice of her
state of suspense. Although only a year younger than her brother,
she had never really known him, for while she was living in
Jerusalem he was being educated in Rome. There was a brief reunion when she accompanied her husband to plead with Claudius

for the custody of the high priest's robes; but it was a tense and agitated period, which allowed little time for family intimacy. Soon afterwards Berenice returned to Chalcis to undertake her duties as queen, wife and mother, while Agrippa stayed on in Rome. The brother who was now to arrive in Chalcis as its new king was virtually a stranger. He might be a merciless tyrant like his Idumaean ancestor Herod the Great, or a mischief-maker like Antipater. As king he was entitled to turn her out of a palace in which she was no more than a guest; as the head of the family he could lay hands on her private wealth inherited from two husbands and pretend to hold it in trust for her sons. Family history had taught her that brothers could be enemies. She must have awaited his arrival with little enthusiasm.

It was probably a rather guarded Berenice who welcomed the young king to his royal residence. Her first impression must have been favourable. At twenty-three Agrippa was gay, lively, full of society gossip and brimming with charm. He may have anticipated some difficulty with the one-time queen, and no doubt set himself to win her over by kindness. The first meeting must have allayed both their fears. Agrippa turned out to be no ogre, while Berenice proved to be no hostile widow. Brother and sister were completely won over by one another. Soon the young king found himself listening with attention to advice tactfully offered by the more experienced dowager-queen. A working partnership was established to the satisfaction of both parties.

A coin that Agrippa struck of himself a few years later may suggest what he looked like at the time of his arrival in Chalcis. He had a good head of hair, a smooth, slightly rounded face, still unworn by care, a dominant nose and a short chin. It was not his looks however that pleased Berenice most but his ways. Having been brought up in Rome, he was sophisticated, smooth of tongue, a skilful diplomat and an entertaining companion. Like Berenice he was thoroughly hellenized in his tastes, fond of good living and splendour. Like her he was a believer in the fundamentals of Judaism and a conformist. The brother and sister found they had a great deal in common.

For Berenice the daily proximity to an attractive young man was a new experience. Until then she had always been surrounded by middle-aged or even elderly men who were her father's con-

temporaries. Marcus, whom she married at twelve and a half, was
mostly away. Herod, whom she married at fifteen, was forty years
her senior. Although the marriage was sound, it could hardly
have been exciting for a young woman. There were mutual respect
and affection, but there could have been no question of love on
her part. Now, for the first time in her life, she found herself in
daily contact with a young man of her own age, who was attractive and who obviously was finding her attractive too. For the
first time in her life she experienced love's awakening. That the
object of her love was her own brother must have appalled her at
first. She had been brought up on the Mosaic law that condemned
incest most vehemently. She must have struggled against it more
desperately than Agrippa, who had spent his formative years in
Rome and had seen incestuous relationships tolerated in the best
of families.

That Berenice was attracted to Agrippa is fairly understandable
in the circumstances. Why he was attracted to her is less so. She
was not only his sister, but a mature woman, a widow, twice a
mother. Yet she fascinated him to such an extent that no Ituraean
maiden could put her out of his mind. What must have encouraged them both to embark on a forbidden relationship was the
fact that they lived in a semi-barbarian society, which, even if it
did not condone incest, at least did not treat it with the same
abhorrence as Judaism. In the event their passion overcame religious injunctions, moral misgivings and plain common sense.
Brother and sister made no secret of their love. They lived openly
together and shared the responsibilities and privileges of royalty.
It became the most enduring relationship of Berenice's career.

Once their personal problem was resolved the queen and king
of Chalcis—protocol laid down that Berenice should take priority
because she had been queen before he became king—could turn
their attention to events outside their tiny kingdom. Things had
been going badly for the Judaeans ever since the return of the
procurators, and in the year 52 they seemed to have reached their
lowest ebb.

The deterioration started in the same year that Berenice lost her
husband, when Ventidius Cumanus was sent to replace Tiberius
Alexander. Unlike his two predecessors, Cumanus did not have

the requisite qualities for dealing with his recalcitrant subjects. With his arrival the delicate balance between political subjugation and religious freedom was upset, and bloody clashes became the order of the day.

The first incident occurred shortly after his arrival in his new province, while Agrippa was still in Rome trying to win the kingdom of Chalcis. In the spring of 49 tens of thousands of pilgrims had gathered as usual in Jerusalem to celebrate the Passover. Crowds spelt danger, so Cumanus left his headquarters in Caesarea and went to Jerusalem to attend personally to the security arrangements. In accordance with the practice established by his predecessors, he posted soldiers from the Antonia garrison at strategic points under the temple porticoes with instructions to keep law and order. While he retired to the royal palace in the upper city, reserved for his use on such occasions, the soldiers were left to contend with the milling crowds who pushed and jostled in their eagerness to perform a rite which their protectors, despised Gentiles that they were, were not allowed to share. Keeping the peace among the worshippers was an odious duty. From his post under one of the porticoes a soldier felt like showing them what he thought of their feast and their religion. He pulled up his uniform to expose his backside to the crowds below, crouched down and farted loudly. The worshippers were aghast. It was an outrageous act of blasphemy. They shouted for revenge and pelted the soldier and his mates with stones. Cumanus was alerted and sent in reinforcements to put down the disturbance. The arrival of more soldiers caused panic among the unarmed pilgrims. They stampeded for the narrow exits, pushing, struggling, kicking, trampling one another. All hell broke loose in the temple courts. Josephus later estimated that when law and order were at last restored thirty thousand dead were counted. The rest of the Passover became a period of mourning and seething hatred.

Although Cumanus could not be held directly responsible for the temple tragedy, the bereaved could not help giving vent to their hate by acts of subversion, or at least of connivance at it. The anti-Roman elements, which during Agrippa I's reign had lain low now raised their heads again. At one time they had been condemned by moderates as no better than bandits and robbers. Now many began to feel that robbing a Roman was not only a non-crime, but a brave act in the struggle for freedom. When an imperial official was robbed near Beth Horon, about twelve miles out of Jerusalem, Cumanus not incorrectly assumed that the neighbouring villages were sheltering the robbers. As collective punishment was thought then as now to be the best deterrent, he had the notables of the villages put in chains and the villages themselves evacuated and sacked. In the heat of the action a soldier got hold of the holy scroll of the law and tore it to pieces. Immediately individual feelings of hatred gave way to a wave of religious fury. Forgetting their arrested notables and their burnt property, the villagers started marching towards Caesarea, seventy miles to the north, to demand justice against the offender. All along the route they were joined by more supporters, many of whom were armed with daggers under their cloaks. By the time the marchers reached Caesarea their numbers had swelled to thousands, all prepared to take the law into their own hands if denied justice. In view of so much fanaticism Cumanus made a conciliatory gesture and had the offending soldier executed. A bloody uprising was averted just in time.

But worse was to come. Agrippa had not long been in Chalcis when news reached him and Berenice of a strife between Jews and Samaritans, which threatened to develop into a long war of attrition.

The town of Samaria, near the modern Nablus or Shechem, was founded by an ancient king of Israel and rebuilt by Pompey. Augustus gave it to Herod the Great who built there a temple for the Greek population and renamed it Sebaste. It was there he married princess Mariamme, and it was there he later had her two sons executed. The town became the capital of the region and a recruiting ground for the royal army.

The natives of Samaria however were not Greeks but descendants of Jews who many centuries earlier had deviated from orthodoxy. They observed the law of circumcision, but disregarded the levirate law of marriage. They kept the Sabbath, but took no notice of the many bylaws worked out by Pharisee scholars. Above all they denied the sanctity of the temple in Jerusalem. They had their own temple on their holy Mount Gerizim, just outside the town of Samaria, and their own high priest. The Jews regarded them as past redemption and would not marry into them. The Samaritans hated the Jews and often indulged in acts of spite. Sometimes they would light beacon-fires on the tops of the hills at the wrong time of the month, to mislead the Jews about the appearance of the new moon which determined the lunar calendar and the dates of the holy feasts. They had little use for a Jewish king and were only too pleased to return to the rule of Roman procurators.

The region of Samaria lay in the direct pilgrims' route between Galilee and Jerusalem, and the Galileans, in spite of their hostility for the Samaritans, used to go right through their towns and villages on their way to the holy festivals. Once, near the modern Jenin, a fight developed between a party of Galilean pilgrims and the Samaritans, in which a Galilean was killed. That was a sign for a free-for-all. Galileans killed Samaritans, Samaritans killed Galileans. The Galileans demanded justice from Cumanus; the Samaritans bribed him to withhold it. The Galileans looked for help elsewhere. A well-known anti-Roman leader from Jerusalem came out with his followers and swooped on Samaritan villages. Cumanus armed the Samaritans and sent out his soldiers to fight the Jews. Many were slaughtered or captured; others, defeated but unable to return to their homes, joined the ranks of the subversive anti-Roman party. In the meantime both Jews and Samaritans lost faith in Cumanus and took their case to the governor of Syria. The governor dealt out summary justice to all. He crucified or beheaded many prisoners and sent to Rome a large party of hostages consisting of both Jewish and Samaritan notables. Cumanus and his military tribune Celer were instructed to follow them. They were all to give evidence before Claudius and await his judgement.

There is no reason to suppose that Agrippa rushed to Rome to act as a self-appointed champion for his co-religionists. His departure for Rome about that time must have been motivated by purely personal considerations. Like his father before him, he may have felt that after nearly two years' absence from the centre of power it was time for him to return and cultivate old contacts with a view to winning new favours. But he was well informed about the happenings in Judaea, and once he learnt that a trial was impending he took the course that was as natural to him as it had been to any other member of the Herodian family. He made himself the ardent advocate of the Jews.

From previous experience he knew the value of preparing the ground before the hearing. Claudius was still fond of him, but he was easily swayed by his freedmen, whose natural reaction was to support Cumanus against his accusers. The most influential freedman at that time was Pallas, once a slave of old Antonia's. Agrippa succeeded in buying his goodwill as well as that of Claudius's wife Agrippina, who was reputed to be Pallas's mistress. But Cumanus had not been idle either. He too had been courting influential freedmen and the outcome of the trial was in the balance. During the hearing Agrippa made a spirited speech in defence of the Jews, and with Pallas and Agrippina backing his case, obtained a favourable verdict. The Samaritans were found guilty and three of them condemned to death. The Jews were released. Cumanus was dismissed and banished, and his military tribune Celer sent to Jerusalem to be executed, so that justice could be seen to be done.

After the trial the whole future of the procuratorship came under review. The province consisted of two distinct elements; the Jews, who were difficult subjects and needed a strong hand, and the hellenized pagans, who were well contented with the Roman administration. Having got rid of Cumanus Agrippa must have used all his influence to try to divert part of the large province to himself. His efforts were richly rewarded. The territories across the Jordan, that had once been his father's and before that formed Philip's tetrarchy, were sliced off and offered to him as a client-kingdom. At twenty-five, Agrippa was king of Trachonitis, Batanaea, Gaulanitis and Abilene, which his father had received from Caligula when he was twice his age. Chalcis was reabsorbed into the province of Syria, but another small territory in the Lebanon was given to him instead. The rest of Cumanus's province, including the difficult Judaea and Samaria, was given to Antonius Felix, brother to Pallas and himself a freedman.

Early in 53 Agrippa returned to Chalcis for the last time, to take Berenice and her sons to his new capital Caesarea Philippi. The family party included the two younger sisters Mariamme and Drusilla whose education in Rome had long been completed and who were in need of husbands.

Caesarea Philippi, where Berenice had lived for a while at the beginning of her father's reign, was an attractive city hugging the lower slopes of Mount Hermon. Herod the Great had received it from Augustus and was the first to rebuild it. Near the cave containing one of the principal sources of the Jordan and a shrine of Pan, he built a temple of white marble, a counterpart to the one he had built in Samaria. But it was his son, Philip the tetrarch, who made it his capital and developed it. It was a place of great natural beauty, green all the year round, with cool mountain streams watering slopes that were covered with fig trees, almond trees, poplars, willows and rhododendrons. Agrippa and Berenice set to work to make it a royal city. They embellished the palace, put up new buildings and built a theatre where gladiatorial games could be held. It became their permanent home, to which they always returned after their various journeys to Berytus, Jerusalem, Athens, Rome.

One of Agrippa's first duties as head of the family was to see his younger sisters safely married. Mariamme's marriage presented no difficulty. Long before her father's death she had been engaged to the son of his military commander Helcias. With her brother's elevation she became a most desirable match, and the wedding took place without delay.

But Drusilla's case was different. When she was three or four years old her father had betrothed her to the son of his old friend king Antiochus of Commagene, who promised to undergo circumcision when the time came. After Agrippa I's death the bridegroom had second thoughts. It was a high price to pay for a wife who, although a princess, had no political advantages to offer. He must have broken off the engagement long before Drusilla's status rose again through her brother's elevation. Now a new husband had to be found for her. Drusilla was over thirteen when she arrived at Caesarea Philippi, strikingly beautiful and knowing her own mind. Having once been engaged to a prince, she was not willing to be married to a commoner. Berenice must have had words with her on the subject, and Drusilla, who was a shrewd young lady and not blind to what was going on in the palace bedrooms, must have stood up to her. The relations between the two sisters became strained. When Berenice eventually produced a royal candidate, Drusilla was not grateful. It was Aziz, king of Emesa, with whom Berenice had been on cordial terms through her husband Herod and her uncle Aristobulus, who had married into the Emesa royal family. Aziz must have been attracted by the prospect of being related to a king whose kingdom was larger than his own, and he accepted circumcision. The marriage was duly celebrated and Drusilla became queen of Emesa. Berenice was relieved to see her go. Not only was Drusilla too outspoken and unafraid of her, but she was beginning to eclipse her with her fresher beauty. The two queens parted without regret.

But not for long. They were to meet at regular intervals in Jerusalem, where the three sisters and their menfolk attended the holy feasts. Agrippa presided as usual over the handing-over ceremony of the high priest's clothes and attended to the temple administration. Like his father and his uncle Herod, he took part in the temple ceremonies, while Berenice found her usual place in the Court of Women, next to her sisters Drusilla and Mariamme.

The pilgrimages to Jerusalem precipitated an unavoidable crisis. What could be tolerated by the pagan inhabitants of Caesarea Philippi could not pass uncriticized by the pious Pharisees of Judaea. The forbidden relationship between the royal brother and sister became a public scandal. There may well have been some hostile demonstrations of popular feeling. Berenice was torn between her passion and her scruples. Agrippa, equally perturbed, also had to reckon with the danger of losing his right to control the temple funds and the holy vestments. After a period of inner wrestling they decided to end their relationship and stop the scandal. Berenice was to find a husband and put distance between her and temptation.

The prospective husband had to be Jewish; and, to be acceptable to the queen of Chalcis, he also had to be royal. A suitable candidate was found in the person of Marcus Antonius Polemo, who had been made king of Cilicia (in Asia Minor) either by Claudius or by Nero who succeeded him in AD 54. Polemo was no stranger to Judaism. Cilicia had a well-established Jewish community whose members brought up their sons in synagogue schools and maintained close links with Jerusalem. It was the birthplace of St Paul, whose trial in Judaea Berenice was to attend a few years later, and who described himself as a true-born Jew, circumcised on his eighth day. Some Jewish ideas had a following among the native population and for several generations there had flourished in Cilicia a sect of non-Jews who observed the Sabbath and worshipped Yahweh. Polemo realized however that he had to go further than the Sabbatists. He had to accept Judaism in full.

There was no question of his paying Agrippa the obsolescent bride-price; it was he who had to be offered every possible inducement to undergo circumcision and marry a widow whose tarnished reputation could not have escaped him. Berenice met his price. Her first two husbands had left her a rich widow, and her brother must have given her a handsome dowry as a further inducement. Both sides to the bargain knew exactly what they were offering and what they were getting. When the negotiations were satisfactorily concluded, Polemo was circumcised, possibly by one of his own Pharisee subjects, and the wedding was celebrated. Berenice left for her new kingdom. As a parting present Agrippa gave her a diamond ring of such unusual size and magnificence that more than twenty years later, when she wore it in Rome, it gave rise to a wave of malicious gossip. Polemo's conversion must have given the Jewish community of Cilicia a tremendous feeling of pride and satisfaction, and when their Jewish queen arrived to join her newly converted husband, there must have been many expressions of loyalty and jubilation.

With his sister far away, Agrippa too made an effort to readjust. He courted the good opinion of the Pharisees and tried to conform to their teachings in all matters concerning daily routine. Once he sent them a query about the performance of a domestic rite concerned with the Feast of Tabernacles, from the phrasing of which it would appear that he too had married. In fact he had taken not one wife but two, which was permissible. One kept house for him in Tiberias, which Nero added to Agrippa's kingdom in AD 54, and the other in nearby Sepphoris (Zippori). Presumably neither was well born or well loved enough to be given the style of queen; certainly neither was allowed to take Berenice's place in Caesarea Philippi.

Agrippa must have kept in touch with his sister and soon learnt that the marriage with Polemo had not effected the expected cure. Self-denial only served to make Berenice regret her concession to public opinion. She grew restless and spiteful. Turning over the

problem in her mind she may well have reflected that in Egypt
marriages between brothers and sisters were customary among
the Pharaohs, and even Cleopatra was once married to a younger
brother. Her own sister Drusilla was named after a sister of Caligula's who had been his mistress; and king Antiochus of Commagene, who just missed being related to the Herodian family,
was married to his own sister Iotape. Obviously incest was acceptable in some parts of the civilized world. But there was hardly any
need to derive encouragement from foreign practices, when the
Jewish religion itself seemed to supply a precedent of tolerance.
Berenice must have remembered the example of old queen Helena
of Adiabene, who was still living in Jerusalem and enjoying great
popularity among the Pharisees. Not only had Helena been incestuously married, but she had produced many sons of that
marriage, all of whom were highly respected in Judaea for their
piety and devotion to Judaism. True, Helena was a widow, and
her husband-brother long dead; but the incest had never been
criticized even when he was alive and Helena already a professing
Jewess. When she came to settle in Jerusalem no Pharisee ever
reproached her with her sinful past, even though her sons were a
constant reminder of it. Berenice may well have reckoned that if
she and Agrippa conformed to all other demands of piety and
showed generosity to the people of Judaea, they too might in
time come to be accepted. She could not have failed to observe
that some originally taboo associations, by no other virtue than
their permanence, ended by acquiring a measure of respectability.
Hope as well as instinct urged her to go back.

Nearly a year passed in longing and indecision, when news
reached Berenice that the high-spirited Drusilla had run away
from Emesa and was openly living in Judaea with a man not her
husband and not of the Jewish faith. Obviously virtue was not at
a premium. Being less impulsive, Berenice decided to end her stay
in Cilicia in a more dignified manner. She asked Polemo for a
divorce, and Polemo, who was no doubt allowed to retain a considerable portion of her dowry, if not all of it, let his wife go.
Josephus later made much of the poor king who had undergone
circumcision only to be abandoned. As it happened Polemo must
have made a handsome profit from the transaction and could not
have been reluctant to terminate a marriage that had nothing

pleasing about it apart from its financial provision. That the experience left him unscathed may be deduced from coins he struck nearly fifteen years later, on which he styled himself, like his predecessors, high priest and ruler of Cennatis, Lalassis and primarily of Olba, with its sanctuary dedicated to Zeus Olbios.[1]

Some modern historians suggest that in spite of appearances no incestuous relationship existed between Agrippa and Berenice and that the case for it rests on the prejudiced accounts of Josephus and Juvenal.[2] Their accounts however seem to be borne out by circumstantial evidence. Only an involvement with his sister could have stopped a family-conscious king like Agrippa from taking a high-born wife and begetting children to continue the Herodian line. Only an involvement with her brother could explain Berenice's failure to remarry at any time after her return from Cilicia, living as she did in a society that attached no stigma to divorce and equated widowhood with unhappiness. Jewish tradition encouraged widows to remarry as soon as possible by allowing them the briefest of waiting periods between funeral and wedding. When Berenice married Herod of Chalcis after her first widowhood and Polemo of Cilicia after her second, she did no more than the expected thing. After her divorce she was free to marry again; indeed such a marriage would have been not only appropriate but virtually a social obligation. If she failed to comply, it was most likely because of her involvement with her brother, which did not admit of any other attachment.

After her return to Caesarea Philippi Berenice resumed cohabitation with Agrippa as if she was his legal consort. That was the real beginning of her remarkable rise to a position of power and authority. Both brother and sister believed in the supreme power of Rome and the desirability of remaining under its aegis. Together they watched out for any internal changes in the imperial set-up and kept up friendships and contacts. Gradually Berenice grew in stature and importance. She became the recognized queen in her brother's court, his acknowledged partner in affairs of state. Official correspondence was sometimes addressed to her as well as to him, and she had a say in the appointment of royal secretaries. She probably had her own private ones who attended to her personal finances and her charities.

Earlier family settlements had left her a rich woman in her own right. Agrippa added to her wealth by allowing her the revenue from some of his corn-growing lands. She lived in royal style and introduced into the capital the fashions and luxuries of the Roman world. Caravans from the east brought fabrics for her wardrobe along with gold and silver for the royal treasury. But wealth and power meant to her more than the gratification of personal pleasures. She continued her father's policy of contributing towards the welfare of other centres of hellenistic civilization, notably Athens itself. The grateful Athenians raised a statue to her, alas not preserved, on the base of which they put an inscription commemorating the great *basilissa* Berenice, daughter of Agrippa and descendant of great kings and benefactors. The statue and inscription, attributed to 61, must have been the result of several acts of generosity and possibly visits to Athens, obviously undertaken independently of her brother.

Jointly with him she showed much interest in Berytus, another traditional recipient of Herodian largesse. She and Agrippa gave the town a theatre, as their father had done before them, and virtually ransacked their own territories in order to adorn it with the most beautiful statues in the land. A Latin inscription commemorated their joint generosity, mentioning the *regina* Berenice before Agrippa.

The title of *basilissa* in Greek and *regina* in Latin indicated the high standing Berenice had achieved in the Graeco-Roman world. Even the ambivalent Josephus respectfully referred to her and her brother as Their Majesties. Time indeed thrust a mantle of respectability over their association. Not until twenty years later was it raked up again, and then not in Jerusalem or in Caesarea Philippi but in Rome, and not on moral grounds but for political reasons. Of Agrippa's two wives no more was heard.

Chapter XI

In-laws to a procurator

WHEN Archelaus the son of Herod the Great was deprived of his tetrarchy in AD 6 and banished to Gaul by Augustus, Judaea became a Roman province and was put under a procurator. Apart from the brief three-year period of Agrippa I's reign, and in spite of the great rebellions of AD 66 and AD 132, it remained a province until the disintegration of the Roman empire itself.

By the beginning of the Christian era the empire embraced most of the known areas within reach of the Mediterranean. Broadly speaking, the boundaries were the Rhine, the Danube and the Black Sea in the north; the Red Sea, Upper Egypt and the Sahara in the south; the Atlantic and the English Channel in the west. As the empire had grown haphazardly, it had no regular or uniform administration. Augustus set out to remedy the situation and organize an efficient system of control. He rationalized frontiers and divided the subject territories, or provinces, into three administrative groups. The first, consisting of the richer and more settled provinces which did not require a garrison, was entrusted to ex-consuls and ex-praetors. The second, consisting of large territories of strategic and economic importance, was administered by members of the senate. The third included the smaller provinces and was ruled by procurators risen from the middle classes.

Judaea, although essential to the Roman defence system against the rival Parthian empire in the east, belonged to the third group, like the small islands of Sardinia and Corsica. Politically it was joined to Syria, which ranked above it as belonging to the second group. Its governor had authority over the procurator and in cases of emergency could over-rule his decisions.

The procurators were usually civil servants who had risen in the administrative hierarchy thanks to their own merit. They were experienced administrators, but they rarely knew what to make of the Jews. At best they thought of them as intractable separatists who clung to a strange religion and made difficulties. They had a somewhat clearer idea of the geography of the province, or Palestine as it began to be called, as may be deduced from Tacitus's description of it:

The country is bound on the east by Arabia, on the south by Egypt, on the west by Phoenicia and the sea, and on the north by Syria. .... The highest mountain in Palestine is Lebanon; surprisingly enough in this semi-tropical climate it is thickly wooded and is covered with snow all the year round. Its slopes feed the tumbling water of the river Jordan. The Jordan does not flow into the Mediterranean, but goes through two lakes [the swampy lake Hula, now drained, and the Sea of Galilee] and is absorbed into a third [the Dead Sea]. The third lake is as large as a sea, but its water is even saltier. Its stagnant water pollutes the air and causes disease among those who live on its banks. Neither fish nor water-fowl can survive in it. The water is so heavy that swimmers and non-swimmers find it equally buoyant. ....

Not far from the lake there is a plain which tradition says was consumed by lightning, though it was once fertile and supported two large cities [Sodom and Gomorrah, near modern Sdom]. It seems that the ruins of these cities can still be traced. ....

One of the rivers flowing into the Mediterranean is the Belius [Naaman, north of Haifa], at whose mouth there are sands which, after being fused with natron, are used to make glass. The beach concerned is small, but its output seems to be inexhaustible. ....

There are many villages in Judaea, and several towns. The capital is Jerusalem.[1]

Of the population Tacitus seemed to know only that 'the health of the Jews is good and their physique sturdy'.[2] He did not seem to know much about their religion, and noted that they lived mostly on agriculture. That was probably the extent of the knowledge a new procurator would be armed with on his arrival in Judaea.

Although Jerusalem was the capital, the procurators resided in Caesarea in the same palace which had been the scene of Agrippa I's death. They went to Jerusalem only to supervise the security arrangements during the holy feasts or during times of emergency. Judicial functions were left to the native courts, and the procurator's assent was required only for capital punishment.

Their tenure of office was usually short and their task ungrateful. They might well have been efficient administrators elsewhere, but Judaea was a trial even for the best intentioned amongst them. As it happened, not many approached their task with any degree of dedication. They preferred to regard it as an easy source of revenue and fleeced their subjects in every conceivable way. Most did not stay more than two years. Tiberius was the first who allowed them to stay longer, either because he could not be bothered to replace them, or, as he once explained, because a settled and satiated procurator was less of a bloodsucker than a ravenous newcomer.

The accepted practice was to draw the procurators from the ranks of the second order of the Roman state, the equestrian order, which consisted at that time of the upper middle classes of Italy. The appointment of Felix, a freedman, caused a wave of indignation in imperial circles. He owed it partly to his brother Pallas, who wielded great power over Claudius, and partly to the former high priest Jonathan, who was one of the prisoners sent to Rome to stand trial before the emperor and who, on his release, thought it politic to repay Pallas by putting in a good word for his brother. Felix in his turn repaid Jonathan by having him assassinated.

Both brothers had been slaves of Claudius's mother Antonia, and both claimed descent from the kings of Arcadia. But while Pallas, having amassed a fortune by all sorts of means, was careful not to drive the senate into open opposition, Felix had no such scruples. He was greedy and corruptible and 'believed that all his crimes could be committed with impunity'.[3] He was described as 'a monster of cruelty and lust, who exercised the powers of a king in the spirit of a slave'.[4] He may have had all sorts of mistresses, but for wives he took only queens. He was once married to a grand-daughter of Antony and Cleopatra and was thus related to Claudius. By the time he arrived in Judaea he had divorced or lost his second queen and was in search of a third. The one who caught his fancy was the beautiful and dissatisfied Drusilla.

They met in Jerusalem during one of the holy feasts, which Felix attended in the line of duty and which the Jewish queen of Emesa and her convert husband attended as celebrants. Felix may have made some overtures to her there and then, but Aziz whisked his wife off to Emesa before the procurator could get very far. He had to woo her by proxy. A certain Cypriot Jew who practised the art of magic was picked for the assignment. He proceeded to the court of Emesa and described Felix's charms in such glowing terms that Drusilla was completely won over. Without much thought for decorum or legal separation, she ran away and joined Felix in Caesarea as his mistress. By Jewish law she was doubly guilty; not only was she an adulterous wife, but the man she was committing adultery with was a Gentile. Aziz however obliged the lovers by dying shortly after Drusilla's desertion, thus enabling her to go through a form of marriage which may have satisfied Felix, but which in the eyes of the Pharisees must have been just as sinful as her previous behaviour.

The tendentious Josephus, describing the event in retrospect, not only refrained from condemning Drusilla, but put all the blame on Berenice, who, he suggested, from her palace in Caesarea Philippi had contrived to make life so unbearable for Drusilla in Emesa, a good hundred and twenty miles away, that she had to run away to put an end to her suffering. What Josephus omitted to mention was that Caesarea Maritima, where Drusilla joined Felix, was considerably nearer Caesarea Philippi than Emesa; and that if her sole object in running away was to put distance between her and her sister, she had somewhat miscalculated. In any case the desertion occurred in the year 53 or 54, when Berenice was most likely in far-away Cilicia.

But the hatchet had to be buried. Agrippa had no quarrel with Felix, and Berenice, on her return from Cilicia, was far too sensible to allow any past misunderstanding she may have had with Drusilla to prejudice her standing with the imperial procurator. Both Agrippa and Felix had their duties to perform in Jerusalem, and both were dependent on the goodwill of the emperor in Rome. The sisters made it up and the two families must have met regularly during the next six or seven years. When Drusilla bore Felix a son she called him Agrippa. It was a subtle way of ingratiating herself with her brother, while at the same time scoring a point against her sister.

About that time the middle sister Mariamme also had a change of partner. Through an arrangement made in her infancy she had married the son of her father's army commander and bore him a daughter whom she named Berenice. But Mariamme too had her fair share of the Herodian temperament. She divorced her husband and married a certain Demetrius who was then the rich *alabarch* of Alexandria. Fortunately he was Jewish, so the marriage was both regular and advantageous. It yielded a son whom Mariamme, having lost the race to Drusilla by a short head, had to call Agrippinus. When Drusilla's son grew up both he and his wife died in the eruption of Vesuvius in AD 79. What became of Mariamme's children is not known, just as nothing is known of the lives of Berenice's two sons by Herod of Chalcis.[5]

When in Caesarea Philippi, among his pagan subjects, Agrippa behaved like one of them. He minted coins with images, erected statues, arranged games and no doubt attended the celebrations in the shrine of Pan. But in Jerusalem he followed his father's example and took great care to observe the religious minutiae of everyday life. As the running of the palace was Berenice's responsibility, it was she who often had to consult the learned Pharisees on points of domestic ritual. The scholars derived much satisfaction from guiding the royal family. When the palace was in difficulties no lesser a personage than the president of the religious council, the *Rabban* of the day, was called upon to pronounce.

A problem once arose in connection with the Passover, which Agrippa and Berenice usually celebrated in Jerusalem. The Paschal offering could consist of either a lamb or a kid; but whichever it was, it had to conform to the instructions of the person in whose name it was made. If a head of a family instructed his servants to go to the temple and offer a lamb in his name, and they offered a kid instead, the offering was invalid. When Agrippa's servants once neglected to ascertain his exact intention and tried to play safe by sacrificing a lamb as well as a kid, both offerings were on the point of being disqualified. Fortunately the tactful *Rabban* found a way out by pronouncing that frivolous persons such as a king and queen might for once be exempt from a ruling that was binding for conscientious observers of the law like himself and his scholarly colleagues.

In a country with a hot climate such as Palestine the Pharisees sometimes legislated with an eye to hygiene. If a dead lizard happened to be found in the slaughter-house, the meat was declared unclean and unfit for human consumption. If however a live lizard was caught, the meat was not considered contaminated and could be eaten. A culinary crisis in the palace was once averted only after Berenice sent an urgent appeal to the Pharisee experts, who approached the problem empirically:

One day a lizard was found in the slaughter-house and the whole meal was about to be declared unclean. The palace servants went and informed the king who told them to go and tell the queen. When they told the queen she told them to go and ask Rabban Gamaliel. So the servants went and asked for a ruling. Said Rabban Gamaliel:

'Was the slaughter-house hot or cold?'

'It was hot,' they answered.

'Then go and pour a glass of cold water over the lizard,' Rabban Gamaliel ordered.

When they returned to the slaughter-house and poured cold water over the lizard it moved, which proved it was alive; whereupon Rabban Gamaliel pronounced the meat clean.[6]

The story, preserved in the Talmud, concluded that since the king was dependent on the queen in this instance, and the queen on Rabban Gamaliel, the entire royal dinner was dependent on Rabban Gamaliel. Berenice's concern with dietary niceties must have been a source of amusement to Drusilla, who also spent her Passovers in Jerusalem together with Felix. But while Berenice, to please the Pharisees, accepted the restrictions of ritual laws, Drusilla could indulge in truly Roman conviviality, having through her marriage with a pagan put herself outside the Jewish religion. She must have also derived immense satisfaction from the fact that she, the youngest of the three sisters, was the only one entitled to reside in her late father's palace in the upper city, while Berenice, the eldest and the most ambitious, had to make do with the unfashionable Hasmonaean palace near the temple. The procurator's wife may well have felt that she scored another point against the queen of Chalcis.

Agrippa's attitude to the Sadducees was less respectful. They still represented the priestly aristocracy, but their way of life had become more aristocratic than priestly. They had acquired the tastes and vices of a secular nobility, and the high priesthood had become no more than a prestigious post, much coveted, but devoid of the traditional aura of sanctity. A Sadducee might aspire to become a high priest just as a Roman politician might aspire to become a consul. He would bribe his way up, make the most of his short tenure of office, then vacate the seat to the next royal favourite. Dismissal was no longer a disgrace. A year's service was often quite enough for a pleasure-loving Sadducee, who would be prepared to put up with the rigid discipline for a limited time, but would not mind going back to a life of laxity. Once, when Agrippa offered the post to a Sadducee who had already served his term a few years earlier, he declined the honour and recommended a brother instead.

Agrippa's choice of a candidate was prompted by mercenary motives. His predecessors appointed high priests according to their political usefulness; he chose them according to their ability to pay for the nomination. He turned the high priesthood into a new source of revenue for the royal treasury. As the aspirants could not be expected to soil their holy hands with bribes, their women-folk sometimes handled the transaction for them. Joshua ben Gamala owed his nomination to his wife Martha, who came from one of the richest Sadducee families in Jerusalem. She paid Agrippa two whole bushels of gold coins. The business was carried out openly, as if it was a legitimate and accepted procedure; the Pharisee scholars referred to Martha's two bushels of gold in a most matter-of-fact way when discussing the difference between election and nomination.

It was Martha again who put wealth before godliness even on the most sacred of the holy feasts. Having succeeded in promoting her husband to the high priesthood, she wanted to give herself the pleasure of seeing him officiate. She decided to do so on the Day of Atonement, when she expected to feel faint with the fast.

To combine duty with pleasure, she did something that no queen would have dared do. She had the whole route leading from her residence to the temple gate laid with carpets, so that she could proceed to the spectacle without exerting herself too much. Her husband somewhat redeemed himself by instituting free education for the young throughout the country.

Other high priests were less conscious of their moral obligations. They were more interested in the social trappings of the post. Since the magnificent sacred vestments could be worn only four times a year, they tried to add glamour to their workaday robes. Again the womenfolk were responsible for what developed into a fashion contest. The mother of one Ishmael ben Phabi made him a beautiful tunic worth a hundred *minas*, which he put on to officiate just once, then cast off. The mother of Eleazar ben Harsom ordered a tunic estimated at twenty thousand *minas*, that was no doubt meant to outshine anything that had ever been worn by any high priest. The fabric was indeed the finest ever seen, and the most transparent. When the high priest put the new tunic on he looked quite naked. He was forbidden to use it again.

Worse than their foppery was their rapacity. Some high priests, possibly taking a leaf from Agrippa's book, regarded their post as a source of revenue. They introduced the custom of sending their servants to the villages at threshing-time to supervise the work of the peasants and collect the tithe on the spot. The tithe was not theirs to claim but due to the lower priesthood. The high priests kept it all the same, sold it and grew rich on it while the common priests, who depended on it for their daily bread, starved to death.

The Sadducees also indulged in bitter feuds. Agrippa's frequent meddling with the high priesthood was not always accepted with good grace. Depending on the circumstances, a dismissal could still be taken as a loss of face, certainly a loss of revenue. Two rival families were so incensed against one another that they each hired gangs of ruffians to do battle in their name. When they met in the narrow lanes they hurled insults and stones at one another. More acts of violence followed until the whole city was plunged into strife and lawlessness. The authorities were unequal to the situation. The Roman procurator had no right to interfere with the work of the local courts; and no Pharisee court could possibly bring to justice a former high priest on a charge of inspiring street brawls.

Felix had his own difficulties to contend with. His newly demarcated province included Judaea, Samaria, Galilee and Peraea; and although it was smaller than it had been during his predecessors' reign, it was just as intractable. Its Jewish subjects might well be divided amongst themselves, but they were unanimous in their dislike of the Romans, the occupation power which had taken over their country and deprived them of their freedom. They resented their presence and gritted their teeth under their ruthlessness, their callousness, their greed. They could see no practical way of overthrowing the enemy and sought comfort in dreams of providential deliverance. The general state of lawlessness and insecurity intensified the longing for a redeemer who would free his people from their misery. Even the sober Pharisees believed in a Messiah, God's anointed, who would establish a better order of things on earth.

In their mood of despondency and longing the people were inclined to clutch at any straw. Any person with some power of persuasion could dazzle the crowds with his eloquence and make them follow him blindly in the hope of finding a better world. There were always the poor, the hungry, the truly unhappy and the gullible, who would put their faith in a self-styled prophet and expect him to make the Romans vanish. Many of those prophets sincerely believed in their mission and divine power. Their expeditions usually met with the same fate. They were hunted down by the Roman soldiers.

One of the first popular manifestations occurred during Cuspius Fadus's term of office, shortly after Agrippa I's death. A prophet called Theudas led a large number of believers, with all their families and belongings, to the bank of the Jordan, which he promised to divide so that they could cross it on foot. That was only by way of proving his divine powers, after which he proposed to turn back and overthrow the Romans with the help of God. Fadus did not wait for the miracle and sent his horsemen after the crowds. Many were killed, many were arrested, and the rest dispersed in fear and hate to await the next divine call. Theudas himself was put to death and his head sent to Jerusalem, but his fate did not in any way diminish the faith of the believers in some future miracle.

Felix had to tackle many such cases. Time and again he executed the visionaries who led these demonstrations and brought their followers back from the desert to Jerusalem, where they joined the ranks of the homeless, the vagabonds, the common thieves and the *sicarii*, the patriotic daggermen. The most disastrous attempt of his reign was made by a Jew from Egypt who persuaded thousands of people to follow him to the Mount of Olives, just outside Jerusalem. He claimed that at his command the city walls would crumble and the Romans would be put to flight. Felix, like Fadus several years earlier, did not wait for the miracle. His horsemen and his soldiers killed several hundred men, arrested a few more hundreds and dispersed the rest. The only miracle the prophet performed was his own escape. He was never caught.

Agrippa and Berenice must have disapproved of the false prophets just as much as Felix, if for different reasons. To a Roman procurator they were simply rebels, mercifully inexperienced in the art of war, who stupidly hoped to crush Roman rule with a few prayers and a mob armed with more faith than weapons. To Agrippa and Berenice they were unrealistic fools who were battering their heads against a stone wall. As Jews they must have felt sympathy for their co-religionists' deep-rooted craving for liberty. But as rulers by the grace of Rome they must have disapproved of misguided leaders who did not have the political sense to realize that national independence was a thing of the past. They may have deplored Felix's ruthless methods, but they could not condemn his policy. They maintained cordial relations with him, saw him and Drusilla whenever the four of them went to Jerusalem for their respective duties, and took care not to make an enemy of a man who had won the favour of two successive Roman emperors.

Chapter XII

From Caesarea to Caesarea

I N the late autumn of 54 news reached Agrippa and Berenice that their old friend and benefactor, the emperor Claudius, was dead.

The rumours of poisoning that came with the news could not have surprised them. From their peaceful capital Caesarea Philippi they had been closely following the turbulent developments in the imperial household and were aware of the family intrigues surrounding the succession. Agrippa knew, from his own successful visit to Rome a couple of years earlier, how much Claudius was swayed by his freedmen and his wife of the day; it was mostly thanks to Agrippina and Pallas that the emperor returned a favourable verdict in the case of the Jews against the Samaritans. That Agrippina intervened in the dispute not for the love of justice but for the love of Pallas mattered little to Agrippa, but it was characteristic of the way things were done in the imperial court.

Claudius had always been susceptible to feminine charm and his old age increased rather than cured his dependence on women. His wives exploited his weakness to their own advantage, and although he was married four times, he was never happily married. He divorced his first wife for adultery and his second for the same reason. His third wife was Messalina, who was more lascivious, cruel and avaricious than either of her predecessors, and who succeeded in scandalizing even the libertine society of imperial Rome. When in AD 48 she made use of Claudius's temporary absence to contract a bigamous marriage with her lover, her enemies accused her of high treason and brought about her death. Claudius was stunned. 'He showed no sign of hatred or joy or anger or sadness, or indeed of any human emotion either in the presence of her triumphant accusers or her weeping children.'[1] When he recovered he declared to his guards that as he had been so unfortunate in his wives, he would never marry again; they could kill him if he did not keep his word.

He did not and they did not either. As soon as Messalina was out of the way a fierce matrimonial contest was waged among a number of ambitious and beautiful matrons who aspired to the power vested in the emperor's wife. It was won by Agrippina, the daughter of Claudius's dead brother Germanicus. Although widowed by one husband and still married to another, she used a niece's privilege to sit on her old uncle's knees and cunningly roused his desire by her seemingly innocent caresses. Roman law, unlike Jewish law, did not permit a marriage between an uncle and his niece. Claudius had it amended. Once Agrippina became empress, she set about assuring the succession for her son by her first marriage. That Claudius had a son of his own was a consideration she did not let stand in her way.

Messalina had borne Claudius a daughter, Octavia, and a son, Britannicus, who was regarded as his father's heir. Agrippina proceeded gradually. She first forced Claudius to break off young Octavia's engagement and marry her instead to her own son Domitius. After Domitius became the emperor's son-in-law, Agrippina asked her husband to adopt him as well. Her lover Pallas, quoting old Tiberius's example as a happy precedent, persuaded Claudius that two heirs-apparent were better than one. Domitius was formally adopted and given the name of Nero. Men of learning noted that it was the first case of adoption in the whole of the Claudian family history, and that never before had the direct line been broken.

Once Nero had gained the unique status of son as well as son-in-law, the question of the succession seemed to be naturally settled in his favour. Britannicus was still a boy. Nero was three or four years older than his step-brother and had no difficulty in asserting himself as the obvious heir. There was however a disgruntled faction that resented Agrippina's power over Claudius and tried to make him change his mind in favour of his real son. Claudius vacillated. Agrippina realized that the only way to stop him altering his decision was to put him out of the way. She arranged to have poison put in his favourite mushroom dish, and when he died had Nero proclaimed emperor.

For Agrippa and Berenice Claudius's death marked the end of

an era. He had been a contemporary of their father and a child-hood friend. During Agrippa I's reign over Judaea, and particu-larly after his death, he brought up young Agrippa in Rome as his own son. He had always treated him kindly, given him a kingdom in the face of a candidate with a better claim, listened favourably to his pleas for the cause of the Jews in Judaea. He had also shown benevolence to Berenice. On his accession he released the impri-soned *alabarch* and so indirectly made it possible for her to marry young Marcus. Claudius may well have attended her wedding feast in Rome and later must have treated her in the same way he treated her second husband Herod of Chalcis, whom he liked and favoured. Although in his last years he could best be approached only through his freedmen and his wives, he never changed towards Agrippa and Berenice. They were always the children of his dashing friend Agrippa I who had smoothed his path to the imperial throne after Caligula's murder. Whatever acts of atrocity Claudius might commit against his officers and his senators, to the children of his dead friend he continued to be a benevolent father. With his death, at the age of sixty-three, their last link with the past was severed.

But with all their sadness at his demise, they were realists. They had little use for sentimentality. They may well have shed a sincere tear at the passing of an old friend but, like their father on the death of Caligula, they lost no time in transferring their allegiance to his successor. Agrippa may have seen Britannicus as a baby and a young boy when he himself was a youth in Claudius's house, but he could not have felt any obligation towards him. Agrippina was after all his benefactress as much as Claudius. It was essential to maintain her good will and win the favour of her son.

At twenty-seven Agrippa was an adroit diplomat, well versed in the art of currying favour. That the new emperor was only seven-teen—an age at which he himself had been pronounced unpre-pared to govern—may well have facilitated his approach. Although there is no record of such a journey, he may well have rushed off to Rome to congratulate Nero and ingratiate himself with him by assurances of loyalty and lavish presents.

Towards the end of 54, when news came that the Parthians had invaded the Roman client-kingdom of Armenia, Agrippa was quick to prove his usefulness. Rome was questioning the ability of a seventeen-year-old boy to rebuff the Parthian threat. Nero's answer was to order the Roman legions in the east to take up positions along the Armenian border, at the same time instructing the client-kings of the east to discharge their duty towards Rome and supply auxiliary troops. Agrippa obeyed the call with alacrity; so did his father's old friend Antiochus of Commagene, and Sohaemus of Emesa who earlier that year had succeeded to the throne vacated by the death of his brother, Drusilla's first husband. The campaign was a success. The Parthians retreated and Agrippa was duly rewarded by the enlargement of his territory. Nero sliced some more choice bits off the province of Judaea and added them to Agrippa's kingdom. They included Tiberias, on the beautiful Sea of Galilee, with its thriving commerce and its mixed population of Jews and Greeks; Tarichaea, also on the Sea of Galilee, which was, as its name denoted, the centre of the salted fish industry and better known to posterity as Magdala (Migdal), birthplace of Mary Magdalene; Julias, or Livias, with fourteen adjoining villages east of the Jordan; and Abila, also across the Jordan.

Tiberias had been Agrippa 1's capital for a short while before he was made king of Judaea. It held some mixed childhood memories for Berenice, who had lived there first as the little daughter of an inspector of markets, then as a young princess. It was less isolated than Caesarea Philippi and far closer to Jerusalem, which she and her brother were constantly visiting. Yet they did not take up their official residence in Tiberias. There were personal as well as political reasons for this. Tiberias had a large proportion of Jews; living amongst them would have meant accepting the same religious discipline that prevailed in Jerusalem and from which only pagan Caesarea Philippi could offer a respite. Moreover, Tiberias was ideal for a brief stay during the winter, when its mild climate and its thermal springs made it a popular centre for visitors; but most of the year round it was unbearably hot and could not compete with the cool green slopes of the north. There was however another reason, more compelling than the others, why brother and sister preferred to stay away. It was in Tiberias that Agrippa had installed one of the two wives he had taken while Berenice was in Cilicia. Small wonder that he did not wish to complicate matters by blatantly living with his sister in the same town. Instead, they increased their efforts to turn Caesarea Philippi into a real haven of hellenistic civilization. With its palace, its baths and its new theatre it became splendid enough to entertain a Caesar. In due course, to please Nero, they changed its name to Neronias and Agrippa commemorated it on his coins. The name however did not strike roots and fell into disuse soon after Nero's death.

Another upshot of the Parthian campaign was that Nero gave Lesser Armenia to Aristobulus, the son of Herod of Chalcis by his first marriage. After his suit to succeed his father had been rejected by Claudius in favour of young Agrippa, Aristobulus stayed on in Rome and waited for a second chance. He had to wait several years, but in 57 Nero made him king. For the second time within fifteen years two Herodians were contemporaneously ruling under the imperial aegis. One was king of large, though disjointed, parts of Trans-Jordan and Syria; the other was king in Asia Minor. It was a tribute to their skill that their Jewishness did not disqualify them from ruling over pagan territories.

With Aristobulus's elevation the house of Herod reached new heights. Five descendants, all cousins, were now royal. The men were kings in their own right; the women, within their limitations, were no less distinguished than their male cousins. Queen Salome, once notorious for her sensuous dancing, achieved such high standing with her husband Aristobulus that he had her head minted on some of his coins; Berenice was a titular queen of Chalcis and a recognized, if unofficial, co-ruler in her brother's kingdom; and Drusilla could still call herself queen of Emesa and was the much-envied wife of the man who held in his hands the prize most coveted by all true Herodians, the province of Judaea.

For several years Felix had been jogging along without any major disaster. He had been putting down sporadic disturbances caused by false prophets, arresting and executing members of the anti-Roman movement, suppressing officious local advisers, imposing heavy taxes and inviting bribes. The country groaned under his rule, but no insurmountable crisis faced him until AD 58 when a strife broke out between the Jewish and Syrian inhabitants of his capital Caesarea.

The cause of the trouble was the question of civil rights which both Jews and Syrians demanded exclusively for themselves. The wealthy Jewish inhabitants claimed preference over the Syrians on the grounds that Caesarea had been founded by their own king Herod the Great. The Syrians, representing the military community, claimed that although Herod was Jewish, he had meant Caesarea to be a Greek city, or else he would not have built there a temple with statues. They also pointed out that the Jewish population consisted of immigrants who had settled there during Herod's time; whereas the Greeks, or Syrians, had lived there before Caearea had ever been thought of.

The dispute followed the usual pattern. When words failed, violence started. Street brawls became so dangerous that Felix had to send his soldiers to control the situation. As the Jews had won the battle of the day, the soldiers took punitive action against them. They routed them, killed anybody who offered resistance and with Felix's authorization looted their property. Living in the same palace which had been subjected to a ferocious mob attack when she was a child, Drusilla must have had some uncomfortable moments. As the procurator's wife she was in no immediate personal danger, but the sight of riots between Jews and Syrians, with the soldiery let loose, would have been painfully reminiscent of the events that followed her father's death fourteen years earlier.

In the end Felix had to fall back on the stock solution and refer the case to Rome. Notables of the two factions were sent off to argue their case before Nero, whose subsequent withdrawal of Jewish civil rights brought about fresh riots on an unprecedented scale. There was a temporary lull while the Caesareans awaited his decision. But there was no peace for Felix, who was being pressed by the Pharisees and the priests of Jerusalem to pronounce the death sentence on a man he had been holding prisoner in Caesarea for nearly two years. He was a Jew from Tarsus in Cilicia, a Roman citizen by birth, whose name was recorded in an official report simply as Paul.

Paul, called Saul until he saw the light, had come to Jerusalem in the early summer of 58 to bring greetings and donations from the Christians abroad to the Christian church in Jerusalem. He took up lodgings with a friend and attended the Pentecost ceremonies in the temple like any other celebrant. No priest or Pharisee had any reason to suspect in that middle-aged and dignified pilgrim from the tribe of Benjamin a disseminator of deviationist ideas. But Paul had been spreading the gospel among the people of the Graeco-Roman world for so many years that he could not long remain anonymous. He was recognized by some pilgrims from Asia Minor who lost no time in denouncing him to the temple authorities as a dissenter from orthodox Judaism and a public danger. There was a general commotion in the temple court. The Roman duty officer thought that at long last he had succeeded in tracking down the elusive Egyptian Jew who had recently led a riotous crowd to the Mount of Olives, and arrested the man pointed out to him. Paul spoke to him in Greek, established his identity, and asked permission to address the crowd. For a few minutes he held their attention because he spoke in Aramaic, but as soon as he mentioned his Christian beliefs, he was attacked. The officer-in-charge removed him to the Antonia, where he soon learned to his consternation that he had arrested a native of Cilicia and a Roman citizen.

However, as a charge had been brought against Paul by the Jewish authorities, he was sent for trial before the *Sanhedrin*, the supreme court, which consisted of both Sadducees and Pharisees. Paul decided to play them off one against the other. He suggested that he was on trial for his belief in the resurrection of the dead, a doctrine that the Pharisees upheld, but which the Sadducees vehemently disclaimed. The hearing degenerated into a theological brawl and the prisoner was returned to the Antonia with nothing decided in his case. A group of fanatics swore to kill him come what may, and the Roman commander who got wind of the plot, decided to refer the whole tricky affair to the procurator. He sent Paul to Caesarea under the most stringent security precautions. No less than seventy horsemen and four hundred infantry were detailed to escort him. Five days later a delegation of accusers came down from Jerusalem. The charges seemed inconclusive and Felix decided to await the arrival of the Roman commander for further evidence. In the meantime he kept Paul in his palace under open arrest and allowed him to receive any of his friends who might wish to visit him and make themselves useful.

Felix was in a quandary. He was aware that he was expected to convict his prisoner not for breach of the peace, but for some theological offence that might well have endangered the unity of

Judaism but not the task of Roman peace-keeping. It was no use turning to Drusilla for advice. With her open defiance of one of the most fundamental of Jewish laws, she could not have felt much sympathy for a delegation of priests who had descended on the palace like a host of militant angels. She must have felt more affinity with Paul, to her way of thinking just another Jew who had dared break away from restrictive orthodoxy. She certainly wanted to hear more about his new faith. Felix too felt it was his duty to hear more about a subject that so exercised his province. He sent for Paul and invited him to speak to him and Drusilla about his doctrine. Paul got so carried away that forgetting his audience he talked ardently of virtue, chastity, self-control and the coming judgement. Felix and Drusilla felt uncomfortable. Paul was dismissed but as a face-saver Felix told him that he would like to hear him again at some future date, when time would permit.

For the next year or two they had several more talks, although not in Drusilla's presence. Felix, 'well informed about the Christian movement'[2] as he was, must have reckoned that the church of Jerusalem could raise enough money to buy Paul's release if offered the chance. He made no secret of his willingness to be bribed and kept sending for Paul from time to time to see whether he would signify his desire to buy his way to freedom. Paul made no such gesture, and Felix kept him on in the palace, fending off the clamouring priests in the hope of eventually settling the problem quietly and profitably. But what with Pallas's fall from grace and his own inglorious handling of the Caesarea troubles, he was recalled to Rome. When early in the year 60 he handed over to his successor Porcius Festus, he left Paul to him.

Within three days of his arrival in Caesarea Festus went to Jerusalem to acquaint himself with the religious capital of his province. He had hardly taken up residence in the procuratorial palace when a Jewish delegation of notables came to pay their respects and ask for the return of Paul to Jerusalem, where he would be tried again before the *Sanhedrin*. Festus instructed them to follow him to Caesarea. Again there was a full gathering in the palace *praetorium*, again the Jewish spokesman accused Paul of having committed offences against the law and the sanctity of the temple, and again the Roman mind boggled at the complexity of what seemed to be an academic argument about someone who had risen from the dead. Paul however sensed that Festus was not going to prolong his detention indefinitely like Felix. The procurator was anxious to hold a trial, and Paul knew that a trial by the *Sanhedrin* could end only in a death sentence. For the first time since his detention two years earlier, he made use of his prerogative as a Roman citizen and demanded to be tried by Caesar himself. Festus consulted his advisers, then gave his consent by pronouncing the formal reply: 'You have appealed to Caesar; to Caesar you shall go.'[3] The Jewish delegation returned to Jerusalem empty handed, while Paul continued under arrest in the palace, waiting to be escorted to Rome.

Felix's recall and Festus's arrival caused a flurry of activity in Caesarea Philippi. It was essential to establish cordial relations with the new procurator from the very start of his term of office. As soon as they heard that he had completed his brief visit of inspection to Jerusalem and returned to Caesarea, Agrippa and Berenice set out in style to present themselves and pay their respects. They covered the seventy-odd miles between their capital and his in good time and arrived in Caesarea only a few days after Festus's own return. As royal guests on a courtesy visit they were offered the hospitality of the procurator's official residence. After sixteen years' absence Berenice was back in the palace where at the age of sixteen she had witnessed, and possibly experienced, the violence of a mob on the rampage.

The visit went off pleasantly. There was no Drusilla to give herself airs as the procurator's wife, no fear of being outshone by a beautiful sister eleven years younger. There must have been suitable entertainment for the royal guests and much discussion of the political problems of the province. The procurator was deferential to the king, and the king was anxious to reassert his position in Jerusalem as administrator of the temple. Festus was apparently a man of integrity, or at least of good intentions. Rightly considering Agrippa as more knowledgeable on the complexities of Jewish religion than he could ever hope to be, he discussed Paul's case with him and confided his perplexity. The Acts of the Apostles succinctly reconstructed the conversation between him and Agrippa, held no doubt in Berenice's presence:

'We have a man' he [Festus] said, 'left in custody by Felix; and when I was in Jerusalem the chief priests and elders of the Jews laid an information against him, demanding his condemnation. I answered them, 'It is not Roman practice to hand over any accused man before he is confronted with his accusers and given an opportunity of answering the charge.' So when they had come here with me I lost no time; the very next day I took my seat in the court and ordered the man to be brought up. But when his accusers rose to speak, they brought none of the charges I was expecting; they merely had certain points of disagreement with him about their peculiar religion, and about someone called Jesus, a dead man whom Paul alleged to be alive. Finding myself out of my depth in such discussions, I asked if he was willing to go to Jerusalem and stand his trial there in these issues. But Paul appealed to be remanded in custody for His Imperial Majesty's decision, and I ordered him to be detained until I could send him to the Emperor.'

Agrippa said to Festus, 'I should rather like to hear the man myself.' 'Tomorrow', he answered, 'you shall hear him.'[4]

The following day a hearing was arranged in the audience-chamber of the palace, to which high-ranking officers and prominent citizens were also invited. It was to be a grand session, with the presence of royalty lending it additional solemnity and style. The audience were conscious that they had not been asked to attend a trial, but to listen to an exposition of faith. In a way it was a command performance, with the chief protagonist acting for his life. Berenice gave much thought to the choice of a dress suitable to the occasion.

The well-to-do ladies of Jerusalem had always been noted for their love of self-adornment, and a rich and beautiful Herodian queen would have considered it her duty to outshine any lady she might meet, whether Jewish or Roman. The Roman procurator and his entourage had to be impressed with the grandeur of the royal visitors, and before she left for Caesarea Berenice had her boxes packed with special care. Her luggage must have contained her most magnificent dresses and shawls, her most splendid jewellery, her best perfumes and cosmetics. Her personal maids travelled with her to groom her for her meetings with Festus and any subsequent formal occasion. The hearing of Paul's declaration of faith required a regal appearance, and Berenice would have given the utmost consideration to every part of her toilet.

In Judaea, no less than in Rome, a lady began it by taking a bath, using a sponge or a brush, with soap produced from soda-yielding plants. Then she rubbed herself with leaves of sweet-smelling rosemary or marjoram. Berenice, whose way of life combined the pleasures of both Jewish and Roman civilizations, would have considered a hot-water bath followed by a cool one an indispensable prelude to dressing up.

Her wardrobe, particularly when preparing to impress the procuratorial society of Caesarea, would have followed the Graeco-Roman fashion which in any case had long been accepted in Judaea, along with its terminology. A lady first put on a light sleeveless under-tunic, a shift and a sort of brassiere. Over them she wore an ankle-length dress with wide sleeves, firmly belted under the bust. This was the Roman *stola,* or *itstalit* in its Hebraized form. Silk was popular in summer, wool in winter. The style of the over-dress hardly ever changed, and the vagaries of fashion were confined to colour. The known colours of the day ranged from purple with its shades of red, dark rose and blue, to sea-green and saffron. The rich colours were rendered even more resplendent by the addition of gold borders. Jewish tradition regarded the wearing of red and purple as indecent in a woman, but in Pharisee-free Caesarea Berenice would have felt above such restrictions.

Jewels were an essential part of a lady's toilet. Diamonds, since they could not be cut, were mostly made up as rings. Pearls were used for ear-rings. Further scope for wearing jewellery was offered by necklaces, bracelets, brooches, studded diadems. Known stones included opals, sapphires, emeralds, beryls, jaspers, carbuncles, topazes, onyxes. A rich and self-assured woman of thirty-two, as Berenice was, would have acquired a collection of jewels to suit all occasions, but her proudest possession was still the large diamond ring Agrippa had given her before her marriage to Polemo of Cilicia.

The question of a hairstyle was difficult to settle. Roman trends were not unknown in Caesarea Philippi, and Berenice would have been one of the first to be given a demonstration of a hairstyle introduced by Poppaea, Nero's beautiful and elegant mistress, who was only two or three years younger than her. But a style had to agree with type of hair, face, occasion. For a wedding the Jewish concept of beauty favoured long hair worn loose over the shoulders with a crown on top. For other occasions Jerusalem ladies used to plait their hair, weaving gaily coloured ribbons into it; or they combed it back and knotted it. Roman hairstyles were more elaborate. Berenice could choose to part her hair in the centre and let it form into tight curls on the temples with big waves at the back; she could have it parted on each side of the head, with a fringe in front and bun at the back; she could have it plaited and arranged on top of the head like snakes; or she could have it closely curled and built up high to look like a globe. She may have preferred a simpler style, allowing her thick beautiful hair to fall in a rippling mass over her shoulders, with a diadem over her head, setting off her jewellery as well as her femininity. Whatever she decided, it would be a long session, with one maid holding a polished metal mirror in front of her, and one or two others performing with gold and ivory combs, curling-tongs, tweezers, hairpins, ribbons, hairnets and jewellery.

Another essential part of her toilet was the make-up. Her cosmetics chest was full of small pots and jars containing the most fashionable concoctions of the cosmetic industry of the day, home-made as well as imported. According to the prevalent taste of the east, Berenice would have applied eyeshade made of antimony; rouge which also did duty as lipstick; and nail varnish produced from the burnt leaves of the henna-blossom.

Last but not least came the scent. It was such an accepted part of the feminine toilet that Jewish women were allowed to spend one-tenth of their dowry on it. The stalls in the perfumers' market offered a rich variety. There were the scents produced from lilies, jasmine or roses; and there were the more expensive ones like balm from Jericho, nard from India, myrrh from Arabia. It was common practice for ladies to secrete a tiny leather vaporizer in their sandals, which would exude whiffs of scent every time they wriggled their toes. A final touch to a meticulous toilet was given by sucking a scented pepper to sweeten the breath.

Bathed, perfumed, combed, made up and dressed, Berenice was ready to grace the audience chamber with her regal presence. Agrippa had also put on his royal robes and they arrived together in full state, followed by the other distinguished guests. Once Their Majesties were conducted to their seats the session could begin.

It was formally opened by Festus who briefly outlined the history of the case, then stated the object of the gathering. It was not to try Paul, but simply to elicit something concrete which might go into a report to the emperor. 'There is no sense, it seems to me', concluded Festus with candour, 'in sending on a prisoner without indicating the charges against him.'[5]

After this introduction Agrippa took over and gave Paul permission to speak. Paul must have realized that he had been summoned to talk to the king rather than to the procurator who had already heard him. Sensing in Agrippa a sympathetic listener, or at least someone sufficiently well informed to have preserved an open mind, he addressed his remarks directly to him, sometimes calling him king Agrippa, sometimes Your Majesty. According to the account in Acts, he did not address himself to Berenice even once, although he must have been aware of her standing with her brother. To him she represented everything he disliked most about women. His definition of a good woman was the very opposite of Berenice's character, trait for trait. She did not dress modestly and soberly, she bought expensive clothes, she indulged in elaborate hairstyles, she decked herself out with gold and pearls. Moreover, she was guilty of a sin most hated by him; she sought to dominate, whereas a good woman should have been retiring, submissive, and a listener rather than a talker.[6] Quite apart from her questionable morals, of which Paul must have heard, he would not have debased himself to address a woman who in her very presence epitomized everything he preached against.

And so he spoke for Agrippa's benefit alone. He was so vehement about his faith and doctrine that Festus thought he had gone out of his mind and tried to silence him. He had to shout at the top of his voice to make Paul take notice of him. When a degree of quiet was restored, Paul made his last plea to Agrippa. There followed the much-quoted exchange:

'King Agrippa, do you believe the prophets? I know you do'. Agrippa said to Paul: 'You think it will not take much to win me over and make a Christian of me.'
'Much or little', said Paul, 'I wish to God that not only you, but all those who are listening to me today, might become what I am, apart from these chains.'[7]

That was the end of Paul's speech. Agrippa rose, and the rest of the audience rose as well. Later Agrippa and Berenice had a private discussion with Festus, during which the king gave his opinion that Paul had done nothing that was punishable by death or even by imprisonment; had he not been so hasty as to appeal to Caesar's court, he could have been discharged. Festus however had no alternative but to follow the correct procedure. He may not have collected enough information to put in his report, but he did send Paul to Rome.

From Agrippa's point of view the courtesy visit to Caesarea was a success. On his return to Caesarea Philippi he could congratulate himself on having consolidated his position with the Roman procurator and won his friendship. It little mattered that his failure to toe the orthodox line against Paul antagonized the temple priesthood. He had acted according to his own judgement, and in that he was in complete agreement with Berenice.

Chapter XIII

Their Majesties' pleasure

THE old Hasmonaean palace which Agrippa and Berenice occupied during their visits to Jerusalem was too small for a royal family who liked to entertain on a grand scale.

Berenice had first lived in it after her father became king of Judaea. As queen of Chalcis she returned to it from time to time with her husband Herod during his official visits to the city in his capacity of custodian of the holy robes. When her brother succeeded to the post she accompanied him on his pilgrimages and presided over his court in Jerusalem just as she did in Caesarea Philippi. The visits to Jerusalem lasted longer than the actual duration of the festivals which necessitated them. Agrippa had duties to attend to which could be accomplished only after the holy days. There were conferences with the temple administrators, consultations about the use of the temple funds, receptions for the city notables, entertainment. A palace built by the dour Hasmonaeans several generations earlier could hardly come up to Berenice's ideas of gracious living. She required a large reception room where she could entertain in the style and state she had been accustomed to. The desire, natural enough in itself, must have been given a sharper edge by her envy of Drusilla's magnificent palace in the upper city. Alterations were decided upon. The building plans were probably submitted while Drusilla and Felix were still in Judaea, but the actual work was carried out and completed during Festus's term of office.

The palace was situated in such a position that expansion sideways had to be ruled out. The royal architects hit on the happy idea of building upwards. They erected another storey on top of the flat roof and turned it into what was later called, depending on the interpretation given to Josephus's description of it, a chamber of unusual size, a banqueting hall, a tower, a dining room, a penthouse. It became Their Majesties' favourite room. They took their

Coins showing

Herod of Chalcis
Berenice's second husband

Polemo of Cilicia
Berenice's third husband

Agrippa I
Berenice's father

Agrippa II
Berenice's brother

Nero

Poppaea, Nero's wife

meals in it and had a pleasant time looking through the large windows at the city that spread below them. Agrippa used to have only one main meal a day, at three in the afternoon, and the royal dinner was therefore no hurried affair. The hosts and their guests reclined on cushions after the hellenistic custom accepted in Judaea and had plenty of time to admire the beauty of Jerusalem in between courses served up at a leisurely pace.

The Hasmonaeans had built the palace on an elevation west of the temple and put a bridge to connect the two. It was a lofty building even in its original form; its new height gave it a perfect view not only of the city beyond but of the temple courts below. Agrippa was charmed with his grandstand view and spent much of his leisure looking down at the Court of Priests which included the sacrificial altar and the sanctuary. Nothing escaped him. No priest could sacrifice or pray without feeling exposed to the royal eyes. Neither Agrippa nor Berenice had ever seen the sacred performance before; by tradition the Court of Priests was out of bounds to the public. Now, without actually trespassing on holy ground, they could see for the first time in their life the mysteries of the daily sacrifice. They must have enjoyed the experience and saw no reason to keep their impressions to themselves. The priests were outraged. The very notion of two outsiders, satiated with food and drink, reclining on cushions like pagans and watching the sacred work, was obnoxious. In particular they must have resented Berenice's share of the view. She was not only a woman, who should have been satisfied with her place in the Court of Women, but a woman of questionable virtue. The situation was insufferable.

There was no legal action they could take against the king. They could not invoke the authority of the *Sanhedrin*, for there was nothing specific in the Jewish law against watching the priestly rites. All they could do was to protest that prying on their duties was contrary to tradition. Agrippa was not the man to be intimidated by a protest, so the priests took a leaf from His Majesty's book. They consulted their own architects and embarked on a building project of their own. When it was completed it turned out to be a high wall in their own court. It completely cut off the view from the royal penthouse.

Their Majesties however were not going to be defeated by a

bunch of priests. Agrippa reported to Festus that the new wall was screening the temple courts from the Roman soldiers on guard duty during the festivals. Festus reacted as expected. He issued a demolition order.

The priests were not daunted. They informed the procurator with all due respect that once the wall was up it became part of the sacred temple; pulling it down would be just as sacrilegious as pulling down the temple itself. Once again Festus found himself caught up in the intricacies of Jewish theology. He neither wanted to offend the religious feelings of his subjects, nor did he wish to embroil himself with the king. He took his time and was probably relieved when the notables of Jerusalem asked him to let them argue their case before Caesar. With his consent a ten-man delegation left for Rome, headed by the high priest Ishmael ben Phabi. It was the same Ishmael ben Phabi whose mother had once made him a tunic worth a hundred *minas*, which he gave away after just one service. Agrippa for his part did not feel the case warranted a personal visit to Rome. He sent a representative and put his trust in Nero's proven goodwill towards him. In that he reckoned without Poppaea's curious religious sympathies and her capricious temperament.

When Nero succeeded Claudius at the age of seventeen, he was already married to Claudius's daughter Octavia. It was a political match, and Nero lost no time in seeking his pleasures elsewhere. In the year 58, when he was twenty-one, he met the twenty-seven-year-old Poppaea and fell in love with her.

Poppaea was high born, rich, beautiful, intelligent, pleasant to talk to. It was said she possessed all the virtues except kindness. She was an ambitious woman and was prepared to go to any lengths to achieve her aim. Although her love life was not above reproach, she was not promiscuous. She was guided by her head rather than her heart. She used her charms to better her position and bestowed her favours for gain rather than pleasure. She divorced her first husband, by whom she had a son, for a dashing young courtier called Otho, who many years later emerged as an emperor for a brief period. At the time of his marriage to Poppaea his chief claim to fame lay in his intimacy with Nero. He introduced his wife to him, and the rest followed quite naturally.

Poppaea conquered without difficulty, displaced the current imperial mistress and had Otho sent away to govern a remote province. Nero's wife hardly counted, but his mother Agrippina fought tooth and nail to retain her power over her son, until he got rid of her by assassination. After a few years as mistress, Poppaea became Nero's consort and empress. Her henchmen were described by Tacitus as 'the vilest tools in the employ of the imperial household'.[1]

It was strange that this pampered and wily woman should be attracted to a foreign religion that put so much stress on feminine virtue; yet she was undoubtedly attracted to Judaism. It was no momentary interest born out of a passing whim, but something real and enduring. Josephus, who was introduced to her in Rome and benefited from her intercession, described her as *theosebes*, god fearing. She was known as a Jewish sympathizer, and the Jewish actor Aliturus had the entry of her house. A Jewish lobby formed round her, soliciting her favour in difficult dealings with the emperor.

It was therefore through her that the priestly delegation from Jerusalem hoped to win Nero to their way of thinking. Agrippa's deputies must have also approached her with the same view, but failed to convince her. Poppaea promised her help to the priests. It is difficult to imagine that she was swayed by their religious arguments in favour of the wall; it is more conceivable that she took their part to gratify a grudge against Agrippina. Agrippa and Berenice had been the dead woman's friends; that was reason enough to reject their suit.

On the appointed day Nero gave the case a full hearing. His idea of a full hearing was entirely his own. Instead of allowing each litigant to present his case as a whole, he heard only one charge at a time, then had it debated separately. After that he withdrew to study the problem on his own, deferring his judgement to the following day. He never consulted openly with his judicial advisers, but made them submit their views in writing. As no one was supposed to know the contents of the written submission apart from its writer, Nero was free to pronounce whatever verdict he fancied, passing is off as a majority opinion.

The case of the priests versus Agrippa must have been conducted in a like manner. After the hearing Nero pronounced the verdict that had been advocated by Poppaea. Festus's demolition order was declared invalid and the wall was to stay intact. The priests were jubilant, but their triumph was not altogether sweet. Nero had no intention of unnecessarily humiliating a loyal client-king. He gave orders to detain the high priest and the temple treasurer in Rome as hostages. Why Jewish hostages were required when the Jews had won their case was not indicated; it was clearly an attempt to soften the blow dealt to Agrippa's pride. The so-called hostages were not treated badly. They were lodged in Poppaea's own house and allowed to live according to the Jewish religion. How long they stayed as her reluctant guests is not known. Poppaea died in 65 after a miscarriage brought on by a kick delivered by Nero in a fit of rage. Ishmael ben Phabi was beheaded in Cyrene (Libya) some time after 70 without ever having regained his position in Jerusalem. An unrepentant Agrippa, relieved not to have to face a high priest who had conducted and won a case against him, found a replacement for him. The wall, however, stayed. All Berenice could do was to rearrange the seating plan of the royal dining room in order to avoid its ugly starkness.

The next clash with the priesthood occurred over the question of the Levites' uniforms.

The Levites, as their name denoted, belonged to the tribe of Levi, as did the priests who were above them. They were divided into two distinct groups, the choristers and the gate keepers. Each group constituted a closed shop, and a member of one was barred under penalty from doing the work of the other. The gate keepers were a rung higher on the social echelon of the temple hierarchy, and the choristers, trained musicians that they were, sought to improve their status. One day when Agrippa was staying in Jerusalem he was informed that a choristers' delegation was seeking audience with him. After many flatteries they came to the point. They wanted to cast off their habitual uniforms and be allowed to wear linen tunics like the priests. They assured the king that such an innovation would commemorate his reign for ever.

Agrippa and Berenice must have been amused to see a point of fashion submitted and debated with so much earnestness. They had no particular interest in the internal rivalry within the tribe of Levi, except perhaps that they were more aware of the choristers than the gate keepers because of their sweet psalm singing accompanied on Greek and native instruments. The dispute however gave them a chance to get their own back on the priesthood. The priests were bound to resent any attempt to take away the exclusiveness of their traditional dress, and that was reason enough to support the musicians' request.

Although the king was the administrator of the temple affairs, his authority was secular; to introduce such an unheard-of innovation a religious body had to be consulted. Agrippa used his scriptural prerogative of convening the *Sanhedrin* and asked them to sanction the change. Not many members attended that particular session; those who did gave their grudging consent. The choristers cocked a snook at the gate keepers, but the worst hit were the priests. Now they were outwardly quite indistinguishable from the lowest group of the Levites. Some of the worshippers did not much like the change either. Although the act had been passed by the *Sanhedrin*, they blamed Agrippa for contempt of tradition. Their Majesties remained unperturbed.

It may well have been in the royal dining room, still commanding a view of the temple precincts if not of the priests' court, that Agrippa discussed with Berenice suggestions put forward for the future use of the temple building fund.

The original temple had been built by king Solomon in the tenth century BC on the north-east side of Jerusalem. It was a magnificent building whose architecture and dimensions were proudly recorded in the scriptures. It later came to be known as the First Temple or Solomon's Temple.

In the sixth century BC it was razed to the ground by Nebuchadnezzar of Babylon, who also sent thousands of Jews into exile and thus created the first Jewish diaspora. Fifty years later, when the Persians took over the Babylonian empire, they allowed the exiled Jews to return to their homes and rebuild their house of God. The foreign population which had settled in Jerusalem during the fifty years resented the return and tried to sabotage the work. The builders were not daunted. The foundations were laid hurriedly, and when their work was finished the result lacked the grandeur that characterized the original edifice. The young generation rejoiced in their new temple; but those priests and Levites and heads of families who were old enough to have seen the first one, mingled tears of sorrow with their cries of joy. Modest and makeshift as it was, it survived many vicissitudes and served its purpose for the next five hundred years, until the middle of Herod's reign.

Herod the Great felt that it was too mean and unassuming; it was certainly out of tune with the beautiful buildings he had put up in the holy city. In 20 BC he embarked on an ambitious reconstruction scheme that was to turn the Second Temple into the most majestic house of God ever dreamed of by a Jew. Whatever fears the Pharisees may have had about the Idumaean's intentions were soon allayed by his obvious concern with tradition. Solomon's original designs were meticulously studied and served as a basis for the enlarged plan. Thousands of priests were trained in the building craft so as not to introduce secular labourers into the holy places. The work progressed with great speed. The sanctuary was ready within eighteen months; the vast outer structure was completed in ten years. Legend has it that throughout that period not one day's work was lost through inclement weather. God in his kindness sent rains only by night, so that the holy work could go on unimpeded by day. In 10 BC the temple was dedicated. Its beauty surpassed anything that had ever been seen in Judaea, combining as it did the best of Solomon's ideas with acceptable elements of Graeco-Roman architecture. Even the pious scholars grudgingly conceded that he who had not seen 'Herod's building' had never seen a really beautiful edifice. It stood up for eighty years; then, shortly after it had received its final touches, it was burnt down by the Romans in AD 70. Thanks to contemporary descriptions and modern research it is possible however to obtain some idea of its construction and size.

It was a large complex of buildings and courts, encircled by the Court of Gentiles which covered some thirty-five acres. This was so called because Gentiles were allowed into it, but forbidden to proceed beyond it into the inner courts. Tablets in Greek and Latin warned them that trespassing was punishable by death.

The Court of Gentiles was brilliantly paved and enclosed by a wall on all four sides, with towers and pinnacles soaring high. It was entered by irregularly placed gates, which were however fairly uniform in construction. The interior of the court was surrounded by colonnades of Corinthian columns. On three sides there was a double row of columns; the fourth boasted a triple colonnade. The eastern colonnade was called Solomon's Portico, as tradition had it that it was the place of his coronation. The ceiling was made of cedar wood, covered with gold leaf and embellished with carvings in high relief.

Within the colonnades of the Court of Gentiles brisk business was conducted. There were vendors of pigeons, the poor man's offering; money-lenders; dealers of all kinds. Jesus's disciples went there for talks and discussions, using Solomon's Portico as their particular meeting place. There were also storerooms, a bakehouse for the twelve loaves of the shewbread that were replaced every Sabbath, the administrative offices, and the chamber where the *Sanhedrin* held its meetings. Somewhere under the colonnades the horn-shaped treasure chests were kept, for people to drop their money offerings to the temple funds. Over those chests Agrippa I had hung up the golden chain once given to him by Gaius Caligula.

Inside the Court of Gentiles a succession of smaller courts began, one behind the other. The first was the Court of Women, so called because it represented the limit beyond which women were not allowed to go. It was surrounded by a fence or grating and entered by three gates. It was from the Court of Women that queen Cypros and her daughters watched Agrippa I make his emotional appeal to the celebrants to forgive him for his foreign ancestry; it was there that Berenice sat as queen of Chalcis; it was there that queen Helena of Adiabene offered her prayers; it was there that every woman, even a high priest's wife, had to stop.

Behind the women's court was the one reserved for men, which was known as the Court of Israel. Only male Jews were allowed into it. Like the women's court, it was intended for the people as well as for royalty.

On the west side of the Court of Israel was the Court of Priests, which housed within its boundaries the sacrificial altar and the sanctuary. It was into that court, hidden away from all eyes, that Agrippa and Berenice could for a while look down from the height of their new penthouse. The sacrificial altar was on the far end. Right behind it there rose a lofty structure reached by twelve steps. That was the sanctuary, purposely built high so as to be visible far and wide from every direction. It was made of white stone and covered with gold; from a distance it looked like a snow-clad mountain, as Josephus recalled after its destruction.

The massive sanctuary was divided into two chambers. One was the Holy Place, which housed the table of the shewbread, the *menorah* or the seven-branched candlestick, and the altar of incense. The other was the Holy of Holies, which contained nothing. None but the high priest was allowed to enter it, and even he only once a year, on the Day of Atonement, after much preparation and purification. Pompey, who had burst into the Holy of Holies during his incursion into Judaea in 63 BC, earned the undying hatred of Jews all over the world.

Although Herod's temple was dedicated in 10 BC, the building work continued for many years, providing employment for successive generations of masons and craftsmen. But after seventy years of alterations and improvements the task was completed. By the time Agrippa started on his penthouse, there was very little for the builders to do. There was certainly not enough to keep busy the eighteen thousand labourers on the temple pay roll. Many had been put on short time; but as Mosaic law guaranteed a full day's pay even for part of a day's work, provided the task assigned was completed, they had no cause for complaint. But eventually the time came when full-time pay for part-time work could no longer be justified and the vast labour force became redundant.

The addition of eighteen thousand unemployed to the ranks of the destitute of Jerusalem was not to be viewed with indifference. Unemployment was conducive to rioting, and in the turbulent anti-Roman atmosphere of Judaea any spark could have started off a conflagration. The temple authorities were well aware of the danger, and so was Agrippa whose business it was to see to temple affairs in the name of the Roman emperor. Fortunately there was no shortage of money in the building fund. It was only a question of channelling it into an alternative project.

There was another consideration which made it imperative to do so without delay. In 62 the well-meaning Festus died and his successor Albinus turned out to be more rapacious than any of his predecessors. Agrippa fully shared the priests' fear that should the money be deposited in the temple chests instead of being put into immediate use, Albinus would find a pretext to lay his hands on it. There was no point in putting temptation in his way. A building project had to be agreed on as soon as possible.

The priests suggested raising Solomon's Portico which had been built over a ravine and was not as high as it could be. Their plan may have looked fine on the drawing tablets, but Agrippa was quick to see its defects. The improver of Caesarea Philippi and Berytus was no mean authority on questions of architecture, expenses, scales, time allocation and general practicability. He pointed out to the disconcerted priests that, before the portico could be made higher, the existing colonnade would have to be demolished and the foundation reinforced. He warned that the demolition work could be accomplished quite easily and quickly, but the actual reconstruction would be slow and expensive. He even hinted that because of troubled times ahead it might never be completed. The project was shelved.

Instead Agrippa put forward an idea of his own, or perhaps of Berenice, who had good cause to know what she was talking about. The royal litter-bearers were finding it difficult to progress along the ill-paved lanes of the city. Some were no more than dirt tracks, caking into soft mud in the winter, crumbling into dust in the summer. Stones serving as steps up and down the inclines had either broken with use or been dislodged. If for royalty it was a momentary inconvenience, for the busy traders in the market-place it was a constant nuisance. Agrippa put up the audacious plan of using the sacred fund for paving the city lanes. Only a generation ago a suggestion on the part of a Roman procurator for spending temple money on public works had created a general uproar. Now it caused hardly a murmur. Perhaps the priests were not as impractical as they seemed to be. They raised no objection, and neither did Albinus, who was probably not sorry to see sacred money freely spent on urban improvements that should have been initiated by him and paid for with tax money ostensibly levied for the imperial treasury. The work was duly carried out, white flag-stones replaced the old surface, unemployment was averted. A remnant of Agrippa's fine paving work may still be seen in the grounds of St Peter in Gallicantu, outside the Zion Gate in Jerusalem.

Shortly afterwards Agrippa embarked on another project, the seeds of which may well have been sown during his hours of illicit prying into the Court of Priests. The foundation of the sanctuary had begun to sink and it became necessary to support it from the base. To meet the contingency no expense was spared. From Lebanon, the traditional supplier of timber for the temple woodwork, Agrippa ordered a large quantity of beautiful planks of unusual size and straightness. Their actual transportation from a foreign land took some time. Before the work could get under way the great revolt had broken out and the precious timber was used for engines of war against the besieging Romans. By that time Their Majesties were no longer in Jerusalem.

Even as they were planning and supervising their peaceful building projects, both Agrippa and Berenice were aware that troubled times lay ahead. Ten years of intimate association with temple affairs gave them a clear insight into the psychology of their co-religionists who, unlike them, saw the Roman occupation as the source of all evil. By the time Albinus took over they knew that a Roman procurator might well weather the ever-recurring quarrels between Jews and Samaritans, Greeks and Jews, Jews and Christians; but he could never extinguish the love of freedom that burnt in every Jewish heart. It was not until 66 that Agrippa and Berenice came face to face with the fanatic wave of nationalism that culminated in the great revolt, but they were not taken by surprise. They had seen it coming. Even as they were pursuing their royal pleasures in their renovated palace in Jerusalem they knew that the real danger did not lie in civil strife and proclamations of new religious doctrines, but in the ever-increasing faction of freedom fighters whom the Romans called bandits, history the Zealots.

Chapter XIV

Towards the brink

Round about the thirteenth century BC, when the Children of Israel were crossing the desert after their exodus from Egypt, there was a young man called Pinchas who was so zealous for the worship of God that he drove his spear through an Israelite who had intercourse with a pagan girl and had prostrated himself before her god.

This Pinchas, a great-nephew of Moses and a hereditary high priest by the will of God, became the national symbol of religious zeal. Tradition gave him the honorary title of Zealot, and his spontaneous action was set up as an example to posterity.

During the long history of the Jewish people in the promised land many more Pinchas-like people rose to strike a blow for God and religion. From their zeal for the purity of the faith there was only one step to the hatred of invaders who interfered with the freedom of worship. During the second century BC the activities of such zealous patriots led to the Maccabean revolt against the Seleucids and the subsequent establishment of the Hasmonaean dynasty.

During the reign of Herod the Great, after the near-extinction of the Hasmonaeans, a new generation of Zealots came into being, who regarded the Idumaean as a foreigner, a risen slave, a usurper. They organized themselves into something like a party and took up arms against him, only to be ruthlessly crushed. In AD 7 they rose against the Romans, who a year earlier had made Judaea into a province. Like later uprisings, it was doomed to failure. Its leader, Judas of Galilee, paid for it with his life and his followers were dispersed. Many took refuge in caves and fortified places in the hills of Galilee, settled down to a rough existence with their wives and children and continued to harass the invaders.

Agrippa I's accession was in a way a fulfilment of their dreams. There was again a Jewish king in Judaea and the laws of God were seen to be observed. But his untimely death in Caesarea in 44 put an end to the brief golden age. Judaea was again made into a province and the rule of procurators was resumed. The spirit of zealotry revived.

The Roman procurators did not need to be particularly ruthless to be hated. Their very presence in Judaea, personifying a rule of occupation, was enough to stir resentment. Even Tiberius Alexander, whose term of office from 46 to 48 was noted for its non-interference with Jewish customs, found that his relatively mild policy cut no ice with the Zealots. Judas's sons, Jacob and Simon, took up where their father had left off and led a new uprising against the Roman authorities. Tiberius Alexander, although a Jew by birth and a brother-in-law of Berenice, had no hesitation in putting them to death.

Far from suppressing the anti-Roman movement, the executions only increased its following among the masses. The Zealots came basically from the poorer classes who suffered most under the Romans. The upper classes, without being necessarily cowards or traitors, had come to terms with the Roman occupation either through political sense or a desire to benefit materially. There were the aristocratic Sadducees, the grabbing high priests, the stewards of the rich families, the petty tax-collectors who showed great zeal for their odious work because they could keep back an undisclosed proportion of what they had collected. The Zealots branded them all as Romanizers. They developed into an aggressive party whose declared aim was the eventual overthrow of the occupiers and the restoration of Judaea into a state of political and religious independence. During Cumanus's administration, from 48 to 52, they became more active. They led the march from Beth Horon to Caesarea to demand justice against a Roman soldier who had profaned the scroll of the law, and sent a contingent of fighters against the Samaritans during their strife with the Galileans. Even those who would not openly side with them gave them food and shelter. What was not freely given was often taken by force. Living outside the law as they did, the freedom fighters could not afford to be squeamish. They left a trail of fear and violence.

None were so violent as a group of extremists who became known as the *sicarii*, daggermen, from their use of the *sica*, a small dagger which could be easily hidden under a cloak. The *sicarii* would mingle inconspicuously with the crowds, particularly at festival times, stab their victims and hide their daggers in a single spring-like movement, then join the hunt for the unknown assassins. With time they became less scrupulous about their targets. They began to mark for political assassination not only Roman officials but also fellow-Jews who were either sympathetic to the Romans or simply irksome to the *sicarii*. In the general state of lawlessness that came in the wake of insurrections and internal strifes their ranks were swelled by hardened fighters who did not scruple to use patriotism as a means to settle a private feud. Things came to such a pitch that no man could consider himself safe from their daggers. If that was their strength, it was also the chink in their armour.

Felix was quick to size them up and make use of them. His appointment as procurator in AD 52 was partly due to the recommendation of the former high priest Jonathan, who was one of the hostages sent to Rome to stand trial before Claudius after the troubles with the Samaritans. When Felix took office Jonathan resumed his position in Jerusalem as an influential Sadducee. Apparently he relied too much on the procurator's gratitude for he took it upon himself to criticize his treatment of his Jewish subjects. He made such a nuisance of himself that Felix decided to get rid of him without actually staining his hands with his blood. The *sicarii* seemed ideally suited for the job. He entered into secret negotiations with them and offered them a handsome inducement to put Jonathan out of the way. The deal was accepted and the assignment carried out with the usual efficiency, if with less than the usual secrecy.

Once the service was paid for, Felix spent the rest of his eight-year term hunting them down and putting them to death. But the daggermen were like a hydra's head; for every one that was cut off two new ones grew instead. When in AD 60 Felix was succeeded by Festus, he left the province in a much more turbulent state than he had found it.

Festus seems to have been more of a soldier than a politician. He led expeditions against the trouble-makers, captured many and executed not a few. Whether he appreciated the difference between *bona fide* patriots and common robbers, he pursued them all as breakers of the peace. He was not corruptible like his predecessor and tried to restore law and order as best he could. He was baffled by the Pharisees' clamour for the blood of Paul, embarrassed by his friend Agrippa's feud with the priests. He was strict, possibly harsh, but not necessarily unfair. His death, which occurred after he had been in office less than two years, was neither lamented nor celebrated. As Roman procurators went, he was not intolerable.

His unexpected death in 62 left a hiatus in Judaea. As his successor, Nero appointed Lucceius Albinus who was then serving in Alexandria. Although Albinus proceeded to his province as soon as he could, he was not quick enough. During the period between his predecessor's death and his own arrival, fresh trouble broke out.

It was the sort of trouble that had been baffling Roman procurators ever since Judaea became a province. At the root of the matter were the Christians. They were holding meetings in the temple precincts, disseminating their doctrines and increasing their following. The temple authorities could not tolerate the situation and decided to act while no procurator was around to stop them. Their main target was James, the brother of Jesus, who was so respected for his virtue and piety that he was popularly known as the Righteous.

In his personal habits he was an ascetic. He drank no wine, ate no animal food, took no baths and did not rub himself with oil. No razor ever came near his hair. He spent so much time kneeling in prayer that his knees were said to have become as hard as a camel's. In recognition of his holiness he was elected by his fellow Christians to be the first bishop of Jerusalem. As far as conservative Judaism was concerned, he was a dangerous influence.

The instigator of the action against him was the high priest Ananus ben Ananus. Taking advantage of the interregnum he convened the *Sanhedrin* and brought James and some of his followers to trial. They were accused of transgressing the law and condemned to death by the traditional method of stoning. Capital punishment usually required the procurator's sanction. Some members of the court baulked at the high priest's audacity; they also feared the consequences to themselves when the new procurator would arrive and find out that his authority had been flouted. They sent messengers to meet him on his way from

Alexandria and report to him on the recent proceedings. At the same time they called on Agrippa to use his influence and stop the execution. Agrippa however had no legal authority over the *Sanhedrin.* All he could do to mark his disapproval was to dismiss Ananus and appoint someone else instead. That did not save James. By the time the new high priest took office James was already dead, ceremoniously stoned in the proper place of execution, or, according to another account, pushed off the temple parapet, stoned by the crowd below and clubbed to death by a fuller. Whatever the manner of his death, Albinus had no desire to probe into it or involve himself with a tedious theological argument among Jews. He considered it enough to send the dismissed Ananus a sharp reprimand and threaten him with punishment.

The *sicarii* had more claim on his attention. During the interregnum they had become bolder than ever, openly confiscating property, living off the land. They had also hit on the happy idea of kidnapping wealthy people and freeing them only against the release from prison of their own members. The hostages were mostly influential Sadducees or their stewards, whose relatives would rush off to Albinus and beg him to barter some of his jailed daggermen against their own kinsmen. Albinus usually obliged, but not before the mediators paid him handsomely for his share in the deal. It may well have been then that he conceived the idea of expanding the business. When there were no more hostages to be exchanged, he released prisoners against a direct payment to him. When there were no more prisoners rich enough to pay his price, he accepted money from the *sicarii* still at large, turning a blind eye to their subversive activities.

Relations between him and Their Majesties followed a very different pattern from the one established with his predecessor. Agrippa's dismissal of the high priest who had independently condemned a man to death cut no ice with Albinus. He had come to Judaea to rule in his own way, not to seek local advice; cultivating Herodians was not included in his programme. There was no feasting of the Jewish king and queen in the palace of Caesarea and not much social intercourse during the simultaneous visits to Jerusalem on the occasion of the festivals. Albinus, on Josephus's evidence, was only interested in filling his purse. He imposed crippling taxes and sanctioned official actions that were just so much daylight robbery. He cheated and dissembled and did not mind who robbed whom as long as he got his rake-off. His parting gift to his province after two years of maladministration was the emptying of its prisons. It was not an act of clemency but a calculated attempt to leave such a mess behind that his own misdemeanour would pass unnoticed.

His manner of administration, and particularly his last act, had the effect of making Roman rule more hated than ever. The yearning for freedom was general. Certainly the Zealots held no monopoly of patriotism. The difference between them and other patriots was over the question of means. People like Agrippa and Berenice, schooled in the history and might of Rome, advocated a *status quo*, possibly hoping against high odds that a grateful emperor would one day add Judaea to their other territories, as Claudius had done in the case of their father. Devout Pharisees strove to preserve the national identity through the world of the spirit. Religious hot-heads led unarmed marches against the troops and prayed for miracles. The Zealots believed in military action and sought to achieve independence by guerilla warfare. Only one more manifestation of Roman brutality was required to spur the majority of the people into open defiance.

Chapter XV

Barefoot

I N Rome there were many aspirants for the post of procurator of Judaea vacated by Albinus's recall in AD 64. The very lawlessness of the province, far from putting them off, served as an additional attraction, for it allowed an imperial agent to extort with impunity any amount of money he set his heart on. The intractability of the people in matters of religion and political obedience was more than made up for by their impotence against exorbitant taxation. A procuratorship in Judaea was a gold mine.

The contest was won by Gessius Florus, a native of Clazomenae, on the central coast of Asia Minor, whose main qualification for the post seemed to be his wife's friendship with Caesar's consort. In AD 64 Poppaea had been legally married to Nero for about two years. When a year earlier she had borne him a child that died shortly after birth, Nero had it deified. She was at the height of her power. Her interest in the Jewish religion had not waned and sometimes manifested itself in acts of kindness to individuals; it did not however develop into concern for the Jews of Judaea. When her friend Cleopatra asked her to recommend her husband Florus for the vacancy, she did so with such good effect that Nero appointed him with no further ado.

Florus's methods of extortion flabbergasted even those who thought they had seen everything. By comparison even Albinus's sins seemed slight. Josephus could not find harsh enough words to describe his behaviour:

Albinus committed most of his crimes in secret; Florus boasted about his quite openly. He acted as if he was a public executioner entrusted with the punishment of criminals. There was no form of robbery or violence he did not indulge in. . . . It was not enough for him to rob individuals. He stripped whole cities, ruined entire communities and made it known throughout the country that anyone could practise brigandage with impunity as long as he himself received this rake-off.[1]

The destitution caused by the combined effect of banditry and official fleecing drove the victims out of their homes in search of food and safer living. Many went into exile in an attempt to re-build their lives, finding more security among strangers than in their own homeland. But those emigrants or refugees were a minority. The majority of the people carried on with mounting exasperation and rebelliousness. By the beginning of 66, after nearly two whole years of Florus, they reached breaking point.

For Agrippa and Berenice the year 66 had begun well. The spring brought them two welcome developments. For one thing, they learnt that Tiberius Alexander, Berenice's brother-in-law by her first marriage, had been promoted to the key post of governor of Egypt. For another, Berenice, who had apparently been suffering from a long unspecified illness, had just recovered. The double event called for celebration. After some consultation the king and queen decided to part company for a while. Agrippa was to go to Egypt to congratulate Tiberius Alexander on his appointment and hold talks with him on topics of common interest; Berenice was to go to Jerusalem and offer her thanks to God for her recovery.

Agrippa hardly knew Tiberius Alexander; Berenice, who did, had not seen him for many years, probably not since 48 when he left the procuratorship of Judaea for another post. At that time Agrippa was still living in Rome and had not had the advantage that his sister had of cultivating the rising man that Tiberius Alexander then was. In fact Agrippa may never have met him, except perhaps in 36, when his mother Cypros was negotiating a loan with Tiberius's father in Alexandria. Agrippa was then only a small boy of eight or nine, while the other was well over twenty.

Tiberius Julius Alexander was born between AD 14 and 16, the eldest son of Alexander the *alabarch* and the nephew of Philo the philosopher. The family possessed Roman citizenship and be-longed to the equestrian order of the empire, but as Jews they were not immune to harassment. After the Alexandrian riots of 37 Tiberius put Judaism behind him. To an ambitious young man in his early twenties the step must have meant no more than the shedding of an inconvenience in order to conform to a state religion that opened up the road to promotion. Even then promotion did not follow immediately. Caligula had put the *alabarch* under arrest, and the son had little to expect from an emperor who had flung his father into prison and turned his uncle's audience with him into a farce. Claudius's accession brought the desired change. The father was released, the young brother Marcus was able to marry Berenice, and in 42 Tiberius Alexander was appointed *epistrategos*, military commander, of Upper Egypt. That was in the middle of Agrippa I's reign over Judaea. If the young Berenice did not take much pride in her marriage to Marcus the merchant, she must have liked being the sister-in-law of Tiberius the military commander. It must have been pleasing to reflect that through her a family alliance existed between the Roman administration of Upper Egypt and the reigning house of the Hasmonaeans.

A couple of years after Judaea had ceased to be a kingdom, the thirty-year-old Tiberius Alexander was appointed its procurator. His two-year term of office was marked by his execution of anti-Roman leaders as well as by his tolerance in matters of religion. That was the time when Berenice and Herod of Chalcis cultivated his friendship and it was probably the last time she had occasion to meet him.

In AD 63 Tiberius Alexander served under the Roman commander Domitius Corbulo in the Parthian campaign in Armenia which had been prosecuted intermittently for the last ten years, and in the opening stages of which Agrippa had lent Nero a helping hand. Tiberius Alexander was one of the highest-ranking personages in the Roman eastern command. When the Parthian king Tiridates agreed to peace talks, Tiberius was one of the two officers chosen to meet him and escort him back to the Roman headquarters, the other being Corbulo's own son-in-law. It was an assignment that required both courage and tact, for the Parthian's intentions could have been treacherous. As it happened Nero did not much like the peace terms accepted by Corbulo and ordered him to commit suicide, which he did. Tiberius's position however remained unshaken.

In the spring of 66 he reached what must have seemed to him the peak of his career. At the age of fifty he was appointed *praefectus* of Egypt. It was a mark of Nero's confidence that he entrusted him with the rich province that was the granary of Rome. Whoever controlled Egypt virtually controlled the fortunes of the empire. Tiberius justified Nero's trust until the latter's death.

The Jews of Alexandria must have looked askance at the new governor who although from their midst was not one of them. In spite of their number and wealth they were always on the brink of a volcano. Their civil rights were constantly in danger and no imperial edict could suppress the hostility of the Greek population. Agrippa, who was always sensitive to the call of Jewish communities in distress, may well have wished to discuss their situation with the new governor. Like his father a generation before, he had personal as well as diplomatic reasons for his concern. His young sister Mariamme was married in Alexandria to the *alabarch* Demetrius and had borne him a son. If Agrippa I had not been prepared to envisage his prospective grandchildren by Berenice and Marcus attacked by an Alexandrian mob, no more was Agrippa II prepared to allow such a mob to endanger the lives of his sister Mariamme and her children, who still had the royal blood of the Hasmonaeans flowing in their veins.

The odd thing about Agrippa's visit to Alexandria was that Berenice was not included in it. She was just as much involved as he in Roman and Jewish politics, just as conscious of the need to form and maintain influential contacts. Moreover, she was the acknowledged queen at her brother's court and his political helpmate. When, several years earlier, he had tried to establish himself with Festus as unofficial adviser on Jewish affairs, she had accompanied him to Caesarea as a matter of course and lent both elegance and weight to his discussions with the procurator. In Alexandria she could have been even more useful. Tiberius Alexander would have welcomed a queen whom he could still call sister-in-law; and the queen, more than her brother, could have brought into play the claims of a past association dating back to the years of their youth.

She too had a personal interest in the visit. Her sister Mariamme was nearer her age than Drusilla, and there had never been any rivalry between them. On the contrary, when Mariamme gave birth to a daughter, she named her Berenice after the queen. A visit to Alexandria would have added the pleasure of a family reunion to the responsibilities of a diplomatic mission that Berenice was well equipped to share.

If in spite of these considerations she decided to give up the idea of accompanying her brother and go instead to Jerusalem, there must have been a compelling reason for her doing so. Its roots may have lain in her basically simple religious belief which was strangely at odds with her general sophistication. Berenice was no profound thinker. Her piety was more a result of conformity than of inner conviction. Like her father and her brother, like her husband Herod of Chalcis, she clung to fundamentals, but for the rest was content with form dictated by time and place. Her lack of depth was compensated by practical observance of the minutest details of the law. It was an investment against divine displeasure, while to infringe the rules was to invite retribution. There was no point in bringing down God's wrath on her head through the non-fulfilment of a vow she had made during the time of her illness. If the performance of that vow coincided with a journey abroad, and if the journey could not be postponed, then it had to be abandoned. God could not be kept waiting for his due.

In Judaism the practice of making vows went back very far. There was a whole set of rules laid down by Moses and crystallized by the interpreters of the law for guidance. Once the object of the vow was achieved—a child born, an illness cured—the beneficiary would observe a period of abstinence before the ritual thanksgiving ceremony in the temple. Abstinence meant no wine, no physical contact with a dead body and no cutting of one's hair for a period decided on by the person concerned. Popular custom favoured thirty days. The performer of the vow was known as a *nazir*, a person in a state of abstinence. Although grammatically the term referred only to men, women too could make a vow. Queen Helena of Adiabene set a royal example when she observed the triple abstinence for many years. For women the most trying part was the care of the hair. Not only were they forbidden to cut it throughout the vow-period, but they were not allowed to comb it either. Only rubbing and scratching were permitted.

At the end of the specified period the *nazir* went to the temple to perform the final rite in a small court reserved for the purpose which was therefore called the Court of Nazirites. There he would present his offering to the Lord, the main items of which were one yearling ram as a whole-offering, one yearling ewe as a sin-offering, and one ram as a shared-offering. The hair which had been dedicated to God would be cut off and burnt under the pot containing the flesh of the sacrifice. Poverty often prevented the completion of the final rite. Many a *nazir* could not afford to buy the sacrificial animals and had to go on with his regime of abstinence even after the period of the vow had expired until he could find the means of discharging his debt. The rich and pious sometimes came to the rescue by paying for so many *nazirs'* sacrifices, thus enabling them to complete the rite and return to normal life. A shorn head was the external mark of a vow ritually completed.

A vow was not taken lightly. It was only after the failure of most human remedies that a person would importune God for help in a personal matter. Berenice must have consulted the best medical advice available before making hers. When her faith was rewarded and her illness cured, her duty was clear. She was to go to Jerusalem, begin a period of abstinence and offer the prescribed sacrifice so as to fulfil the obligation she had undertaken in her time of need. Failure to do so might have brought a relapse, or even worse. And so she let Agrippa go on his own to what must have looked like an exciting round of talks and festivities, while she made her way to Jerusalem, escorted by her household and the royal guards. Once settled in the palace, she began the thirty-day period of abstinence. For the first time in her life she was in Jerusalem without a royal companion—father, husband or brother. If she felt lonely, as she may well have done, she probably consoled herself with the thought that at least her brother would not be there on the thirty-first day to wince at her shorn head. But within days of her arrival all thoughts of feminine vanity gave way to grave concern over a political development that was to culminate in a bloody massacre.

As often in the past, the trouble started over a Roman attempt to interfere with religious tradition. While Berenice was in Jerusalem she learnt with indignation, as did the rest of the people, that Florus had ordered the temple treasurers to hand over seventeen talents, claiming that the money was owing to the emperor. Whether this was a new way of collecting tax arrears or just another excuse to put more money in his purse, the procurator's order caused an uproar. Laying hands on the sacred fund was sacrilege. From her penthouse Berenice could see the mass protests in the city below, with bold young men passing round collection boxes, pretending to beg alms for the poor starving procurator of Judaea. Abuses and threats were shouted, feeling ran high and the demonstrators were clearly in an ugly mood.

When the imperial messengers brought back to Florus nothing better than a report of the mock collection held on his behalf, he was touched on the raw. He marched to Jerusalem at the head of a small force of cavalry and infantry and stationed them about his fortified palace in the upper city. The day after his arrival he had a dais erected outside the palace and the notables of the city summoned to appear before him. Priests, scholars, eminent citizens, Sadducees and Pharisees lined up before this tribunal, most of them well-meaning moderates who were prepared to go a long way towards humouring the procurator, though not to let him have the sacred treasure. Florus ordered them to surrender the ringleaders of the protest. The notables argued that they could not identify individuals but assured him that the masses were loyal to Rome. Florus reacted by ordering his soldiers into action. Out of the fortress they burst, rushing into the market place below, sacking, killing and looting. There was a stampede through the narrow lanes and many people were trampled down while trying to escape. When the soldiers had cleared the market they turned to the neighbouring houses. Those who were not killed on the spot were captured, scourged and crucified.

The news of the carnage round the market place spread in no time to other parts of the city and a number of notables rushed off to the royal palace to ask Berenice to intervene. The request was natural. As a Heiodian and a descendant of the Hasmonaeans she was the highest-ranking Jewish personage then in Jerusalem. She was a queen, sister to an influential king and, last but not least, a Roman citizen. It was inconceivable that a Roman procurator— strictly speaking far lower than her in the social hierarchy—should ignore a plea from her. Without delay Berenice despatched the commander of her small unit of household cavalry with her compliments to Florus and an appeal to stop the killing of innocent unarmed people. Florus refused to listen. Berenice then sent the commander of her personal bodyguard. Florus did not listen to him either. After several futile attempts to reach him through a messenger it became evident that the only way to gain his ear was to go to him in person.

Confident as she may have been of her immunity as a queen and a Roman citizen, it still required courage to venture into Florus's presence, within a stone's-throw of the rampaging soldiers. Yet there could have been little hesitation, if any, on her part. Standing up for co-religionists in times of distress was part of her proud Herodian heritage. Recent family history could offer several instances of princes and kings who had risked their position, even their life, for the sake of fellow Jews. Now it was up to her to discharge the duty that was incumbent upon highly placed personages in times of national emergency. It was her turn to live up to her name, her station, her family tradition.

There was no time to lose. Not stopping to change into royal robes, her hair uncombed since the beginning of her period of abstinence, she called for her litter and had herself conveyed to the upper palace, accompanied by her cavalry and bodyguard. In front of the dais the litter stopped, and the proud queen, unkempt, barefoot, careful not to trip over dead bodies in consideration of her vow, walked towards the procurator like a suppliant. Florus was not impressed; if anything, the presence of a royal Jewish spectator drove him to a further display of authority. On his instructions the soldiers brought their prisoners up to the dais and tortured them to death before Berenice's very eyes. Florus must have been driven to such a fury of revenge that when his soldiers, taking their cue from his disrespectful attitude to royalty, made an attempt on Berenice herself, he did nothing to stop them. The royal bodyguard fought back while retreating until the queen was in her palace again. Even then her safety was not assured. All that night the guards stood by to rebuff a possible attack by Florus's men. The soldiers however preferred the easy killing and looting in the market area. By the end of the day they had killed more than three-and-a-half thousand men, women and children. It was the sixteenth of Iyar by the Jewish calendar, the third of June AD 66 by modern calculations. It was only the first stage of Florus's punitive policy.

Apparently the lives of the notables who had been summoned by the procurator had been spared, for the day after the massacre

Florus sent word that he required a further assurance of their loyalty. He wanted them to organize a peaceful procession which was to salute a small detachment due to arrive from Caesarea. After the events of the previous day it was extremely difficult to persuade the people to obey. In a desperate attempt to prevent further bloodshed the moderate leaders called for a public meeting. The priests brought out in procession the holy vessels of the temples, the choristers in their new tunics came out carrying their harps and other instruments. They tore their robes, heaped dust upon their heads and begged the people to accept Florus's demand for the sake of peace. Confronted with so much religious pressure the activists were silenced. The crowds went out to welcome the Roman soldiers as instructed, but once face to face the inevitable happened. The soldiers charged and killed, the horsemen trampled and pursued. This time the Jerusalemites were not wholly unprepared. Armed Zealots rushed off to the temple precincts and pulled down the colonnade and staircase connecting it with the Antonia fortress. The Roman garrison was deprived of its easy access to the temple and the first act of armed resistance could be regarded as a success.

At this juncture Florus changed his tactics. He informed the still co-operative notables that he was withdrawing from Jerusalem and making them responsible for law and order. He returned to Caesarea without the seventeen talents and immediately sent his report to Cestius Gallus, the governor of Syria, who was his administrative superior.

Chapter XVI

A time to weep

FLORUS's retreat left the people of Jerusalem more divided than ever. Broadly speaking they fell into two groups; the peace party, which advocated loyalty to Rome in spite of the procurator's misdeeds, and the war party, which called for the total overthrow of the Roman rule. The peace party consisted of the official leadership, the Sadducee aristocracy, the well-to-do and a body of Pharisees who objected to war in principle and directed their energies and hopes to spiritual matters. The war party consisted of the Zealots, whose patriotic call for freedom and their successful sabotaging of the staircases between the Antonia and the temple had won them followers outside their traditional recruiting ground. While the peace party, with the *Sanhedrin* at its head, tried to pursue a policy of appeasement, the war party did its best to rouse the people to rebellion. The city magistrates had great difficulty in persuading the activists to hold their hand while they awaited the result of their own report to the governor of Syria.

By conviction and tradition Berenice was a supporter of the peace party, but her status in Jerusalem was such that she could be no more than a committed outsider. Still acting as an intermediary, she wrote to Cestius Gallus and gave him her own eyewitness account of Florus's atrocities. In fact she wrote several times, no doubt adding her personal grievance of the way she had been handled by the procurator's men to her general charge of maladministration. She must have met Cestius Gallus during the previous year, when he paid an official visit to Jerusalem; she may even have entertained him in her palace. She was certainly in a better position than the magistrates to bring the charges to his notice. At the same time she informed Agrippa in Alexandria of the recent developments and probably asked him to cut his visit short.

Confronted with Florus's report, the magistrates' accusations and Berenice's letters, Cestius Gallus found it difficult to make up his mind. He already had some first-hand information of the situation from his visit to Jerusalem the year before, when he was besieged by huge crowds demanding justice against Florus. At that time he allowed himself to be persuaded that the complaints were unfounded, but in view of the fresh charges before him he felt that an enquiry was called for. He appointed the tribune Neapolitanus to go to Jerusalem on a fact-finding mission.

On his way to Judaea Neapolitanus learnt that Agrippa had left Alexandria and was also making his way to Jerusalem. They met in Jamnia. Jamnia was in no way on the direct route either from Syria, which was Neapolitanus's point of departure, or from Caesarea, where he may have called on Florus. He must therefore have made a considerable detour in order to have a preliminary consultation with a person whom he, like the late Festus, had every reason to consider the best pro-Roman authority on Jewish affairs.

The Jamnia talks were not hurried; they lasted long enough to allow members of the *Sanhedrin*, the chief priests and the notables of Jerusalem to arrive in force and ask Agrippa to be their spokesman. Agrippa had every reason to desire the downfall of a procurator who had not only taken little notice of him in the past but had also encouraged the near-killing of his sister. All the same he did not allow personal considerations to divert him from the course of political wisdom. He played his hand coolly. Like king Archelaus of Cappadocia when called upon to arbitrate between Herod the Great and his son Alexander, he pretended to take the side of the wrong-doer. As a result the impassioned delegates were pulled up short, while Neapolitanus was favourably impressed with their apparent moderation.

As the combined procession of tribune, king and notables approached Jerusalem, a vast demonstration came out to meet them, headed by widows in mourning, all sobbing, lamenting, shrieking, denouncing Florus and calling for punishment. They did not disperse until they had taken the tribune and the king round the scene of desolation in the upper city.

While Neapolitanus put up in the procuratorial palace-fortress with its perfect view of the ruined market place, Agrippa joined

Berenice in the Hasmonaean palace. By then she had had time to get over the fright and horror of the sixteenth of Iyar and was able to review the situation soberly. Apparently she made no plea for revenge; at least none was left on record. She must have curbed, and not for the first time, a natural urge for satisfaction so as not to obscure a more important issue.

Proving Florus's atrocities was easy enough; the evidence lay right on Neapolitanus's doorstep. Convincing him of the loyalty of the people to Rome was more difficult. It took all Agrippa's eloquence and persuasiveness to induce him to walk round the city without a bodyguard in order to satisfy himself that the people wanted justice rather than war. Bravely the tribune made the tour of the city with only one armed escort, came to no harm and ended up in the temple. Once in the Court of Gentiles he addressed the pressing crowds, praised them for their loyalty and urged them to keep the peace. Then, to show his goodwill, he paid homage to the sanctuary.

No sooner had he departed to submit his findings to Cestius than reaction set in. The war party became clamorous again, and even the peace party demanded the immediate dismissal of Florus. As such a dismissal could not be effected without Caesar's authority, to Caesar they proposed to go. In vain did Agrippa argue that Nero would never listen to a Jewish deputation preferring charges against a procurator of his choice, that rather than take their side he was more likely to detain them and send a punitive expedition against Jerusalem. His advice was ignored. The agitation grew daily. With the moderates planning to go to Rome to denounce Florus and the extremists calling on the people to forget Florus and declare war against Rome, the situation became explosive. Agrippa called a mass meeting in a last attempt to bring the people to reason.

The idea must have been carefully discussed with Berenice. Now that he was back in Jerusalem she stepped aside to allow him to resume his unofficial role of mediator which had been thrust upon her in his absence. But although not the central figure in the Herodian peace campaign, she was an essential part of it. Her popularity with the people of Jerusalem at that moment was beyond question. She was the acknowledged heroine of the sixteenth of Iyar, the courageous queen who had risked her life in an attempt to stop the massacre. If anyone had a chance with the crowds, she had.

Both brother and sister were well versed in the art of histrionics; it had formed part of their early education and came easily to the children of Agrippa I. They must have planned every move, calculated every gesture likely to make the best dramatic effect. Agrippa was to use eloquence and logic; Berenice was to play on the people's emotions. The message they wished to convey was simple and unequivocal. There must be no war with Rome, for war meant national suicide. That was the gist of Agrippa's speech, probably the most important of his career and one which, had it made the intended impact, may well have changed the course of history.

The text of his speech, as quoted by Josephus, may be regarded as basically authentic. Classical authors often put their own concept of an argument into the mouth of a protagonist as if they were his actual words. On the other hand, if they happened to be in close contact with the person they were writing about, the speech they attributed to him was probably nearer to the original, as recollected in retrospect. In Agrippa's case the speech must have belonged to the second category. For one thing Josephus probably heard it delivered, for in the spring of AD 66 he was in Jerusalem, a highly thought of young scholar and a rising leader. For another he almost certainly let Agrippa see his reconstruction of the speech when, some years later, he began to write the history of the Jewish–Roman war. He had an extensive correspondence with the king on the subject and let him check his manuscript. If in the process some of the wording was perfected and polished, the general construction must in the main have remained the same. It epitomized the Herodian political *credo*. It was a clear exposition of *realpolitik*, cleverly argued, irritatingly wise, inevitably out of tune with the mood of the people.

On the appointed day the public assembled in the colonnaded gymnasium facing the Hasmonaean palace. Berenice, her Nazirite vow probably completed by then, placed herself conspicuously beside her brother on the flat roof of the royal penthouse. From their vantage point they could see and be seen, and Agrippa's voice could carry without difficulty. It was not recorded in what language he spoke, but it was most likely Aramaic, the popular language of the people, rather than Hebrew, which was the language of the learned. Having asked the forbearance of potential hecklers, Agrippa came straight to the point:

I am aware that many orate against the insolence of the procurators and rhapsodize about the wonders of liberty; but before I go into the question of who you are and whom you are planning to fight, I must first sort out your jumble of pretexts. If you are trying to avenge your wrongs, why do you prate about liberty? If on the other hand slavery seems unbearable, it is a waste of time to blame your rulers; if they were the mildest of men, it would still be a disgrace to be slaves.

Consider these pretexts one at a time, and see how feeble are your grounds for war. First, the charges against the procurators. . . . I grant that the ministers of Rome are unbearably harsh; does it follow that all the Romans are persecuting you, including Caesar? Yet it is on them that you are going to make war! It would be absurd because of the trifling misdemeanours of one man to go to war with a whole nation. Our grievances can be easily put right; the same procurator will not be here for ever, and his successors are almost sure to be more reasonable. But once set on foot, war cannot easily be either broken off or fought to a conclusion without disaster.

As for your new passion for liberty, it comes too late; you ought to have made a supreme effort to retain it long ago. . . . The time when we ought to have done everything possible to keep the Romans out was when the country was invaded by Pompey [in 63 BC, nearly a hundred and thirty years earlier]. But our ancestors and their kings, with material, physical and mental resources far superior to yours, faced a mere fraction of the Roman army and put up no resistance; will you, who have learnt submission from your fathers and are so ill provided compared with those who first submitted, stand up to the whole Roman Empire?[1]

Agrippa then proceeded to outline the history of those peoples who had tried to stand up to the whole Roman empire. He mentioned the Athenians, the Spartans, the Macedonians, all experi-

enced fighters who were forced to accept Rome's supremacy like
many other freedom-loving nations. He then pointed out how
short of conventional war resources Judaea was:

Where are the men, where are the weapons you count on?
Where is the fleet that is to sweep the Roman seas? Where are
the funds to pay for your expeditions? Do you think you are
going to war with Egyptians and Arabs? Look at the far-flung
empire of Rome and contrast your own impotence. Why, our
forces have been worsted even by our neighbours again and
again, while their arms have triumphed over the whole world!
And even the world is not big enough to satisfy them; Euphrates
is not far enough to the east, or Danube to the north, or Libya
and the desert beyond to the south, or Cadiz to the west; but
beyond the Ocean they have sought a new world, carrying their
arms as far as Britain, that land of mystery. Why not face facts?
Are you richer than the Gauls, stronger than the Germans,
cleverer than the Greeks, more numerous than all the nations
of the world? What gives you confidence to defy the power of
Rome?[2]

Accepting for argument's sake that enslavement was a terrible
thing, Agrippa went on to say that it was a common lot, shared
not only by the proud Greeks, but also by five hundred cities of
Asia, by the Colchians round the Black Sea, the Taurians in the
Crimea, the people near the Sea of Azov. His list was inexhaustible. It included Bithynia, Cappadocia, Pamphylia, Cilicia, Thrace,
Illyria, Dalmatia, Gaul. He spoke of the cloud-capped Pyrenees
that failed to check the Roman advance into Spain and the Rhine
beyond which the fierce Germans sought refuge from the Roman
legions. He then brought up the clinching example of a false sense
of invincibility:

Consider the defence of the Britons, you who feel so sure of
the defences of Jerusalem. They are surrounded by the Ocean
and inhabit an island as big as this continent; yet the Romans
crossed the sea and enslaved them, and four legions keep that
huge island quiet.[3]

Agrippa argued that if the Judaeans went to war they would find themselves completely isolated. Even the Parthian empire, the traditional ally against Rome, had at last come to heel. It was no use looking up for help from co-religionists in the dispersion; they were in a vulnerable position and their host-countries would never allow them to take up arms against Rome.

Having crushed all hope in human aid, Agrippa proceeded to demolish the deepest hope of all, that of divine intervention:

> So there is no refuge left except to make God your ally. But He too is ranged on the Roman side, for without His help so vast an empire could never have been built up. Think too how difficult it would be, even if you were fighting feeble opponents, to preserve the purity of your religion, and how you will be forced to transgress the very laws which furnish your chief hope of making God your ally, and so will alienate Him. If you observe the custom of the Sabbath with its complete cessation of activity, you will promptly be crushed, as were your ancestors by Pompey, who was most active in pressing the siege on the days when the besieged were passive. But if in the war you transgress your ancestral Law I don't see what you have left to fight for, since your one desire is that none of your ancestral customs should be broken. How will you be able to call the Deity to your aid if you deliberately deny Him the service that is due?[4]

Not only did Agrippa assure his audience that the result of armed resistance to Rome would be defeat, but that defeat meant total annihilation. From his first-hand knowledge of Roman war practices he warned:

> Possibly some of you suppose that you are making war in accordance with agreed rules, and that when the Romans have won they will be kind to you, and will not think of making you an example to other nations by burning down your Holy City and destroying your entire race. I tell you, not even if you survive will you find a place of refuge, since every people recognizes the lordship of Rome or fears that it will have to do so. Again, the danger threatens not only ourselves here but

The Beirut Inscription, apparently the only surviving mention of Berenice's name. It records: 'Queen Berenice daughter of the great King Agrippa and King Agrippa her brother adorned with marbles and columns the building which their ancester King Herod had made, after it had fallen into decay through age.'

Titus,
Museo Capitolino, Rome

Vespasian
Uffizi Gal.
Florence

also those who live in other cities; for there is no region in the world without its Jewish colony. All these, if you go to war, will be massacred by your opponents, and through the folly of a few men every city will run with Jewish blood. There would be an excuse for such a massacre; but if it did not take place, think how wicked it would be to take up arms against such kindly people! Pity your wives and children, or at least pity your mother city and its sacred precincts. Spare the Temple and preserve for your use the Sanctuary with its sacred treasures. For the Romans will no longer keep their hands off when they have captured these, since for sparing them hitherto they have received no thanks at all.[5]

And Agrippa ended with an impassioned plea:

I call to witness all you hold sacred, the holy angels of God, and the Fatherland we all share, that I have not kept back anything that is for your safety; if you make a right decision you will share with me the blessing of peace, but if you are carried away by your passions you will go without me to your doom.[6]

It was a long speech. With its rhetorical questions and dramatic pauses it must have taken the best part of an hour. Josephus recorded that towards the end Agrippa seemed so overwhelmed by his emotions that he broke down in sobs. Berenice too was visibly moved and burst into tears. At the sight of so much sincerity even the most incensed began to have second thoughts. They turned to one another and murmured that they had no quarrel with Rome, only with Florus. The loudest amongst them shouted that much up to Agrippa. He called back that the best way to prove their loyalty was to rebuild the colonnade joining the temple with the Roman garrison in the Antonia. Not giving them a chance to shake off the impact of his speech, he and Berenice descended quickly from their penthouse, put themselves at the head of the crowd and marched off to the temple where, symbolically, the work of reconstruction was put in hand there and then.

While the work progressed in the temple, the magistrates acted on another suggestion of Agrippa's and went out to the villages round Jerusalem to collect tax arrears. Before long they got together forty talents. But the submissive mood of the people did not last long. The realization came upon them that they had been hoodwinked by Their Majesties. They had been made to reconnect the Roman garrison with the temple, they had been induced to part with their meagre earnings to fill the imperial treasury, yet Florus had not suffered any punishment. They were exactly where they had been. Restraint had not paid. It was better to use force.

Again Agrippa called a meeting. This one was dominated by supporters of the war party. They booed his suggestion that they should wait patiently until Florus was quietly relieved by Nero as a matter of routine. They told him a few home truths, reminded him that he did not belong in Jerusalem and ordered him to be off. Even the consolation of a dignified retreat was denied to him. He was followed with words of abuse and stones all the way to the palace.

Clearly there was nothing for it but to leave Jerusalem while the going was good. After some final words of advice to the leaders of the peace party Agrippa and Berenice left for Caesarea Philippi. Before the summer was out their palace was set on fire and Jerusalem was in the throes of war. They were never to enter it again.

Chapter XVII

Imperial allies

JOSEPHUS's writings as well as rabbinical sources suggest that throughout the Jewish–Roman war of 66–70 there was no unanimity of purpose among the Judaean leadership. Some tried nearly to the last to surrender in order to avert a greater catastrophe. Others would not accept anything short of total liberation. But it was not a straight fight between the peace party and the war party. Even the war party was bitterly divided. It had its moderates and its extremists, its reckless and its hesitants, its Zealots and its *sicarii*. The enemy without was Rome; the enemy within was the absence of a one-track policy.

After Their Majesties' enforced departure from Jerusalem the war party proceeded to press home its advantage. It found a leader in the person of a young aristocrat called Eleazar, son of a former high priest and commander of the temple guard, the only organized Jewish armed force in Jerusalem. Eleazar was widely respected for his integrity, and his authority was only second to the high priest's. His throwing in his lot with the cause of liberation represented a significant shift in the traditional political pattern. For the first time in the history of the freedom movement an aristocratic Sadducee ranged himself on the side of the low-class rebels. Hundreds of priests were swayed by his gesture, although within his own family it caused a rift as his father and his brother went on advocating submission.

True to his background Eleazar showed his defiance of Rome in the best of priestly traditions. He called for the cessation of the daily sacrifice offered on behalf of the emperor, a custom that had not been deviated from since it was first introduced by Augustus some eighty years earlier. In vain did the high priests and his followers try to oppose the call. The lower priesthood cheered Eleazar's boldness and stopped the imperial sacrifices. It was a theocratic act of defiance which symbolized the breakdown of

Roman rule. To all intents and purposes it was a formal declaration of war.

It was not however a declaration sanctioned by the official leadership. The peace party appealed secretly to Florus in Caesarea and to Agrippa in Caesarea Philippi for troops to quell the revolt before it became a revolution. But the first armed force to enter Jerusalem was neither Florus's, who had sent none, nor Agrippa's, who had sent a detachment of cavalry. It was a unit of triumphant *sicarii* who had successfully eliminated the Roman garrison in the fortress of Masada, on the Dead Sea, helped themselves to the enormous arsenals prepared by Herod the Great, and made it their own headquarters. They were headed by Menachem, a descendant of an illustrious line of freedom fighters. He was the last surviving son of Judas of Galilee who had led the Zealots' revolt in AD 7 and the younger brother of Jacob and Simon who were crucified by Tiberius Alexander in AD 46–48. Menachem joined forces with Eleazar and when Agrippa's three thousand horsemen from Batanaea, Auranitis and Trachonitis arrived to lend their support to the peace party, Zealots and *sicarii* attacked them together.

Both Agrippa and the peace party had underestimated the utter dedication of the freedom fighters who were driven by an internal force far superior to the mercenary motivation of the royal cavalry. After a fierce battle Agrippa's horsemen surrendered and were allowed to retreat. But the Roman soldiers left in various strategic points of the city were surrounded and butchered nearly to a man. With them many of the Romanizers were killed, among them Eleazar's own father and brother. The residence of the arch-Romanizers Agrippa and Berenice was set on fire, its offensive penthouse crumbling down first. In the general turmoil nobody stopped to reflect that the ancient palace of the Hasmonaeans, whose name had become synonymous with national independence, was burnt down for the very cause that had made it possible to put it up.

Once the city was clear of Romans and invaders a savage scramble broke out between the fiery Eleazar and the ambitious Menachem. Menachem was ignominiously killed and his *sicarii* put to flight. They returned to Masada where they held out against the Romans long after the rest of the country had been subdued and where in AD 73, to escape the disgrace of surrender, they committed their heroic mass suicide.

In spite of the initial success of the revolt Agrippa never seriously doubted its outcome. He was convinced, as indeed were many people in Jerusalem, of the invincibility of Rome and the necessity of sacrificing a few lives in order to save the many. Together with Berenice he went to Antioch to see the governor of Syria and offer him whatever help and advice he had in him to give. In that he was acting not only out of concern for Judaea, but in accordance with his prescribed duties as a client-king of Rome.

In view of the staunch support he gave the Romans throughout the war, it was often suggested by modern historians that he was a traitor to his people, a Jew who collaborated with the enemy in order to save his throne. It is not unlikely that a refusal to offer military assistance would have resulted in his being replaced by a more co-operative king; yet it seems somewhat naïve to suggest that his all-out effort to help the Romans was due entirely to his desire to keep his position. His real reason must have been more complex. A fresh scrutiny of his career from boyhood to maturity suggests the possibility of a different motivation.

As the eldest son of king Agrippa I, young Agrippa was brought up to regard himself as his potential heir. His likeness appeared on coins minted by his father and he had every reason to think of himself as the future king of Judaea. He was liked by Claudius, in whose house in Rome he was being educated, and he could have little doubt that the emperor would confirm his succession when the time came. It must have been a bitter blow when at seventeen, on his father's premature death, he was pushed aside and denied the diadem he had long regarded as his due. Although with true Herodian skill he later manipulated Claudius into giving him a kingdom, it was not that of his ancestors. He became a Jewish king, but not a king of Judaea. The nearest he ever got to a position of authority in his homeland was as administrator of temple affairs. To a frustrated heir it must have seemed little more than a consolation prize. Agrippa probably never reconciled himself to the loss of his inheritance. Outwardly he might court the procurators and seek their favour; inwardly he could have never accepted the low-born officials who had usurped his birthright.

His equivocal position in Jerusalem must have whetted rather than satisfied his ambition. There were two important factors that he may have borne in mind. The first was that the reign of procurators had proved an utter failure not only from the Jewish point of view but also from the Roman point of view. The second was that there had already been a precedent of revoking the procuratorial regime in favour of a Jewish kingship dependent on Rome. Agrippa must have considered himself eminently suitable to the post of king of Judaea. Thanks to his ancestry and his record he was more acceptable to the Jews than any foreign procurator, while in Rome he was *persona grata*. It was only a question of biding his time and finding the right moment to broach the subject in imperial circles.

He must have been encouraged when after the Parthian campaign of AD 54 Nero rewarded his military assistance with the addition of Tiberias to his territories. It was no barbarian village in a remote area, but a thriving city in the heart of Galilee and one which had once formed part of his father's Jewish kingdom. It could be interpreted as an auspicious precedent.

When at the beginning of hostilities Agrippa went to Syria to offer his help to Rome against the Jewish rebels, he was therefore playing for high stakes. That was his long-awaited chance to expose the inadequacy of the procuratorial system and hint that the best way to keep the truculent Jews under control was to give them a ruler from amongst their own people. At no other time in his career was he so near his life's ambition. If he put so much zeal into the Roman campaign, tried to persuade the rebels to desist and even risked his life under their attack, it was not in order to safeguard his position as king of unruly natives in Batanaea or Auranitis; far less would have convinced the Romans of his loyalty. If he went to such extraordinary lengths it was because he was desperately trying to prevent the devastation of a country he was hoping to be awarded as a prize. Agrippa was not fighting a Roman war. He was fighting for the restoration of the kingdom of Judaea to the house of Herod as personified in himself. That was why a prince who since his Roman boyhood had stood up for his co-religionists began to behave in a manner seemingly so contrary to his previous record, and why his sister, who a few weeks earlier had risked her life in an attempt to stop a Jewish massacre, gave her support to a policy that on the face of it looked like betrayal. To the Herodian way of thinking it was more than a means of saving Judaea from inevitable destruction; it was a chance to bring nearer the realization of a personal dream of royal grandeur in their own household.

In Syria Their Majesties met old friends and allies who had taken part in the Parthian campaign twelve years earlier. The reunion with Antiochus of Commagene must have been cordial as usual, but the meeting with Sohaemus of Emesa could have been awkward. During one of Agrippa's recent absences from Caesarea Philippi his non-Jewish regent had plotted to overthrow him and actually instigated a massacre of the king's Jewish subjects in the capital. In the ordinary way he would have been put to death when caught, but as it happened he was a relative of the king of Emesa. Rather than alienate Sohaemus by executing his kinsman and thus jeopardizing the unity of the allies and with it his own secret scheme, Agrippa allowed the treacherous regent to go unpunished. His immediate object was to help Cestius Gallus to subdue Judaea as quickly as possible with as few losses as possible. A large allied army was formed, consisting of Roman legions reinforced by cavalry and bowmen supplied by the three client-kings. With Cestius as commander-in-chief—Florus had faded out altogether—the allies began their advance towards Judaea. In the autumn they reached the outskirts of Jerusalem and pitched their camp on Mount Scopus.

Cestius tried to take the walled city by direct assault, but met with no significant success. When winter set in, with its threat of bitter cold and possibly snow, he lost confidence and gave the order to retreat. The defenders of the city came out after him and carried out a spectacular mopping-up operation. Only remnants of the vast allied army managed to reach the safety of Antioch. The first round ended in a resounding success for the freedom fighters. Judaea was clear of Romans and for the first time since the days of the early Hasmonaeans the country was entirely free of foreign domination. The end of AD 66 marked the beginning of a new era. A national government was set up and silver coins were struck to commemorate the first year of liberation.

It was the first time within living memory that a national

government was entrusted with the conduct of state affairs, without a Hasmonaean high priest or king having the last word. It was basically a war coalition which included representatives of the Zealots, but was still top heavy with aristocrats whose attitude to an all-out war was cautious. One of their first actions was to divide the country into defence zones and appoint governors to command them. Jerusalem was entrusted jointly to a former high priest and a secular leader, while Eleazar, the original instigator of the revolt, was relegated to a secondary position as governor of Idumaea. Galilee, the most important region outside Jerusalem, was entrusted to a twenty-nine-year-old priest called Joseph the son of Mattathias, better known to posterity as Josephus the historian.

Josephus was born in AD 37 of a father who was a priest and a mother who was descended from the royal house of the Hasmonaeans. He could therefore claim a distant relationship with Agrippa and Berenice. According to his own testimony he was somewhat of a child prodigy, for when he was fourteen he was consulted on points of law by the great scholars of the day. He made himself thoroughly familiar with the doctrines of the Pharisees, the Sadducees and the Essenes, the ascetic hermits of the desert. He also became fairly proficient in Greek although, by his own admission, he never quite mastered its pronunciation. With his outstanding academic achievements he combined a zest for public life. He became an active participant in Judaean politics, and in his mid-twenties was sent to Rome to try and obtain the release of some fellow-priests who had been languishing in prison for several years. He was introduced to Poppaea and through her good offices accomplished his mission with success. On his return to Jerusalem, in the early spring of AD 66, he was an established public figure.

By conviction he was as much a believer in the might of Rome as his royal kinsmen. He probably heard Agrippa's peace speech in the early summer of that year and must have been in complete agreement with it. Indeed, had not Agrippa been its more likely author, Josephus himself could have written it. He would have preferred a continued existence under Roman rule, but when hostilities broke out he put himself at the head of the queue for military posts. Why he was given the important region of Galilee is puzzling. Perhaps he impressed the coalition government with his proven resourcefulness and his first-hand knowledge of Roman tactics, gained during his recent stay in Rome. His appointment was not a wise one. Josephus was no zealot dedicated to freedom unto death. He was primarily dedicated to self-preservation. While proceeding to fortify Galilee against the expected Roman attack, he kept the door open for retreat by making secret overtures to Agrippa and Berenice who had already allied themselves with the enemy.

He carried his ingratiatory policy to such lengths that on at least two occasions he nearly got caught out by simple-minded patriots. The first instance occurred when the national government in Jerusalem instructed him to pull down the Herodian palace of Tiberias, which its founder Antipas had decorated with animal carvings contrary to Mosaic law. Tiberias had belonged to Agrippa, but when the revolt broke out it went over to the rebels. Josephus showed no alacrity in carrying out his orders. He was hoping to save the royal valuables and send them to Their Majesties in Caesarea Philippi as proof of his open mind. His delaying tactics were not popular with the people. At the instigation of a rival rebel leader they set fire to the palace and burnt it down. All Josephus could recover was the molten gold from the rich ceilings, some Corinthian bronze candelabra, a few finely wrought tables and a quantity of silver. These he put in a safe deposit until such time as he could return them to their royal owners.

The second instance of his middle-of-the-road policy nearly cost him his life. The route joining Agrippa's kingdom with the south ran beneath Mount Tabor in Galilee. One day Josephus's Galilean garrison ambushed a royal convoy and looted its silver plate, gold coins and rich garments probably intended to restock Berenice's wardrobe. The soldiers dutifully took their loot to Josephus, trusting he would use it for the war effort. Instead he made arrangements to return it to Their Majesties. His decision was correctly interpreted as collaboration with the enemy and the mob demanded his death. It required all his wiliness to reverse the tables on his accusers, have them put to death and remain in charge. But in return he was forced to give up his suspect understanding with Agrippa and promise to spend the booty on defence.

The news of Cestius's defeat and Judaea's secession from the Roman empire reached Nero in Achaia in Greece, where he was busy beating the Greeks at their own games. He sang to the lyre, recited, drove a chariot and was predictably awarded the winner's laurels. When he realized the extent of the danger in the east, he appointed one of the most experienced generals of his entourage to take over the conduct of the war.

Titus Flavius Vespasian was born in AD 9 and under Claudius achieved distinction in the conquest of Britain, when he 'fought thirty battles, subjugated two warlike tribes and captured more than twenty towns, beside the entire Isle of Wight'.[1] At the time of the Greek tour Vespasian was in semi-disgrace because he had failed to appreciate Nero's artistic genius. He was known to leave in the middle of an imperial song-recital, or, when forbidden to do so, to fall asleep. But his military ability tipped the scales and at fifty-eight he was given the task of reconquering Judaea. His predecessor Cestius mercifully died before Nero could punish him for his defeat, and his post as governor of Syria was given to Mucianus.

As his second-in-command Vespasian appointed his son Titus who was also on the Greek tour. While Vespasian left for Antioch by land, Titus went to Alexandria by sea, each with the purpose of taking over the Roman legions available. In Antioch Vespasian was met by Agrippa and Berenice who had been waiting in Syria all this time, and accepted the auxiliary army the king put at his disposal. From there they proceeded together to Ptolemais where in due course they were joined by Titus and the other eastern allies. In the early months of 67 Ptolemais saw the foundation of a grand alliance that was to play an important part in Vespasian's bid for imperial power two years later. It consisted of four client-kings whom Josephus listed as Agrippa, Antiochus of Commagene, Sohaemus of Emesa and Malchus of Arabia. Dio referred to them briefly as 'the barbarian kings',[2] while a rabbinical reference, worth quoting more for its quaintness than for its historical accuracy, described them as 'prince of Arabia [Malchus], prince of Africa [?], prince of Alexandria [Tiberius Alexander, who later became Titus's commander-in-chief] and the prince of Palestine [Agrippa]'.[3]

It took several months to organize the army and co-ordinate its many components. It was not until the spring of AD 67, nearly a whole year since the outbreak of war, that Vespasian was ready to take up where Cestius had left off. His plan was to conquer Galilee first, then besiege Jerusalem. His sixty-thousand-strong army was in fine fettle and set out towards Galilee in the usual Roman marching order which Josephus the commander must have dreaded, but which Josephus the historian later described with admiration:

The light-armed auxiliaries and bowmen formed the vanguard, with orders to repel sudden enemy rushes and reconnoitre woods suspected of concealing ambushes. Next came a body of heavy-armed Roman troops, mounted and unmounted. These were followed by ten men from every century carrying, besides their own kit, the instruments for marking out the camp-site. After them came roadmakers to straighten out bends in the highway, level rough surfaces, and cut down obstructive woods, so that the army would not be exhausted by laborious marching. In the rear of these the personal baggage of the commander and his senior officers was concentrated under the protection of a strong cavalry force, behind which rode Vespasian himself with the cream of his horse and foot and a body of spearmen. Next came the legionary cavalry; for each legion has its own troops of one hundred and twenty horse. These were followed by the mules that carried the batterers and other mechanical devices. After them came the generals, cohort-commanders, and tribunes, with a bodyguard of picked troops; next the standards, enclosing the Eagle which is at the head of every legion, as the king of birds and most fearless of all: this they regard as the symbol of empire and portent of victory, no matter who opposes them. The sacred emblems were followed by the trumpeters, and in their wake came the main body, shoulder to shoulder, six men abreast, accompanied as always by a centurion to maintain the formation. The servants of every legion marched in a body behind the infantry, looking after the soldiers' baggage carried by the mules and other beasts. In the rear of all the legions marched the bulk of the mercenaries, followed by a protective rearguard of light and heavy infantry with a strong body of cavalry.[4]

Whatever opposition the army encountered on its advance through Galilee it crushed without difficulty. Josephus and a force of dedicated fighters retreated to the city of Jotapata (Yodfat) which was almost entirely perched on a precipice, protected on three sides by deep ravines and strongly fortified on the fourth. The siege lasted forty-seven days. The Galileans fought with dauntless courage and inflicted considerable losses on the Romans. In the end they were overpowered and the last forty, headed by Josephus, hid in a cave. When they realized that there was no way out except surrender they killed one another by lots. The only one to survive, by miracle or by sleight-of-hand, was Josephus. He surrendered and was brought before Vespasian. As soon as he saw him he was touched by divine inspiration and prophesied that Vespasian would become emperor of Rome. Vespasian was astonished, then hooked. He spared Josephus's life and put him in prison. It is not unlikely that Agrippa put in a good word for him, repaying his past overtures. Although the prisoner was kept in chains he was treated with forbearance; either because Titus and Vespasian took a liking to him, as Josephus would have his readers believe, or, more realistically, because as the former military governor of Galilee he was able to part with useful strategic information. His collaboration was so highly valued that after the Roman victory he was allowed to settle down in Rome, given a pension and permitted to add the imperial family name to his own, thus going down to posterity as Flavius Josephus.

After the conquest of Jotapata Vespasian left the mountains of Galilee for the coast. The port of Joppa (Jaffa, near Tel Aviv) had fallen into the hands of the rebels and, although it had no natural harbour, served as a launching point for naval guerilla operations. The whole sea traffic between Syria and Egypt was harassed by the freedom ships based at Joppa. Vespasian occupied the city without difficulty and forced many of the defenders to seek refuge in their ships. As the luck of war would have it, a fierce gale broke out and smashed the entire fleet against the rocks.

It was still summer and the heat on the coastal plain was not conducive to further exertions. When Agrippa suggested that Vespasian and Titus should go north with him to recuperate in the cool climate of Caesarea Philippi, his invitation was accepted. Part of the army was left in Caesarea on the coast, while the rest marched with its commanders to the royal capital. The three-week stay in Caesarea Philippi set the seal on the relationship between Titus and Berenice that had begun a few months earlier and was to last for more than twelve years.

Chapter XVIII

Kingmakers

W^HAT made Titus fall under Berenice's spell is as hard to explain as the chemistry that had enslaved Antony to Cleopatra a hundred years earlier. It could not have been Berenice's beauty alone; at thirty-nine, attractive and well preserved as no doubt she was, she could hardly have competed with younger and prettier rivals who had their eye on the unattached twenty-six-year-old Titus. It must have been her personality rather than her looks that helped to captivate a popular officer whose age suited him to be a companion to her own two sons rather than to herself.

It was not however a case of a mature and scheming woman laying a trap for an innocent young man in order to further her own political ambitions. At twenty-six Titus had already had more than a taste of the vices of imperial Rome. He had been a boon companion of Nero's and did not shrink from emulating some of his excesses. While Nero, after Poppaea's death, had had a youth called Sporus castrated and had gone through a form of marriage with him, Titus amused himself with a whole troupe of eunuchs. When his first wife died he married another, only to divorce her as soon as she gave birth to a daughter whom he took away from her. If he succumbed to Berenice's charms it was not because he was unworldly.

Her background must have played an important part in his courtship. Titus must have regarded her, as his father did when he first met her, primarily as the influential sister of a useful client-king. She was known to have a say in Agrippa's politics and to be a wealthy princess in her own right. Vespasian was not the man to spurn money whatever the source. It was quite possibly on his instructions that Titus was assigned the pleasant duty of cultivating Berenice.

Although Titus was no stranger to an emperor's court, he had not been used to hobnobbing with royalty, certainly not with royalty whose pedigree could be traced back for generations. His own family background was none too aristocratic, and he may well have been intoxicated with Berenice's long line of royal descent, her majestic bearing, her graciousness, her sophistication and her breeding. Courting a desirable woman for her political influence rather than her feminine charms must have given an added fillip to Titus's awakening interest. Whatever the reason and the circumstances, he fell under her spell and made no bones about it.

Titus Flavius Vespasian, so named after his father, was born at the end of AD 41. Earlier that year Gaius Caligula had been murdered, Claudius became emperor, Agrippa I was given the kingdom of Judaea and a thirteen-year-old Herodian princess called Berenice was married in Rome to a merchant from Alexandria. Young Titus was brought up in court together with Britannicus, Claudius's son by Messalina. The two boys were such close friends that when Britannicus drank his fatal dose of poison, Titus impetuously seized the cup and drained its remains, making himself seriously ill. While he was in the imperial palace he probably met the young Agrippa who was still living in Claudius's household and trying to win a kingdom from him.

From early youth Titus showed a remarkable aptitude for the arts of war and peace. He was a good marksman and an accomplished horseman. After winning military distinction in Britain and Germany he returned to Rome and practised law for a while. He was a good orator in Latin and Greek, composed verses in both languages, sang and played the harp. He was only four years younger than Nero and, unlike Vespasian, was not averse to praising the emperor's artistic skill and taking part in his orgies.

At the time of his meeting with Berenice, most likely during the allied manoeuvres around Ptolemais in the early months of AD 67, Titus must have been in the prime of youth. Although not tall and showing a distinct tendency to paunchiness, he was athletic and bore himself well. He was considered handsome and had an inborn charm that even his stern father found disarming. Berenice, who until his arrival had been making herself agreeable to Vespasian, now set out to win his son. Agrippa tactfully stepped aside.

There is no telling whether Titus ever suspected the existence of anything more than brotherly love between Agrippa and Berenice. Whether he did or not, he was not likely to be repelled or inhibited by it. Roman society was not much perturbed by incest. It condoned it in Caligula and treated it as respectable in foreign royalty. It is however possible that by the time Titus met Berenice, her relationship with her brother had undergone a change. No youthful passion, however ardent, can keep at boiling point if regularly gratified. Theirs, after years of fulfilment, may have evolved into affection and tolerance, as with many a settled couple. It would have been most unusual if Agrippa, in the prime of life, had not succumbed from time to time to the charms of other women; while Berenice, approaching forty, would have hardly expected the continuation of their relationship on its original terms. There were other things to bind them together; their perfect understanding of each other, their similar tastes and interests, their Herodian attitude to Rome and finally their shared dreams of grandeur. Both brother and sister were supreme realists. Without being amoral, they could bend their consciences to suit their will. If their secret aim at this stage was to win Judaea for services rendered, an affair with one of its would-be conquerors could be regarded as an added string to their bow. Their own relationship, whether still amorous or not, would have facilitated rather than impeded the acceptance of an attachment which in the ordinary course of events they would have regarded as immoral.

It must be remembered that both Agrippa and Berenice were conformists as far as religion was concerned. Agrippa had always insisted that his sisters' husbands should be either Jewish by birth or circumcised by consent, and when his sister Drusilla associated with Felix she did so without seeking his approval. He could hardly have encouraged another sister to have intercourse without marriage, and with a Gentile at that, had she not already been guilty of a sin in comparison with which this liaison seemed only a slight one. As for Berenice, whose respect for convention was such that, unlike Drusilla, she preferred a costly divorce to an impetuous escapade, she could hardly have embarked at near-forty on what she had been taught to regard as a sinful association, had she not been lax at some earlier stage. She was not an impulsive woman. At her age she was not likely to be swept off her feet by a dissipated Roman officer, however charming. Her affair with

Titus must have been made morally easier in the light of earlier permissiveness.

That permissiveness must have helped in another way as well. To win and maintain Titus's love Berenice needed every feminine guile she could think of. Had she been living in a state of abstinence ever since her mid-twenties, she would at forty have been far too diffident and lacking in feminine know-how even to attempt to charm a self-indulgent young Roman thirteen years her junior. Her approach to him suggested on the contrary that self-confidence which could have been born only out of the proven power of her charms.

The visit to Caesarea Philippi gave Berenice a chance to consolidate her relationship with Titus who during the preceding months could not have spared much time for pleasure. For twenty days she and Agrippa exerted themselves to make their guests happy. The calm of the capital was disrupted by banquets and spectacles, gladiatorial games and hunting expeditions. Berenice showed her hospitality as well as her acumen by plying the elderly Vespasian with splendid gifts; his reputation for cupidity must have preceded him. For his part he raised no objection to his son's infatuation with the queen. He had every reason to be well disposed towards her brother who had been prompt with his military assistance and who was the only person who could conceivably persuade the Jews, even at that late stage, to lay down their arms. In return for past and future services Vespasian agreed to send his army against the main towns in Agrippa's own kingdom which had gone over to the rebels, namely Tiberias and Taricheae on the west shore of the Sea of Galilee, Gamala on the east shore and Gischala (Gush-Chalav) in the north of the Galilee mountains.

After a twenty-day interlude Titus said a temporary goodbye to Berenice and went back to Caesarea to fetch the main body of the army. Vespasian and Agrippa must have stayed on to allow him to cover the seventy-odd miles between the two Caesareas, then set out to meet up with him about half-way. Berenice probably went with them and took up quarters in the Roman encampment near Tiberias, where she could receive immediate reports about the progress of the fighting and the well-being of the two men whose safety concerned her most, her brother and her lover.

But there was no fighting yet. The elders of Tiberias took fright at the sight of the encamped army and hurriedly sent Agrippa a message of loyalty. While a few hardened anti-Romans fled to nearby Taricheae, the city gates were thrown open and the Roman army took over without resistance. Vespasian was pleased and instructed his soldiers to refrain from looting so as not to cause damage to his friend's domain. Agrippa turned a blind eye to past disloyalties and was even persuaded by Berenice to spare the life of a young aristocrat who had been one of the ringleaders of the Tiberian war party.

Justus the son of Pistus, or Justus of Tiberias, was a well-known figure on both sides of the Sea of Galilee. During Josephus's governorship of the region he had frequent quarrels with him and set himself up as an independent leader, attacking the predominantly Greek villages on the east shore of the lake. Like Josephus he seemed to be more concerned with his own safety than with the cause of independence, and like him he made secret overtures to Agrippa while openly inciting the people of Tiberias to disown him. When the Romans encamped within reach of Tiberias he did not wait to be caught. He went over to the king and threw himself on his mercy. Vespasian felt that his forays into Greek villages warranted a death sentence, but out of deference to Agrippa, whose subject Justus was, he left the case to him. Justus, again like Josephus, was a man of many parts who could wield a pen as well as a sword. He so impressed Berenice with his superior knowledge of Greek and Latin that she not only obtained his pardon from Agrippa but also secured him the post of royal secretary. Her benevolence towards him became one of Josephus's main reasons for turning against her. She had no business being kind to an enemy and a rival while he, a kinsman and a proven well-wisher, was still in chains. Years later, when Justus wrote his own version of the Jewish war, alas not preserved, Josephus accused him of falsifying history and even of betraying Agrippa while in his service. Berenice however seemed unaware of Justus's alleged shortcomings and remained his patron for many years to come.

The next Roman target was Taricheae which was well fortified on three sides and flanked by the lake—the Sea of Galilee—on the fourth. The Taricheaeans had a sizeable fleet, and when Titus's cavalry attack cracked their defences, they took to the lake. Vespasian ordered his engineers to build heavy rafts and with them sent troops after the boats. In the savage naval battle that followed the Romans scored a resounding success. There was massacre by land and water, and the lake turned red with blood. Of the survivors Vespasian sent six thousand to dig the Corinth Canal which Nero had just started, sold another thirty thousand as slaves, and allowed Agrippa to do the same with his share of the captives. The battle of Taricheae was the fiercest so far, and to commemorate it, as well as the Joppa victory, Vespasian and his sons later struck bronze coins bearing the legend *Victoria Navalis*.

Titus had fought valiantly, showing the same youthful impetuosity that had once driven him to drain Britannicus's poisoned cup. The story went round that when his horse was slain under him, he unseated and killed an enemy rider and leapt on his mount unscathed. Another story told how, when he was too impatient for the city walls to crack, he rode his horse through the lake and came up on the defenders from behind. Berenice may not have been altogether sad to learn that he was ordered to go to Syria for talks with the governor Mucianus.

Gamala, the third city on Agrippa's list, was on the east shore of the lake and naturally fortified. As Vespasian could not easily take it without a long siege, he asked Agrippa to speak to the Gamalaites and offer them peace terms. In her quarters at the new encampment Berenice learnt that while her brother was standing under the fortifications and speaking to the defenders above, a slinger took aim at him and hit him on the elbow. He would have been hit again had the Roman soldiers not rushed to his aid and formed a protective wall around him. A month later Titus returned from Syria and rejoined the offensive. Again there was fierce fighting followed by carnage, and of the entire population only two women survived. Shortly afterwards Gischala surrendered. By the end of the year Galilee was in Roman hands and Vespasian led his army into winter quarters in Caesarea. Titus went with him and it may be assumed that Agrippa and Berenice did the same.

The news of Vespasian's victories in Galilee and the arrival in Jerusalem of survivors from Gischala threw the non-too-united leadership into disarray. The Zealots denounced the aristocracy-dominated government as ineffectual and carried out what may be described as a *putsch*. The moderates were ousted and the extremists took over. For the first time since the beginning of the revolt power passed entirely from the hands of the upper classes into the hands of the lower classes. The Sadducee high priest, Agrippa's last nominee, was dismissed and his office given to a non-practising country priest who was hastily instructed in his holy duties. Aristocrats suspected of conciliatory leanings towards Rome were summarily executed.

But the new leaders, although unanimous in their determination to resist the Romans, were unable to act in unison. Each military commander tried to establish his ascendancy over the others and before long civil war broke out. The fighting was fierce and the fortified temple precincts became a battlefield. One faction went so far as to call in help from the outside and invited the blood-thirsty natives of Idumaea to enter the capital and fight the opposition. The Idumaeans obliged with a will. Thousands of people were killed. In their attempt to overpower one another the Zealot leaders seemed to lose sight of the main danger. There was no organized military command, no check on the thousands of refugees who kept flocking into the capital, no co-ordinated plan to lay in provisions for the oncoming siege.

With so much of his work done for him by the rebels, Vespasian stayed in Caesarea and advised those of his officers who were eager to fight that it was best to let the Jerusalemites kill one another without interference. He limited himself to cleaning-up operations and took his time closing in on Jerusalem. The news of his slow but inexorable advance towards the capital had a disheartening effect on the people within. While traffic in and out of the city was still possible many deserted to the Romans and were allowed to go unharmed.

A desertion case that had a far-reaching effect on the future of Judaism was that of the Pharisee scholar Rabban Yochanan ben Zaccai. He was so revered for his learning and piety that even in his lifetime he was referred to by his students as Father of Wisdom and Light of Israel. Intellectually he belonged to a school of thought that dissociated itself from politics and sought solace in the world of the spirit. Jerusalem still had its Pharisees who objected to war on principle. Wars waged by Hasmonaeans, Herodians, Romans or Zealots were to them an expression of human arbitrariness which had little to do with God's rule as promised by the prophets. In a sense these Pharisees were the conscientious objectors of the day. Rabban Yochanan was one of the most outspoken amongst them.

At the beginning of the siege he tried to persuade the Zealots to stop fighting and come to terms with the Romans. He prophesied defeat and warned them that continued resistance would result in the destruction of the temple. When he realized that his warnings were falling on deaf ears he stole out of Jerusalem and went over to the Romans. Vespasian had already heard from his spies inside the city that Rabban Yochanan was a 'Lover of Caesar';[1] Agrippa and Berenice for their part must have spoken to him approvingly of the scholar's philosophy of dissociation. It may well have been partly on their recommendation that Vespasian allowed Rabban Yochanan to retire to Roman-ruled Yavne (Jamnia) and there found a centre of Jewish learning. It was one way of showing the rebels that the Romans could be generous to people who put godliness before military resistance.

In view of Yavne's subsequent importance as the centre of Judaism after the destruction of the temple, Rabban Yochanan's defection to Vespasian has been hailed by posterity as providential. No one has questioned the behaviour of a spiritual leader who in the middle of the siege found it in his heart to leave his brethren to their fate and make his peace with the enemy. His motives were not those of Josephus's, yet he took a similar step. Oddly enough, the account of Rabban Yochanan's meeting with Vespasian, as preserved in rabbinical sources, is reminiscent of Josephus's story of his own meeting with Vespasian and his divine foreknowledge of the latter's future grandeur.

According to one version Rabban Yochanan decided to go over to the Romans when he realized that the besieged, living on a starvation diet of boiled straw, were too weak to defend the city. According to another, his decision was due to an unhappy chain of events. It began when the three wealthiest notables of Jerusalem put their well-stocked silos at the disposal of the besieged. It was estimated that between them they could keep the city going in wheat, barley, wine, salt, oil and firewood for twenty-one years.

But a section of the armed defenders set fire to the entire stock, hoping that the resulting famine would force the people to fight harder. As it happened the commander responsible for the fire was a certain Ben Batiach, the son of Rabban Yochanan's own sister. When he heard that the illustrious scholar had heaved a deep sigh at the news of the fire, he had him brought before him to explain his reaction. The rabbinical version goes on with a wealth of fascinating detail:

'It was not a sigh of distress but a sigh of relief', said Rabban Yochanan ben Zaccai. 'I knew that as long as there was plenty of food in the city the people would not put up a brave fight.'

But when they were left alone Rabban Yochanan chided his nephew for the folly of his policy. 'How long are you going to carry on in this way and starve the people to death?' he said.

'What can I do?' replied Ben Batiach. 'If I as much as mention peace talks my men will kill me.'

'In that case find a way to get me out of here', said Rabban Yochanan. 'Perhaps I may be able to do some good outside.'

'Nobody can get out', said Ben Batiach. 'Only the dead are carried out for burial outside the city walls.'

'Well then, pass me for dead', said Rabban Yochanan.

The nephew agreed. 'Pretend to be ill', he instructed, 'and let all your friends come to visit you. Then put something smelly next to you so that they take you for dead. Let none but your students carry your coffin, for a living body is lighter than a corpse.'

Rabban Yochanan followed the instructions and two of his most reliable students carried him away in a coffin, with Ben Batiach following behind as a mourner. There must have been complicity all round to enable the coffin of the Father of Wisdom to go virtually unescorted on its last journey. The story goes on:

When they reached the city gate the armed guards wanted to put a lance through the body to make sure it was dead. Ben Batiach stopped them. 'Do you want the Romans to say that we have pierced to death one of our own scholars?' he said. The guards wanted to give the corpse a hard shove just to make sure, but again Ben Batiach objected. 'Do you want the Romans to say that we have shown disrespect to the dead body of our great scholar?' he asked.

The guards then opened the city gate and let the funeral procession through. According to one version the mourners put the coffin down in the cemetery and returned to the capital, leaving Rabban Yochanan to make his own way to the Roman camp. According to another only Ben Batiach returned, while the students went on carrying the coffin all the way, only opening it in Vespasian's presence. Whichever way he appeared before Vespasian, Rabban Yochanan called him king and addressed him in Latin: '*Vive domine imperator.*'

'You call me king', admonished Vespasian, 'yet I am not. If the emperor gets to hear of it he will put me to death.'

'If you are not king yet you will be one day', replied Rabban Yochanan, 'for it is written in our books that the temple will fall only into the hands of a king.'

When three days later messengers came from Rome with the news that Nero was dead and that Vespasian had been proclaimed emperor, he sent for Rabban Yochanan and said to him:

'I am leaving now and will appoint someone else to take over. But I will grant any request you wish to make.'

'Raise the siege of Jerusalem', asked Rabban Yochanan.

'Do you think the Romans made me emperor so that I let go of Jerusalem? Ask something else.'

Said Rabban Yochanan: 'Leave the west gate of the city leading towards Lydda unguarded until ten o'clock tonight and let all those who wish to escape do so. And let me found a seminary in Yavne.'[2]

Rabban Yochanan ben Zaccai's story, embroidered as it is, sheds an added light on the divisions within Jerusalem. What with civil war and desertions, Vespasian could well afford to take his time. In the summer of 68 he was still doing no more than tightening his grip when news reached him at his Caesarea head-quarters that Nero was dead and that Galba had been proclaimed emperor. He immediately suspended operations pending new instructions from Rome.

Nero's death was mainly due to his abuse of power. His excesses had alienated senate and people to such an extent that when it was rumoured that the great fire of Rome in AD 64 had been started on his orders to pander to his sense of the dramatic, the accusation was widely credited. Even before the senate plucked up enough courage to declare him a public enemy the legions in Spain revolted and proclaimed their seventy-one-year-old commander Galba emperor. Nero ran away in panic with his eunuch-wife Sporus, botched an attempt at suicide and was despatched having uttered his famous last words: 'What an artist perishes in me.'[3]

Vespasian waited several months before sending Titus to swear allegiance to Galba. When he did, it was with the hope of diverting the imperial throne to his own son. Galba was old and child-less; Titus was young and enterprising. His object, approved by Vespasian, was to try and get himself adopted by Galba so as to be designated as his heir. Agrippa too set out for Rome, planning as usual to further his interests with a new emperor. But hardly had they reached Corinth, at the beginning of AD 69, when news reached them that Galba had been killed and that the imperial throne was disputed by two new claimants. One was Otho, Poppaea's former husband, who was recognized by the senate in Rome; the other was Vitellius, the son of a governor of Syria who had shown kindness to Judaea under Tiberius, and the favourite of the legions in Germany. Titus was discomfited. Not only had he been cheated of a chance to become emperor, but he also became an obvious target for both Otho and Vitellius. In the circum-stances he decided to put distance between him and the successful contestant, whichever he might be, and rejoin his father in Caesarea. It was rumoured that his decision was partly prompted by his longing for Berenice whom he had left behind.

Agrippa however continued his journey to Rome, trusting his instinct to back a winner. His decision too may have been partly prompted by private considerations. In spite of his acquiescence he may well have preferred not to be a constant witness to his sister's amours. He stayed in Rome for several months, first swearing allegiance to Otho, then, on his defeat and suicide, to Vitellius. He was not the only one to transfer his allegiance with such smoothness. Tiberius Alexander, the powerful governor of Egypt, did the same and so did Vespasian in Caesarea. In Agrippa's absence Berenice kept a sharp eye on developments likely to be of use to either of them. It was through her that he got his first inkling of what was brewing up in the Flavian camp.

Vespasian's soldiers, taking their cue from the legions in Spain and Germany, fancied themselves too in the profitable role of kingmakers. They informed Vespasian that he was their choice of emperor. Vespasian bowed gracefully to *vox populi* which confirmed divine prophecies and fitted in with his ambition and particularly with his son's. Titus had already come to an understanding with Mucianus, the governor of Syria, who expected to reap a rich reward for his part in putting the Flavians on the throne. In Berenice Titus had an invaluable helpmate. She threw herself heart and soul into the campaign and freely used her wealth to back her diplomatic overtures. She already had the ear of some of the client-kings of the east and more importantly of Tiberius Alexander. It was an acknowledgement of her political sense that the whole of the eastern group, including the shrewd governor of Egypt, accepted her analysis of the situation and followed her lead.

As soon as things started moving she sent Agrippa a secret message through reliable agents to inform him of the stand she had taken in his name and urged him to come back and take over. It was the second time within three years that circumstances had forced her to take a bold decision independently of her brother. But the working relationship between them admitted of no rivalry or jealousy. Agrippa endorsed his sister's judgement in full. Without rousing suspicion he took his leave of Vitellius and hurried back east. He was too late for the swearing-in of the legions in Caesarea and Alexandria and made straight for Berytus where Vespasian was receiving delegations from all over the east. All the provinces of Asia Minor had declared themselves for him. There were representatives from Pontus, Armenia, Cappadocia and Achaia. Mucianus and Tiberius Alexander reported with their choice troops, as did Antiochus, Sohaemus and Agrippa. Berytus became a dazzling scene of military parades and royal splendour, with the allies vying to outshine one another before the new emperor. After the ceremonies it was decided that Mucianus should go ahead to Rome to clear the way, Vespasian would stop in Egypt to consolidate his position and Titus would return to Judaea to resume the war. As Titus had more courage than experience, the veteran Tiberius Alexander was appointed his chief-of-staff while Agrippa was reaffirmed as strategic adviser on local conditions.

For Agrippa and Berenice the developments of the past few months had created a situation beyond their wildest dreams. Judicious backing had opened up before them a breathtaking prospect in comparison with which their life-long ambition of achieving royal status in Judaea must have seemed pedestrian. The imperial throne was beckoning. There is little doubt even at that early stage that they hoped to make Berenice, through a regularization of her relationship with Titus, the future empress of Rome.

Chapter XIX

The world's darling

NEARLY three years had passed since the crushing of the revolt in Galilee and more than a year since Vespasian's last operation in other parts of Judaea. With Titus's appointment as commander-in-chief the period of comparative inactivity was over. The siege of Jerusalem was to begin in earnest.

The army at his disposal was even larger than the one which Vespasian had commanded. It consisted of four legions, five thousand picked troops from Alexandria and the Euphrates, and the auxiliary forces provided by the allied kings of the east. Altogether it amounted to more than seventy thousand. In the spring of AD 70, shortly after the ceremonies at Berytus, the army arrived outside Jerusalem and encamped on the surrounding hills. From their own camp quarters Berenice and Agrippa commanded a perfect view of the city they still hoped to save from total destruction.

Jerusalem was a natural stronghold fortified by generations of rulers. On three sides it was surrounded by precipices, while on the fourth it was protected by three walls, roughly one behind the other, each marking the expansion of the city towards the north. The most ancient of the walls enclosed the old city and was flanked by Herod's fortress-palace on the west and the temple with the Antonia fortress on the east. The newest and most northerly was the one begun by Agrippa I during his brief reign over Judaea and later finished by the Zealots. In between there was a middle wall with flourishing suburbs on either side of it.

Titus was more venturesome than his father; or perhaps he relied on the cumulative effect of three years of semi-siege and civil strife. He decided on a direct assault and ordered the battering-rams into action. It took fifteen days of hard pounding to demolish part of Agrippa's wall and five more to breach the middle one. But when the soldiers rushed in through the breach they encountered fierce resistance. There was house-to-house fighting and the Romans were made to pay dearly for their victory. Even Titus did not escape unscathed. As he was leading the attack a stone caught him on the left shoulder and caused him considerable injury. Although Berenice and the camp physicians must have nursed the wound carefully, he never recovered the full use of his arm and for the rest of his life remained slightly handicapped.

Once the two walls were breached and the northerly suburbs razed to the ground, the Romans came face to face with the inner one, the oldest and most formidable of the three. Titus's plan was to breach it like the other two. His engineers were ordered to build high ramparts on which battering-rams were positioned and siege-towers constructed. So confident was he of a quick victory that he allowed himself to be persuaded by Berenice to offer the Zealots a last chance to surrender without further bloodshed. Josephus was sent out on the ramparts to parley. But the Zealots hurled stones at him and shouted back that they would rather die fighting than live in slavery.

As Titus found out to his cost they meant exactly that. They fought with the desperation of people who had nothing more to lose. They were daring, unpredictable, resourceful and absolutely fearless. Led by experienced guerilla fighters like John of Gischala and Simon Bar-Giora they harassed the Romans and impeded their progress every step of the way. They set fire to the wooden supports of the ramparts and rolled down heavy missiles to crush the siege-engines. They lured a detachment of soldiers into a colonnade stacked up with pitch and timber and set it alight. They annihilated a force of heavy infantry commanded by the son of Antiochus of Commagene. They performed such spectacular feats of heroism that simple-minded Roman soldiers began to regard them as undefeatable. Some changed sides. The besieged shared their rations with them in the hope of preserving the myth of their invincibility.

When it became evident that Jerusalem would not succumb to a direct assault, Titus decided to starve it out. His engineers built a stone circumvallation topped by thirteen watch-towers which were manned day and night. The city was completely cut off. Now the real agony began.

During the past three years the population of Jerusalem had

increased several times over. Tacitus put it at six hundred thousand, Josephus at over a million. All this time the city had been kept open to refugees from the outlying villages and to pilgrims who had been flocking in until just before Titus's arrival. Now they were all trapped. The war leaders had not laid in adequate food supplies, and what stocks there were had long been used up or destroyed in the fighting. With no more coming in from the outside, famine started. The warriors were allowed to requisition whatever food they could lay their hands on, but even they were reduced to a starvation diet. A rabbinical legend relates how Vespasian, who is often confused with Titus in the siege stories, once came upon excrement dropped by the besieged from the city wall. When examination revealed that it contained no grain substance, he was awestruck. 'If this is the way they fight on a diet of boiled straw', he said to his soldiers, 'imagine how they would fight if they were as well-fed as you are.'[1]

But the worst hit was the civilian population. For them even boiled straw could not be found. Women and children swollen with hunger haunted the refuse dumps of the city and dropped down with faintness. Men went about snarling like dogs and robbing others of their few grains of wheat or barley. Some ate their leather shoes and belts. Thousands died in the streets and were left to rot until the stench reached the Roman camp outside. Blood-curdling stories circulated through the city; a mother was reported so demented with hunger that she cooked and ate her own baby.

Perhaps the most pathetic story of the famine was that of Martha, the wealthiest woman in Jerusalem, who had once thought nothing of bribing Agrippa with two bushelfuls of gold or of carpeting the whole length of the road between her house and the temple so that she should not hurt her dainty feet. Now she had to go hungry like the rest. One day, a rabbinical legend tells us, she ordered her steward to go to the market and get her some fine white flour. The story goes on:

> By the time the steward got there the fine white flour was sold out. He returned to Martha and said: 'The fine white wheat flour had gone but there is still some sifted white flour available.' 'Go and get some,' she said.

But by the time he got there the sifted white flour had also sold out. He returned to Martha and said: 'The sifted white flour had gone but there is still wholemeal flour available.' 'Go and get some,' she said.

But by the time he got there the wholemeal flour had also sold out. He returned to Martha and said: 'There is no more wholemeal flour but there is still some barley flour available.' 'Go and get some,' she said. But by the time the steward got there the barley flour too was sold out.

So Martha took off her shoes to look like a woman of the people and said: 'I'll go and scavenge round, perhaps I'll find something to eat.' While she was scavenging some dung clung to her feet and she died. According to another account she became ill and died because she had picked up and eaten the skin of a fig which had already been sucked dry by Rabbi Zadok. . . . In her agony of death Martha flung all her silver and gold into the street saying: 'What use is it to me?'[2]

In mid-summer, when traditionally the Feast of the First Fruits would have been celebrated, Titus judged the besieged sufficiently weakened to renew his assault. One of his main targets was the Antonia fortress which controlled the entry into the outer courts of the temple. For many days it seemed as if the battering-rams were making no impact, when one night part of the wall suddenly crumbled. The Roman soldiers burst in only to discover that another wall had been built behind. Their dismay and their losses were such that it took all Titus's eloquence to exhort them to further action. But the end was near. The Zealots, exhausted by hunger and unremitting fighting, could not hold back the numerically superior legions. Step by step they were forced to retreat from the Antonia into the precincts of the temple. On the seventeenth of Tammuz, the hottest month of the year by the Jewish calendar, the Antonia was levelled to the ground. That day the daily sacrifices in the temple were suspended, never to be resumed.

The temple was defended by its own system of fortifications and was used by the Zealots to bar the Roman advance into the city below. Titus had new ramparts built, more battering-rams brought into action. The outer courts were taken after fierce resistance, but the inner ones still held fast. Titus changed his tactics. He gave orders to stop the battering and set fire to the gold and silver-covered gates separating the Court of Women from the inner courts. The order was probably passed on through Tiberius Alexander whose late father the *alabarch* had donated the money for the gilding. The heat melted the metal and the exposed woodwork was consumed by the flames. The way to the inner courts and the sanctuary was open.

At this stage Titus took the most momentous decision in the history of the war.

The temple was the cause and purpose of the Jewish freedom movement. It was the source of all religious and national aspirations. Only its total elimination could bring about the collapse of the revolt. Several hundred years earlier it was destroyed by Nebuchadnezzar of Babylon for precisely the same reason. Now it was up to Titus to do the same and bring the war to a satisfactory conclusion.

There were however some considerations that made him waver. Herod's temple was a unique work of art which commanded admiration even in the hearts of pagans. Titus was no barbarian. The thought of destroying so much reputed beauty held no charm for him. Furthermore, like many of his fellow Romans he had a superstitious fear of antagonizing a foreign god by desecrating his temple. But above all he could hardly turn a deaf ear to Berenice's pleading. He called a council of war and put some of the conflicting arguments before them.

Of the six generals who made up the council only Tiberius Alexander could have possibly had a sentimental reason for wanting the temple spared. On the other hand he was not a man to put sentiment before duty, as his ruthless handling of a Jewish riot in Alexandria a few years earlier amply proved. Two other generals, possibly anticipating Berenice's rancour, suggested that the temple should be destroyed only if used to harbour rebels. The remaining three were for expedience. Even as the pros and cons were being debated Titus must have made up his mind to destroy the temple, to judge by a fourth-century account probably based on a lost work by Tacitus. Josephus claimed that Titus made no such decision and that the subsequent burning was due to the uncontrollable fury of the legionaries. It is difficult to see though how a commander-in-chief, having given the order to spare a target, would have allowed such a flagrant breach of discipline to go unpunished. It is more plausible that, having made up his mind to destroy the temple, he gave instructions to make the act look like an accident of war, for which nobody could be held to blame. It was perhaps a ruse to forestall Berenice's anger. Jewish tradition had no hesitation in holding Titus solely responsible for the catastrophe. Whatever the machinations behind the decision, the die was cast.

And so the battle of Jerusalem reached its final stage. The gates were still burning when the legions were ordered to blast their way in. They threw firebrands into the inner courts and the entire structure became a mass of flames. While the fire was raging the fighting went on, savagely, unremittingly, indiscriminately. Josephus gave an eyewitness account of the happenings of that day, the ninth of Ab, which remained for ever a day of mourning in the Jewish calendar.

While the sanctuary was burning, looting and killing went on left and right. The soldiers showed no pity for age, no regard for rank. Old people and young children were butchered alike, laymen as well as priests, fighters as well as those who surrendered. Everybody was caught up in the fighting. The groans of the wounded could be heard above the roar of the flames as they swept on. The temple was so vast and the hill on which it stood so high that from the outside it looked as if the entire city was on fire. The noise was shattering. There were the war-cries of the Roman legions as they converged; the yells of the besieged as they were hedged in by flames; the shrieks of the people above as the soldiers ran them through. The cries from the temple precincts were answered by the wailing from the crowded streets below. Even people faint with hunger found strength enough to moan and wail the burning of the sanctuary. Their voices reverberated like thunder round the surrounding hills all the way to Peraea and back. Far worse than the din was the sight. The temple mount, engulfed in flames from top to bottom, appeared to be boiling from its very roots; yet the sea of flame was nothing to the ocean of blood, and the number of the dead far exceeded the living. The ground could not be seen for corpses and the soldiers climbed over heaps of dead bodies in pursuit of survivors.[3]

The legions ran amuck. They rekindled the fire under the gates and burnt down the treasury chambers under the colonnades. They smashed columns and brought down the remaining porticoes. Herod's magnificent creation, the pride and glory of the Jewish people all over the world, was no more. When the flames subsided and the last of the fighters had been mown down, the Roman legions put up their standards over the smouldering ruins and sacrificed to the gods. Titus was hailed as *imperator*, the title bestowed on a commander-in-chief after a resounding victory. The siege of Jerusalem was virtually over.

Latin sources described Titus as the kindest, gentlest and most affable of emperors. In wartime he mixed with the common soldiers, in peacetime he made a habit of going into the public baths to allow the people to meet him. His concern for his fellow men was such that he never sent a petitioner away without giving him hope. A day without a good deed was to him a day lost. He was lenient even to proven traitors and never put a senator to death. He was pronounced with one voice *amor ac deliciae generis humani*, the world's darling.[4]

In Hebrew sources he lived on as the world's villain. He was the destroyer of the temple, the desecrator of the Holy of Holies, an evil-doer more wicked than Nebuchadnezzar and Pompey put together. His name was hardly ever mentioned without the epithet *harasha*, the Wicked. Even that was not strong enough to express the depth of hatred he roused in generations of Jews. He was *rasha ben rasha*, a wicked man descended of a wicked man, whose wickedness was traceable all the way back to Esau the Wicked, whom biblical tradition regarded as the forefather of the Edomites, the most hated of all ancient pagans. Titus's war against the Jews was regarded as a war against God. Assaulting the temple was megalomania; burning it was blasphemy. When the Roman victory was assured, a rabbinical legend tells us, Titus's insolence knew no bounds. Just before the flames spread to the sanctuary he got hold of a harlot and dragged her into the Holy of Holies, where no human being was allowed except the high

priest on the Day of Atonement. Titus spread a scroll of the law
on the altar and using it as a bed copulated with the harlot in the
face of God. According to another version one harlot was not
enough to express his contempt of God, so he dragged in two
and copulated with both over the altar. Only a wicked man
descended of generations of wicked men could have used the
house of God as a brothel. Titus's premature death at the age of
forty, only eleven years after his act of blasphemy, was regarded
as God's vengeance.

There is no record of what Berenice felt about the destruction.
It must have been a shattering experience and one that temporarily
strained her relations with Titus. But it is unlikely that either she
or Agrippa blamed him for what happened. If anyone was to
blame it was the fanatics who used the sacred precincts as a base
of operations and who had in fact started the war. For years
Agrippa and Berenice had been trying to wean the people of
Judaea from their unrealistic dreams of independence. Throughout the war they pressed Titus time and again to offer the rebels a
chance to lay down their arms and accept a tolerable peace. It was
the fanatics, not the Romans, who had brought about the destruction of the temple and the death of thousands of people who, like
Their Majesties, had been willing to accept political subjugation
as the price of religious toleration. As much as Agrippa and
Berenice lamented the catastrophe, they had little sympathy with
its victims.

But whatever they felt, they had to put a good face on it.
Agrippa's post as administrator of temple affairs had become
redundant, while his hopes of attaining some other position of
authority in Judaea were frustrated when a new procurator was
appointed. All he could do was to keep on the right side of Titus
and press home his claim for a reward. Berenice too had to see
that nothing should jeopardize her standing with Titus now that
he was ready to return to Rome to take up his position as the
emperor's son and heir. She had already heard, like the rest of
the world, that Vitellius was dead, that the senate had proclaimed
Vespasian emperor, and his sons Titus and Domitian both
Caesars. It was as Titus Caesar that the victor of Jerusalem was
asked again to Caesarea Philippi to attend the celebrations arranged for him by Their Majesties. The summer was nearly over

and a sea voyage to Italy could not be contemplated during the rough season. Titus accepted the invitation and spent several weeks in Berenice's company, watching thousands of prisoners-of-war die in the arena and arranging for the disposition of those still awaiting their fate in Jerusalem.

He also had to see to the shipping to Rome of the temple trophies which included the golden table of the shewbread, the seven-branched candlestick, bowls studded with precious stones, incense cups, trumpets, a scroll of the law. Some prudent priests had buried them in a safe place before the fighting reached its climax and later surrendered them to the Romans in exchange for their lives. According to the unforgiving Jewish tradition it was Titus in person who looted the sanctuary. After he had copulated with his harlots over the altar he apparently pulled down the curtain which hung over the Holy of Holies, wrapped it round the sacred vessels and sailed with them to Rome. The story goes on:

While he was sailing a storm broke out and was about to wreck the ship. Said Titus: 'Obviously the strength of the Jewish god is only in water. When Pharaoh pursued his people he drowned him in the Red Sea; when Sisera fought them he drowned him in the Kishon river. Now he is trying to drown me too. But when I was in his own temple and in his power he was too weak to do anything to me. If he is really mighty, let him come and fight me on dry land.'
Then a voice from heaven answered him:
'Wicked man descended of a wicked man, descendant of Esau the Wicked. There is a tiny insect among my creatures which is called a mosquito. Go out on dry land and wage war on it.'
When Titus arrived in Rome the whole city turned out to meet him and hailed him as the Vanquisher of the Barbarians. He was taken to the public baths and a hot bath was prepared for him. When he came out he was given a cup of wine. As he was drinking a mosquito flew into his nose and entered his brain. It tore at it for seven years. One day, as Titus was passing by a blacksmith's, the mosquito heard the noise of the hammering and stopped. Said Titus:

'So there is a cure after all.'

From then on he had a blacksmith brought before him every day to stun the mosquito with the sound of his hammering. If the blacksmith was a Gentile he was paid four *zuzim*; if he was a Jew he was told that it was enough for him to see his enemy in pain. After thirty days the mosquito became immune to the noise and started torturing Titus again.[5]

Unaware of the punishment God held in store for him, Titus made the most of his victory. From Caesarea Philippi he returned to his headquarters in Caesarea where more gladiatorial games were held in his honour. He then set out with Berenice on a grand tour of the east, taking in Berytus, Antioch, Zeugma on the Euphrates and the cities of Egypt. His progress was royal. He was escorted by two of his legions, surrounded by client-kings, acclaimed wherever he stopped. The east beguiled him with its traditional obsequiousness, its opulence, its temptations. In Zeugma the king of Parthia presented him with a golden crown. In Memphis, on his return from the north, he was encouraged to put a diadem on his head, ostensibly in honour of the Apis bull. In Alexandria the faithful legions refused to part with him and hailed him as emperor. A court, presided over by Berenice, formed around him. Titus was drunk with power. Instead of returning to Judaea to crush down the last of the Zealot resistance, notably in Masada, he lingered on in Egypt and Syria, living like an eastern potentate, intoxicated with the adulation of his legions and his queen. The months passed. The winter gales gave way to the mild breezes of spring. The Mediterranean was navigable again, but Titus stayed in the east.

In Rome his behaviour caused uneasiness. It seemed as if the history of Antony and Cleopatra was re-enacting itself. For the second time in the last hundred years an eastern queen was holding a Roman general in thrall, beguiling him with her beauty and wealth, tempting him to make himself ruler of the east to gratify her own ambition. Even before Berenice set foot in Rome, she was represented there as a danger to the empire. She was prompting a dutiful son to usurp his father and disturb the peace so dearly bought during the bloody Year of the Four Emperors. She was a second Cleopatra.

Eight or nine months passed in this fashion when a hint from Rome gave Titus to understand that he would not be allowed to go on with impunity. Suddenly he came to his senses. In the early summer of AD 71 he bade a hasty farewell to Berenice and taking Josephus with him he boarded the first available ship to Italy. Vespasian had not been expecting him and was completely disarmed when Titus rushed towards him calling: 'Here I am, Father, here I am.'[6] The air was cleared. Father and son settled down to work out the details of the triumphal procession for the victory won ten months earlier, while in Caesarea Philippi Berenice began to prepare for her own journey to Rome, which she did not doubt would take place soon.

Chapter XX

Rome and exit

IT was perhaps unusual for staunch allies to absent themselves from the celebration of a victory they had helped to win, but Their Majesties could not have been altogether disappointed at not being able to attend the triumphal procession commemorating the fall of their homeland. For the time being they contented themselves with following Titus's progress from afar.

The senate had proclaimed the whole Flavian family *imperatores*: Vespasian and Titus for their conquest of Judaea; Domitian, Titus's twenty-year-old brother, for his part in putting down a rebellion in Gaul. Each *imperator* was voted a triumphal procession of his own; it must have been Vespasian, with his characteristic stinginess, who insisted on a joint one. Eyewitness reports of the splendid occasion must have reached Caesarea Philippi shortly after it had taken place, in the summer of AD 71.

It started with Vespasian and Titus spending the night in the temple of Isis in Rome. At dawn they came out, clothed in purple and crowned with laurels, to acknowledge the greetings of the senate and the notables. There was a military parade which they watched from a high dais provided with ivory chairs. After the traditional prayers and sacrifices they changed into triumphal robes and treated the soldiery to a ceremonial breakfast. Then the pageant began, in anticipation of which the populace of Rome had been lining the processional route since the night before.

Seven hundred handsome young men had been brought over from Judaea to grace the procession, including the Zealot leaders John of Gischala and Simon Bar-Giora. Dressed in their national costumes to cover up any deformities caused by maltreatment, they were marched behind floats three or four storeys high, hung with rich curtains and framed in ivory and gold. There was a dazzling display of gold and silver vessels, rare jewels and Babylonian tapestries. Artistically executed tableaux depicted scenes from the war: a countryside laid waste; men put to the sword; walls pulled down by engines; cities on fire.

The temple trophies were given pride of place in the pageant, with the heavy golden table and the seven-branched candlestick carried high in spite of their great weight. The holy scroll of the law, Their Majesties heard, had suffered further ignominy by its closeness to the statues of the goddess of victory which were carried right behind it. Undisturbed by the sacrilege, Vespasian and Titus followed in their chariots, while Domitian rode alongside on a magnificent charger. The celebration reached its climax with the ritual execution of Simon Bar-Giora.

If the details of the occasion must have been received with mixed feelings at Caesarea Philippi, the news of Titus's increasing popularity in Rome was wholly welcome. Titus had completely re-established himself with Vespasian and the senate and proceeded to take an active part in the business of government. He made himself his father's secretary, dealt with official correspondence, drafted edicts and read out the imperial speeches to the senate when Vespasian was not disposed to do so himself. Last but not least, he was given the command of the praetorian guards, a post which put him in a position of unprecedented strength and which he did not hesitate to abuse. Vespasian encouraged his son's participation in the government and treated him like a colleague. Titus became a co-emperor in all but name.

Although his ascendance was not achieved overnight, the trend of events was clearly favourable to Berenice's travel plans. The date of her arrival in Rome is however uncertain. It is a matter for conjecture whether she had to accept a long enforced separation, or whether she was able to achieve a quick reunion.

The only clue is given in Dio's *Roman History*, written some hundred and fifty years after the event. Describing the reign of Vespasian, Dio wrote that 'Berenice was at the height of her power and consequently came to Rome along with her brother Agrippa'.[1] Dio gave no date; but in a preceding paragraph he mentioned that Vespasian dedicated his Temple of Peace in the sixth year of his consulship, which was AD 75. The implication is that Berenice's arrival, recorded after the story of the dedication, took place at about the same time. This date is favoured by most modern historians and its acceptance leads to the theory that it took Titus all of four years to overcome the opposition to his mistress's settling down in Rome.

The theory of the four-year enforced separation is however not altogether satisfactory. The first argument against it is provided by Dio's own style, which can by no means be described as slapdash. Dio clearly stated that 'Berenice was at the height of her power' when she came to Rome. The only period when this description could have fitted her was at the beginning of AD 71, when she presided over Titus's eastern court, or very shortly afterwards. Had she been forced to stay away from him for four whole years, she could not possibly have been described as a woman at the height of her power, but rather as a neglected mistress hoping to reassert herself. Dio's description therefore suggests that she must have arrived in Rome not long after Titus's own return to it, when her hold over him was at its strongest.

The second point to consider is Berenice's character. She was a realist. When Titus left for Rome in the spring of 71 he was thirty; Berenice was forty-three. She must have appreciated, like any sensible woman in her forties, that time was not on her side. She would not have risked an indefinite separation from a young lover known for his sexual instability. Absence could easily mean supplantation, and Berenice was not the woman to wait timidly for a call that might never have come. She was a woman of action and, as her past career had shown, not lacking in resourcefulness. There was no law to stop a Roman citizen, and a queen at that, from visiting Rome on what could legitimately be described as a congratulatory mission to an emperor in whose bid for power she had played a part. It would have been more in character for her to have set out for Rome as soon as she heard of Titus's reconciliation with his father, ready to brave any opposition she might have expected to encounter.

Another point to remember is Agrippa's stand with the Flavians. Agrippa went to Rome together with Berenice; but Agrippa had no reason to put off his visit for four years and risk losing the reward for his loyalty. His obvious course was to go to Rome while his services were still fresh in the emperor's mind. Moreover, Agrippa was not the man to stay away from the centre of power while things were on the move. In AD 69 he went to Rome to swear allegiance to Galba, Otho and Vitellius; in 71 he had all the more reason to reaffirm his allegiance to the Flavians. The most propitious moment to do so would have been immediately after the victory celebrations, when he could expect to find the emperor in an expansive mood. It must surely have been that year, and not four years later, that he presented himself with Berenice before Vespasian and was indeed handsomely rewarded.

The last argument in favour of Berenice's early arrival in Rome is provided by Titus's character. Titus was aware that the part his mistress had played in his eastern court made her suspect in senatorial circles, but once he had cleared himself with his father Berenice too must have been exonerated. Besides, Titus was an impetuous young man and there is no reason to suppose that he was more prudent in love than in war. It was not like him to wait four years for the arrival of a desired mistress, nor could he have been intimidated, with the power he was beginning to wield, by senatorial frowns. He must have encouraged Berenice to join him as soon as possible and endorsed whatever plans she may have made for a quick reunion. Taken all in all, the year AD 71 seems to be the more likely date of her arrival in Rome, thus presenting an almost unbroken continuity in her association with Titus.

As in the past, Their Majesties travelled together in a style befitting the occasion. Rome was very conscious of their presence. Like his father thirty-four years earlier, Agrippa was given the rank of praetor and more territory to rule over, though alas not in Judaea but in north Lebanon. Berenice was formally addressed as queen of Chalcis and installed in the imperial palace on the Palatine hill, which Vespasian rarely occupied and which Titus had taken over. As before, Titus and Berenice lived openly together as if they were legally married. Vespasian showed no objection. He himself had been living for many years, since the death of his wife, with a freedwoman called Caenis. She looked after his interests, received petitions in his name, accepted bribes and granted favours. She was absolutely loyal to him and he treated her as a wife in all but name. He may well have expected Berenice to be to Titus what Caenis was to him.

But Berenice was no freedwoman. She was a queen, a scion of a royal house and a descendant of a proud race. Having put aside her virtue and her religion, she expected to rise higher than any

Jewish queen before her. Titus was divorced; so was she. Nothing should have stood in the way of a legal marriage. Berenice took marriage so much for granted that she began to behave in public as if she was already Caesar's wife and the future empress of Rome. The palace on the Palatine hill became an eastern court. Berenice entered Titus's political life and no doubt instigated some of his misuses of authority to accommodate her own protégés. She lived like a queen and stunned even the most ostentatious of Roman matrons with the magnificence of her jewellery. She was deferred to and fawned upon, yet marriage seemed no nearer than when she first arrived. Titus was dependent on the support and loyalty of the senate, and the senate was dead set against the interference of an oriental queen. Living openly with her was reprehensible enough; contracting a legal alliance was too risky. Titus temporized. The idea of a marriage was shelved, although, as far as Berenice was concerned, not totally abandoned. She went on hoping, failing to realize that for the first time in [her] life she was up against something which neither cajolery nor force could ever resolve.

Basically the opposition to Berenice was motivated not so much by the traditional hostility for an oriental queen, but by the hatred for a corrupt and venal system of government of which she was the symbol.

Vespasian's administration was in fact less corrupt than that of his immediate predecessors. He himself had always been a man of simple tastes and hardly changed his way of life after his accession. Instead of living grandly in the imperial palace on the Palatine hill, he set up house in a villa in the Gardens of Sallust, sharing it with Caenis. His habits were frugal, his manner unassuming. He received senators without ceremony and kept the gates of the villa unguarded to allow petitioners a free entry. He was good natured, fond of a coarse joke, shy of ceremonial and careful with public spending. He was not vindictive when people failed to address him formally by his imperial style, and he relaxed the censorship of free speech.

Yet his mildness achieved what he least intended. Free speech began to be used against the very institution which had made it possible. Monarchy became the butt of virulent attacks. Its chief detractors were the philosophers who were the political thinkers and revolutionaries of the day. Sophists, Cynics and Stoics were united in their fundamental hatred of tyranny.

Broadly speaking they regarded wealth and power as detrimental to virtue. They affected simple ways, wore rough cloaks, walked barefoot and left their chins unshaven. They preached moderation and self-restraint in all things and dreamed of a republic where tyranny would be unknown. They denounced monarchy as the embodiment of corruption, social injustice and moral decrepitude. Vespasian's rule confirmed their judgement, for it encouraged graft and iniquity. Caenis sold governorships, procuratorships, generalships and priesthoods; she discharged the condemned for a consideration and even altered imperial decisions if adequately bribed. It was not long before critical voices were raised. The most notable anti-monarchist during Vespasian's first year as emperor was Helvidius Priscus, a man of distinction who had risen to the rank of praetor. He had been inspired by the doctrines of the Stoics and made use of the newly introduced freedom of speech to call for a return to democracy. He incited the people to overthrow the monarchy, depose Vespasian and disown his heir. When his speeches became too inflammatory he was arrested and committed to trial, during which he again spoke out against the evils of monarchy. Suddenly it came home to Vespasian that it was not Helvidius Priscus who was on trial, but his own right to rule and name an heir. He left the senate chamber much agitated and declared that if his son was not allowed to succeed him, no one would.

Berenice's participation in public affairs gave the philosophers more reason to denounce monarchy. Now there were two imperial mistresses interfering with the course of justice; and a queen was more likely than a freedwoman to perpetuate the wrongs of the institution. Titus too was beginning to show his true colours. He had no compunction about using his praetorian guards to dispatch potential enemies without as much as a formal charge. For the next few years he behaved like the real tyrant of the philosophers' nightmares. Far from being intimidated, they intensified their campaign. A philosopher called Demetrius spoke in public against the corrupt rule of emperors and demanded its overthrow. There was nothing for it but to put the entire movement out of action. After several years of hedging, the arch-revolutionary Priscus was put to death and the rest of the leading philosophers, whatever their school, were banished from Rome under penalty of death. The Flavians could breathe more freely, but Titus thought it wise not to antagonize the remaining mal-contents by marrying a queen with a will of her own.

By that time life on the Palatine had fallen into a pattern not uncommon in imperial circles. Berenice was Titus's acknowledged consort; as such she had to turn a blind eye to his occasional deviation from the routine of a permanent union. Apparently he was never unfaithful to her with other women, but at some point or other in their life together he resumed his association with eunuchs. His desires were easily roused at the sight of pretty eunuchs dancing in the theatre, and the orgies that followed were the talk of Rome. Berenice must have been too wise to protest. Her hold over Titus remained unchallenged. When in AD 75 Vespasian dedicated his Temple of Peace and deposited in it the trophies brought over from Jerusalem, it must have been thanks to her that the scroll of the law was left behind in the Palatine palace, under her own roof, together with the beautiful purple curtain that had been torn down from over the Holy of Holies. On at least one occasion she was allowed to preside over a court case where, not without precedent in Rome, she was the plaintiff as well as the judge.

The case was briefly alluded to by Quintilian, the distinguished teacher of rhetoric whose students included two of Titus's nephews. He was a successful pleader in the courts and published a book of practical tips to aspiring lawyers. Discussing courtroom techniques he dwelt on the delicacy of a situation where a plain-tiff or a defendant could be his own judge. Quintilian wrote:

> Some have been judges in cases where their own interests are involved. I note for instance in the books of observations pub-lished by Septimius that Cicero appeared in such a case, while I myself, when I appeared on behalf of Queen Berenice, actually pleaded before her.[2]

His advice, which he himself had no doubt followed with pleasing results, was shrewd:

The opponent of the judge will emphasize his confidence in the justice of his client's cause, while the advocate of the judge's interests will express the fear that he [the judge] may be influenced by a quixotic delicacy.[3]

Quintilian never specified the nature of the case in which he represented Berenice before Berenice, but there is little doubt that he won it for her from her. No other outcome would have been acceptable. Titus's queen was too powerful to be crossed. With the expulsion of the philosophers, followed by the death of the elderly Caenis, her position seemed unshakeable. She may well have been thinking of pressing Titus again for marriage, when the tide turned against her with renewed force.

The undercurrent of hostility towards the Flavians had not disappeared with the suppression of the anti-monarchists. Less idealistic people were ready to take their place and sow discontent among the troops in order to further their own ambitions. It must have been with the connivance of some such intriguers within the imperial circle that two philosophers were allowed to return to the capital and encouraged to resume their campaign against the Flavians. By that time Caenis was dead, Vespasian was getting on in years, Titus was the effective ruler of Rome. The campaign was directed entirely against him and Berenice.

The first manifestation of the new mood occurred in the theatre. The philosopher Diogenes came on the stage and delighted the audience with his eloquence; when the theatre was full and the audience under his spell, he switched over into a long diatribe against Titus and his queen, perhaps the most damning title in the republican vocabulary. It was not recorded whether Titus and Berenice were actually present at the theatre during the performance, but the news must have reached them without delay. Titus tended to make light of it, passed over Diogenes's unauthorized return from exile and contented himself with having him flogged. His mildness was ill-judged. Heras, the second philosopher returned from exile, expecting no harsher punishment than flogging, took up where Diogenes had left off and delivered another virulent attack in public. Titus was accused of immorality with eunuchs and young boys, of a dangerous association with an eastern queen, of taking bribes in his father's name, of warping the course of justice. He was called a monster of vice. He was compared to Nero, Berenice to Poppaea. This time Titus took a serious view of the matter and had the speaker beheaded. Public speeches ceased forthwith, but the political climate remained unfavourable to the Flavians' dynastic aspirations. Things came to a head towards the beginning of 79.

That year Vespasian caught up with a rebel leader who nine years earlier had claimed to be a descendant of Julius Caesar and led an army against the Flavian usurpers. He was put to death together with his wife. Such an extreme measure against a helpless fugitive nine years after his defeat was unnecessary, unless meant as a warning to others. The warning went unheeded. Two of Vespasian's most trusted friends and councillors, Alienus and Marcellus, secretly planned to overthrow him. Titus got wind of the plot and proceeded to undermine it in a way that smacked of the east.

One night he invited the venerable ex-consul Caecina to dine with him at the palace. It is not clear whether Caecina was an accomplice of Alienus and Marcellus, or whether Titus simply wished to use him. Caecina accepted the invitation and enjoyed himself in the company of Titus and Berenice. He was already on the point of departure, outside the dining hall, when Titus's praetorian guards pounced on him and stabbed him to death. Titus then had him searched and produced the text of a disloyal address to the troops which Caecina was purported to have written. Armed with the manuscript Titus went to the senate, explained that he had executed a traitor and accused Alienus and Marcellus of being party to the plot. In view of such conclusive evidence the senate pronounced them guilty. The unsuspecting Alienus was dispatched during another palace feast, while Marcellus was granted the courtesy of a suicide.

Rome was staggered and rumours began to fly round. Caecina's guilt was not generally credited and it was said that he had been killed not for treason but for lechery. He had got so drunk during the feast that he made indecent overtures to Berenice, and Titus was forced to avenge her virtue with his sword. Some said that Caecina was strangled. Whatever the version credited, it was obvious that Berenice had something to do with the murder of an elderly statesman. Her name was linked with plots and counter-plots, old accusations were raked up, stories of incest revived.

It is quite likely that the main aim of the anti-Berenice campaign was to embarrass Titus. The senate had been shaken by the summary execution of three distinguished Romans who must have had considerable following. It was too dangerous to criticize Titus's methods overtly, so Berenice was used as a scourge against him. She was accused of being the cause of all the political discontent in Rome and her expulsion was demanded. Whether the senate really believed that she was a threat to the peace of the empire is questionable; but they certainly used her to break Titus's spirit. In vain did he try to resist pressure. Berenice became a test-case. It was made quite clear to Titus that he had to choose between his queen and dynastic stability. He chose dynastic stability.

And so, after eight years of uninterrupted rule over the Palatine court, Berenice was formally banished from Rome. Her last few weeks in the palace must have been painful, for there seems to have been a genuine attachment between her and Titus. They parted in sorrow, very much against their will; in Suetonius's famous words *invitus invitam*, he reluctantly she reluctant. The expulsion order must have been sanctioned by Vespasian. The emperor had no personal grudge against his son's mistress, but he had set his heart on the foundation of a Flavian dynasty. The queen had to be sacrificed.

But at fifty-one Berenice still had a lot of fight left in her. She must have realized, like everybody else in Rome, that Vespasian was old and failing and that it was only a question of time before Titus would succeed him. She decided to stay close at hand in case a change of circumstances should warrant her return. She probably went no further than Athens, where she was popular for her past generosity. She did not have long to wait. In the summer of 79, within months of her expulsion, news reached her that Vespasian was dead and that Titus had succeeded him without opposition. Berenice hurried back to Rome, trusting that the new emperor would be able to force his will on the senate and resume his former relationship with her.

But the Titus who succeeded to the throne was not the Titus she had known.

The change in him must have begun while he was still fighting to retain her, though its full extent became apparent only after his accession. During his father's last few months he learnt that it was not possible to hold the reins of government without the support of the senate. Now that he had achieved his ultimate ambition and become sole emperor he found that absolute power continued to elude him. He was as dependent as ever on the loyalty of senators and friends. It was imperative to win their trust and improve his public image. Titus became a reformed character. He abandoned his practice of executing suspects without trial, never put a senator to death, was lenient with the odd conspirator. He spent large sums of money on public welfare and worked so hard at being considerate and accessible that Rome was completely won over. It was then he began to be known as 'the World's darling'. He even dropped his eunuchs and stopped going to the theatre to avoid temptation. He became a slave to his image.

By the time Berenice returned to Rome Titus was well entrenched in his new way of life. Nothing was going to make him risk the throne. In vain did Berenice seek audience with him. He refused to see her, perhaps not trusting himself in her magnetic presence. The expulsion order was not revoked and Berenice, after a brief stay, was forced to leave. She never saw Titus again. She went away, leaving nothing for the people of Rome to remember her by, except society gossip and her valuable diamond ring, which she must have sold in a moment of need.

Chapter XXI

And their place knows them no more

Even in defeat Berenice was still feared. The second expulsion
order was therefore made more specific than the first. She was
instructed not only to leave Rome, but to 'return to her own
country',[1] presumably to Caesarea Philippi. The senate was not
taking any chances.

But the senate need not have worried. Titus continued to be a
model emperor. When in the summer of 79, possibly while
Berenice was still in Rome, Vesuvius erupted and buried Pompeii
and Herculaneum under its lava, he gave generously to the survivors from his privy purse. After a three-day fire that ravaged
a part of the capital he spent wisely on relief and reconstruction.
In the second year of his reign a grateful senate, in the name of
the Roman people, dedicated an arch of triumph to 'the emperor
Titus Caesar, son of the divine Vespasian, Vespasian Augustus,
high pontiff, in his tenth year of tribunicial power, seventeen times
imperator, eight times consul, father of the country, for having,
under the instructions and guidance of his father, and on his
authority, vanquished the Jewish people and destroyed the city
of Jerusalem, which many generals and kings have assaulted, but
which none before him had ever conquered'.[2] But the 'father of
the country' was only a shadow of the boisterous conqueror of
Judaea who eleven years earlier had triumphantly toured the east
with a queen at his side and a crown on his head. He was all
tameness and mildness, good works and forbearance. He even
pardoned his brother Domitian for his repeated attempts to usurp
him. He seemed to have lost the zest for life; perhaps, as the
Jewish rabbinical legend seems to suggest, he may have been
suffering from a brain tumour. He died in the autumn of 81, just
over two years after his accession. He was not quite forty.

His death was surrounded by rumours and speculations. According to one account he died of fever. According to another he was

dispatched by Domitian who, pretending to have found a cure for fever, had him put in a crate full of snow and left him to freeze to death. Yet another account suggested that Titus had not been ill at all, but given poisoned wine to drink after his bath. The most detailed account was given by Jewish sources, the reliability of which was vouchsafed by well-known rabbis of the day.

According to these accounts Titus had been ailing for eleven years, ever since God had sent a mosquito to suck the blood of his brain as a punishment for his destruction of the temple. A Jewish rabbi who was living in Rome in 81 and who, inexplicably, seemed to have the entry of the imperial palace, has left an eye-witness account of what must surely be one of the earliest post-mortems on record. His name was Pinchas the son of Aruva, and he was quoted as saying:

I was present, with the other notables of Rome, when after Titus's death his head was cut open to reveal something like a sparrow, two *selas* in weight. . . . It had a beak of brass and claws of iron.[3]

According to another account the tumour on Titus's brain was as large as a full-sized pigeon. Titus apparently knew that his premature death was a punishment for his wickedness in Jerusalem. Just before he died he gave instructions for his body to be burnt and for his ashes to be scattered over the seven seas so that 'the God of the Jews' should not be able to find him and sit in judgement on him. A nephew of his, presumably one of the two who had been taught rhetoric by Quintilian, was so awed by his uncle's death that he decided to go over to Judaism. Before taking the final step he raised Titus from the dead and asked him:

'What punishment has been meted out to you in the other world?'

'What I have meted out to myself,' replied Titus's ghost.

'Every day my ashes are collected so that I can be brought to trial before God. Then I am found guilty and condemned to having my ashes scattered over the seven seas.'[4]

Whereupon the nephew, a son of Titus's sister, was convinced of the might of God, embraced Judaism and became one of the leading Jewish scholars of the age.

Roman sources did not record a dying wish but a death-bed confession. Just before he died Titus apparently said that he had only one regret. What it was he never explained. Some people present suggested that he regretted having seduced his brother's wife; but others, doubting that she had any attraction for him, thought he regretted not having put Domitian to death and thus pre-empted his own. If the story of the death-bed confession ever reached Berenice, she may well have flattered herself that Titus's last thought could have been for her and his only regret not having married her. Whatever the speculation, Titus's confession became an integral part of his history. In the fourth century it found poetic expression in a four-line tribute by Ausonius:

> Your short reign was happy and free of blood,
> We called you the World's Darling.
> Dying, only one fault you claimed,
> Yet even from your own mouth you shall not be condemned.[5]

The news of Titus's death must have dealt the final blow to Berenice's hopes. It is not known by how long she survived him, but an indirect reference in Josephus's *Life*, published after AD 100, suggests that she may have lived on for many years. Trying to discredit his rival Justus of Tiberias, Josephus wrote that Justus had put off publication of his own—biased—account of the Jewish war until after the death of Vespasian, Titus and Agrippa, whose 'entire family'[6] could read Greek and could have been asked to go over the original manuscript. This entire Greek-speaking family of Agrippa's must have included Berenice who, like her brother, had a first-hand knowledge of the events that had led to the fall of Judaea and could be relied on to check the facts, as indeed Agrippa had done—and presumably she with him—for Josephus's draft of *The Jewish War*, prepared during Vespasian's reign. As Josephus mentioned Agrippa and his 'entire family' in one breath, and as Agrippa is known to have lived until AD 100, it may be inferred that Berenice too survived until fairly near that date. It must also be remembered that she came of a long-lived family, and that those of her ancestors and relatives who had not been drowned, strangled or poisoned often lived into their sixties. Unfortunately nothing is known about her life after her final expulsion from Rome. Her role in history was played out. It can only be assumed that she resumed her former way of life in Caesarea Philippi and that she continued to be her brother's trusted colleague until death, probably hers, brought to an end a life-long association which frustrations and disappointments had left unscathed. If she was still alive in 96, when Titus's brother and successor Domitian was murdered, she may well have reflected that the Flavian dynasty, for whose continuity she had been sacrificed, had ceased to exist within seventeen years of the sacrifice. She must have died sadder and wiser, though not necessarily embittered.

Agrippa survived Titus by nearly twenty years. He never lost his talent for retaining imperial favour, although from time to time he had to accept a modification of boundaries. In AD 85 he apparently had to give up Tiberias; in 93 or 94 part of Batanea. But the adjustments to his boundaries did not mean loss of prestige. He was client-king to no fewer than eight emperors: Claudius, Nero, Otho, Vitellius, Vespasian, Titus, Domitian and Trajan. His formula for survival was realistic: 'You should flatter the powers that be, not provoke them.'[7] Years after the fall of Judaea he was still commemorating the Roman victory over it. He minted coins bearing the head of Titus and the figure of Nike, the goddess of victory; then, after Titus's death, of his brother Domitian and Nike. But he never realized his ambition of winning Judaea. It remained a province and was administered, independently of Syria, by governors of praetorian or even consular rank.

Agrippa took his duties seriously. His territories were inhabited by semi-barbarians, and his task was to civilize them according to the Roman concept. In Trachonitis, Auranitis, Batanea and Arca—his newest territory—there were few villages and fewer cities. The population was nomadic and there were still brigands living in caves. Agrippa built fortifications, maintained troops and cavalry, appointed administrators and even interpreters to help them communicate with the natives, many of whom still spoke only Syriac and Arabic dialects. A Greek inscription found in Batanea suggests that he took the natives to task for continuing to live in their lairs like animals, and ordered them to abandon their nomadic way of life in favour of a settled existence. He called himself, like his father Agrippa I, 'The great king Agrippa, the friend of Caesar, the pious, the friend of the Romans'.[8] It was no empty claim. At a time when client-kingdoms were becoming a thing of the past, Agrippa held on to his until his death.

He died in the third year of Trajan, in AD 100, at the age of seventy-three. He had ruled for fifty years, the longest reigning client-king of the century. He had seen more political upheavals in his lifetime than any of his contemporaries, and died as he had lived, convinced of the inevitability of Roman domination. On his death his kingdom was incorporated in the province of Syria. He was the last Jewish king of the Herodian line.

His cousin Aristobulus, whom Nero had made king of Lesser Armenia in AD 57, died a few years earlier. In 71 Vespasian turned Lesser Armenia into a province, as a better safeguard against a potential Parthian encroachment; but he compensated Aristobulus, who had proved himself an able administrator, with the small kingdom of Chalcidene, in northern Syria. Aristobulus was the son of Herod of Chalcis by his first marriage and thus, incongruously, Berenice's step-son, although probably older than she was. His wife was another Herodian cousin, Salome the dancer. They had three sons whom they named, in the best family tradition, Herod, Agrippa and Aristobulus. Nothing is known of them.

Nothing is known of Berenice's sisters Mariamme and Drusilla, except that Drusilla's son by Felix the procurator, also an Agrippa, went to live in Pompeii and met his death in the eruption of Vesuvius in 79. The disaster roughly coincided with Berenice's last attempt to regain her position in Rome, and her grief for her dead nephew must have been mingled with the anguish over the crumbling of her own life.

Nothing is known about Hyrcanus and Berenicianus, Berenice's two sons by Herod of Chalcis, although it is quite likely that they achieved some position of influence in the Roman administration, as must have done Drusilla's son who lived in Pompeii. A Latin inscription found in Baalbek might offer a possible clue. It is attributed to the second half of the second century and is dedicated

to 'Tiberius Claudius Antonius Calpurnius Atticus Julius Berenicianus'.[9] This person could have been a descendant of Berenicianus, named after his royal ancestress Julia Berenice. This is
probably the last known trace of the Herodian queen whose life
had been lived against the background of one of the most eventful
periods in classical history. What better epitaph to Berenice and
the people in whose fortunes she shared than the psalmist's:

> Man's days are like the grass;
> he blossoms like the flowers in the field:
> a wind passes over them, and they cease to be,
> and their place knows them no more.

Appendix

The other Berenice

Some historical characters seem to be a natural choice for writers of fiction, either because their life story is dramatic in itself, or because it lends itself to dramatic interpretation. Berenice is a case in point. She disappeared from the pages of history after her final expulsion from Rome, only to reappear, romanticized and ennobled, in the writings of novelists and dramatists.

My own introduction to her as a heroine of fiction was through the yellowing pages of a Hebrew novel which came into my hands when I was still a child. I hope I will be forgiven for not being able to recall either the book's title or the author's name. But I do recall the plot, which I found tremendously moving. Berenice was represented as a beautiful and noble princess of Judaea, with glowing red hair, a majestic bearing and an indomitable love of freedom. Titus fell deeply in love with her, but the proud Jewess turned her back on him and rejoined her brethren inside the besieged city of Jerusalem. After its fall she was taken prisoner and led to Rome in chains like the rest of the surviving Zealots. In Rome she prevailed upon a kind gaoler to let her come before Titus to plead, not for her liberty, but for her people. Titus watched her progress with amazement. The woman who was approaching the imperial throne still had the same noble features, the same glorious hair; but her majestic walk, the source of her attraction for him, was no more. The heavy prison chains had impaired her bearing, and now she walked ordinarily, without majesty or beauty. The spell was broken. Titus turned away in indifference while Berenice, the champion of Judaea, was condemned to prison and oblivion.

The pleasing feature about that novel was its treatment of Berenice as a virtuous patriot who, like queen Esther of the Bible, was prepared to yield to the embraces of a wicked Gentile in order to save her people. Oddly enough, the detail about her impaired walk was given a prominent place in the trilogy about Josephus by the German writer Leon Feuchtwanger, which was published in the 1930s.

Feuchtwanger, with the sure touch of a potential film script-writer, made Titus and Berenice meet in Agrippa's palace in Tiberias. They failed to be impressed by each other. It was only after a tedious formal dinner, when Berenice had bidden her guests goodnight and was beginning to ascend the stairs, 'her hand slightly resting on her brother's shoulder',[1] that Titus was struck by the beauty of her walk and fell in love with her there and then. Even during their bitterest altercations, usually about the fate of Judaea and the temple, Titus would melt at the sight of her 'cele-brated walk'[2] and give in. They parted because of Vespasian's antagonism, but their love endured. On Vespasian's death Bere-nice returned to Rome, certain that Titus would marry her. Un-fortunately, only a few weeks earlier, she had been thrown off her horse during a hunting party and fractured her leg. The accident was kept secret, but when at long last Berenice arrived in Rome and ascended the steps of the Palatine, at the head of which Titus was waiting to receive her, she no longer walked in beauty. By the time she reached the top of the steps Titus had ceased to love her. They spent the night together, but they both knew that it was all over. Within two days Berenice left Rome for ever, heartbroken, but dignified even in her hour of grief.

It is difficult to assess when Berenice first began to exercise the imagination of fiction writers as distinct from historians. There seems to have been a lapse of many centuries before her name was rescued from oblivion, and it looks as if it was seventeenth-century France that brought her back to life. In 1641 Georges Scudéry published *Les Femmes Illustres,* which consisted of a series of speeches put into the mouths of illustrious women of antiquity. The speech put into Berenice's mouth was an impassioned plea to Titus to keep her in Rome, culminating in a touching farewell. That must have been the beginning of the tradition depicting Berenice as a self-sacrificing heroine.

According to Scudéry Titus and Berenice had legally married in Judaea and were happily living in Rome when Vespasian died and left the throne to his son. At that juncture the hidden hatred of the Roman people for a foreign queen broke out with violence. Berenice could not understand them. 'Are they afraid I might persuade you to rebuild the walls of Jerusalem?'[3] she asked Titus. In the end she realized that Titus had to choose between his love for her and his future as emperor of Rome. Wishing to spare him the agony of such a decision, she made up her mind for him. She went out of his life of her own accord, preferring to sacrifice her love rather than the man she loved.

In 1646 a brief reference to Berenice, who had to leave Titus for 'reasons of state'[4] was made in a play by Le Vert, called *Aricidie et le Mariage de Tite*. Aricidie was a young Roman girl whom Titus wanted to marry against his father's wishes. Berenice was mentioned only *en passant*, as someone who had played a part in Titus's earlier life. It fell to Jean Segrais, in a rambling novel which appeared between 1648–50, to make Berenice into a real heroine of fiction, with no regard for any of the known facts of history. His story started with Berenice and Titus on board a ship bound for Rome after the fall of Judaea. Titus was deeply in love with her, but Berenice was faithful to her sweetheart Izotes who had disappeared during the war. In Rome she was introduced to Titus's brother Domitian, who also fell in love with her. But while Titus was virtuous and respectful, Domitian was lustful and wicked and, to gain his end more quickly, put poison in Titus's food. Mysteriously Izotes turned up in disguise and saved Titus's life. Later, when Berenice was on a pleasure cruise on the Tiber, an attempt was made to kidnap her. The ubiquitous Izotes valiantly fought to save her, but died in the attempt. Berenice disappeared and Titus was dejected.

Segrais never finished his *Bérénice* which, even up to that point, had stretched over four volumes. Apparently 'he was so depressed by the boredom engendered by his own narrative that he did not have the courage to take it any further'.[5] His novel however may well have inspired a five-act play by Jean Magnon which, in 1660, was performed under the title of *Tite*.

Like Scudéry some twenty years earlier, Magnon set the scene of the play immediately after Vespasian's death, when Titus was about to ascend the throne. Berenice, who had been forced to leave Rome during Vespasian's lifetime, did not dare return openly. She therefore returned in disguise, pretending to be Cleobule, an obscure young prince of Iberia. Titus was struck by the young prince's resemblance to the absent Berenice, and made him his companion and confidant. Cleobule of course used all his influence with Titus to remind him of Berenice and bring about her recall. On his advice Titus refused to marry the Roman girl chosen for him by his mother. The jilted girl swore revenge and incited the Romans to rebel against their misguided emperor. While Titus remained helpless in his palace, Cleobule bravely went out to the mob, revealed himself as Berenice and called on the rebels to lay down their arms. In the face of so much courage and loyalty the mob was won over, cheered Berenice as the champion of the empire and authorized her marriage to Titus. The jilted girl was forgiven and found a husband, and a double wedding was celebrated without delay.

It was ten years after Magnon's *Tite* that French society became more widely and continuously aware of the story of Berenice. French scholars are still perturbed by the coincidence of two new plays on the same subject having been performed within one week of each other. On 21 November 1670 the company of the *Hôtel de Bourgogne* put on *Bérénice* by Racine; on 28 November Molière's company put on *Tite et Bérénice* by Corneille. The first was a hit, the second a miss. Who had borrowed the idea from whom, if at all, will never be certain. It is however certain that both playwrights used Suetonius's *invitus invitam* as the leitmotif of their tragedies.

Corneille made Berenice queen of Judaea, who during the war had offered Titus assistance against the rebels. Rome was duly grateful to such an ally, but would not allow Titus to marry her. For his part Titus was not prepared to go against the laws of his country which he, as its emperor, should have been the first to uphold. Rather than betray his country he was prepared to renounce it altogether and follow Berenice to Judaea. In the end it was not the magnitude of his sacrifice that made Berenice give him up, but the senate's decision to raise her to the status of a Roman citizen. She was now prepared to sacrifice her love for the good of a country that had acknowledged her as a subject.

Racine's Berenice had more tenderness than pride. She was all woman, blind to the call of reason, confident that love would triumph. She could not understand that for Titus the laws of his country could outweigh personal happiness. It was only when Titus declared that he would rather die than be disloyal to Rome, that Berenice understood his conflict and resolved it by leaving him of her own free will; not majestically like Corneille's heroine, but tenderly and with utter resignation.

Two hundred and forty years after the tragedies of Corneille and Racine, another Berenice made her appearance on the French stage. *L'Herodienne*, by Albert du Bois, was put on by the *Comédie Française* in 1911 and was judged by a contemporary critic as the greatest event of the season. The house was sold out night after night and hundreds of people had to be turned away from the box-office.

In *L'Herodienne* Berenice had ceased to be a woman of flesh and blood and became the reincarnation of a lofty ideal. The clash between her and Rome was interpreted as a clash between pacifism and war-mongering. She preached justice, love and peace on earth; and although her ideals seemed more early Christian than Jewish, Titus was accused of being enslaved by the spirit of the very people he had conquered. Titus however was a loyal convert to pacifism and it was Berenice who had to accept that Rome's tradition of war could not be eradicated by a message of universal love. Not betraying her cause, she left Titus to save him from being murdered. Her final 'my beloved', uttered three times in a shattering crescendo, must have been one of the most memorable *coups-de-théâtre* of the period.

It is outside the scope of this appendix to list all the known Berenices of fiction; it is enough to say that throughout the generations she has fired the imagination of creative artists in many countries. In England, shortly before the First World War, Maurice Baring gave a short account of her last days in Rome in his witty fantasy entitled *From the Diary of the Emperor Titus*, while more recently the American Howard Fast spun a new yarn in his novel *Agrippa's Daughter*. In the early eighteenth century the Italian composer Porpora brought out a three-act opera called *Berenice*; and in May 1737 Handel produced in London his own opera *Berenice*, which unfortunately had to be taken off after only four performances. In 1911 the French composer Alberic Magnard produced yet another opera by that name which ended with Berenice leaving Titus in order to save him from sinking into a life of lies and compromise. This seems to be the final apotheosis of a woman whose career had made her one of the most intriguing figures of her time.

References

Introduction
1 E. Schürer, *History of the Jewish People.*
2 T. Mommsen, *The Provinces of the Roman Empire.*
3 J. Derenbourg, *Essai sur l'histoire et la géographic de la Palestine.*
4 A. Hausrath, *History of the New Testament Times.*
5 H. Lockyer, *All the Kings and Queens of the Bible.*
6 C. J. Ellicot, *Commentary on the Whole Bible.*

Chapter I
1 Babylonian Talmud, Baba Bathra p. 10, in *Sefer Ha'agada*, book I, vol. I, p. 229.

Chapter II
1 Josephus, *Antiquities*, vol. VIII, pp. 250 and 252.
2 Josephus, *The Jewish War*, vol. II, pp. 216 and 218.
3 Josephus, *Antiquities*, vol. VIII, p. 534.

Chapter III
1 Josephus, *The Jewish War*, vol. II, pp. 262 and 264.
2 Josephus, *Antiquities*, vol. IX, p. 126.
3 *Ibid.*
4 *Ibid.*

Chapter IV
1 Philo, *The Embassy to Caius*, pp. 123 and 125, paras. 276–9.
2 *Ibid.*, p. 125, paras. 281–4.
3 *Ibid.*, p. 127, para. 290.
4 *Ibid.*, pp. 135 and 137, paras. 326–9.

Chapter V
1 Josephus, *Antiquities*, vol. IX, pp. 310 and 312.

2 *Ibid.,* pp. 306 and 308.
3 Dio, *Roman History,* vol. VII, p. 369.
4 Tcherikover, V., *Corpus Papyrorum Judaicarum,* vol. II, p. 213.

Chapter VI

1 Babylonian Talmud, Bikkurim III 3, 4, in *Sefer Ha'agada,* book I, vol. I, pp. 237–8.
2 Deuteronomy, 17, 15, *The New English Bible.*
3 Babylonian Talmud, *Sota,* p. 202.
4 Deuteronomy, 23, 8, *The New English Bible.*

Chapter VIII

1 Josephus, *Antiquities,* vol. IX, p. 380.

Chapter IX

1 Ecclesiasticus, 45, 7–12, *The New English Bible.*

Chapter X

1 D. Magie, *Roman Rule in Asia Minor,* vol. II, p. 1407.
2 Grace Macurdy, *Julia Berenice.*

Chapter XI

1 Tacitus, *The Histories,* vol. V, paras. 6–8.
2 *Ibid.*
3 *Ibid., Annals,* vol. XII, p. 54.
4 *Ibid., The Histories,* vol. V, p. 9.
5 Cf. Chapter XXI.
6 Babylonian Talmud, *Pesachim,* p. 469.

Chapter XII

1 Tacitus, *Annals,* p. 110.
2 Acts, 24, 22, *The New English Bible.*
3 *Ibid.,* 25; 12.
4 *Ibid.,* 25; 13–22.
5 *Ibid.,* 25; 27.
6 1 Timothy, 2; 9–12, *The New English Bible.*
7 Acts, 26; 27–29, *The New English Bible.*

References

Chapter XIII

1 Tacitus, *The Histories*, p. 195.

Chapter XV

1 Josephus, *The Jewish War*, vol. III, pp. 430 and 432.

Chapter XVI

1 Josephus, *The Jewish War*, tr. G. A. Williamson, pp. 148–9.
2 *Ibid.*, p. 150.
3 *Ibid.*, p. 151.
4 *Ibid.*, p. 154.
5 *Ibid.*
6 *Ibid.*, p. 154.

Chapter XVII

1 Suetonius, *The Twelve Caesars*, p. 275.
2 Dio, *Roman History*, vol. VIII, p. 265.
3 *Midrash Rabba Echa*, in J. Derenbourg, p. 291.
4 Josephus, *The Jewish War*, tr. G. A. Williamson, p. 189.

Chapter XVIII

1 Abot Derabbi Nathan, in J. Derenbourg, p. 284.
2 Based on Bereshit Rabba, Eicha Rabba, Abot D.N., Vayikra Rabba, Kohelet Rabba, Gittim 56a–b, in *Sefer Ha'agada*, H. N. Bialik and J. H. Rawnitzky, vol. I, book I, pp. 255–9, and J. Derenbourg, pp. 281–2.
3 Dio, *Roman History*, vol. VIII, p. 193.

Chapter XIX

1 *Abot Derabbi Nathan*, in J. Derenbourg, p. 285.
2 Babylonian Talmud, *Gittim* 56a, *Sefer Ha'agada*, book I, vol. I, pp. 256–7.
3 Josephus, *The Jewish War*, vol. III, pp. 454 and 456.
4 Suetonius, *The Twelve Caesars*, p. 320.
5 Babylonian Talmud, Gittim 56b, *Sefer Ha'agada*, book I, vol. I, p. 258.
6 Suetonius, *The Twelve Caesars*, p. 289.

Chapter XX

1 Dio, *Roman History*, vol. VIII, p. 291.

2 Quintilian, *Institutio Oratoria*, IV, I, 19.
3 *Ibid.*

Chapter XXI
1 Aurelius Victor, *Epitome*, p. 338.
2 *Corpus Inscriptionum Latinarum,* vol. VI, No. 944.
3 Babylonian Talmud, from *Sefer Ha'agarda*, vol. I, book I, p. 258.
4 Babylonian Talmud, ibid., p. 259.
5 Ausonius, *de XII Caesaribus*, vol. I, p. 340.
6 Josephus, *The Life*, vol. I, p. 132.
7 Josephus, *The Jewish War*, vol. II, p. 458.
8 Waddington, vol. III, No. 2365.
9 Rey-Coquais, J. P., No. 78, No. 2784 and footnote.

Appendix
1 Feuchtwanger, L., *Josephus*, p. 277.
2 *Ibid.*, p. 225.
3 Scudéry, G., *Les Femmes Illustres*, vol. I, p. 148.
4 Mireaux, E., *La Reine Bérénice*, p. 148.
5 *Ibid.*, p. 198.

Bibliography

Primary Sources

AURELIUS, VICTOR   *De Caesaribus*, Latin and French, tr. M. N. A. Dubois, 1846, Paris; *Epitome*, Latin and French, tr. M. N. A. Dubois, 1846, Paris

AUSONIUS, DECIMUS MAGNUS   *Works*, Latin and English, 2 vols, tr. H. G. E. White, 1919, London & New York

BABYLONIAN TALMUD, 35 vols, tr. I. Epstein, 1935–52, London

CORPUS INSCRIPTIONUM GRAECARUM, A. Boekhius, vol. I, 1828–77, Berlin

CORPUS INSCRIPTIONUM LATINARUM, G. Henzen and I. B. de Rossi, vol. VI, 1876, Berlin

CORPUS PAPYRORUM JUDAICARUM, V. A. Tcherikover and A. Fuks, 3 vols, 1952–64, Cambridge, Mass.

DIO CASSIUS   Dio's *Roman History*, Greek and English, tr. E. Cary, 9 vols, 1914–27, Cambridge, Mass. & London

EUSEBIUS   *The History of the Church*, tr. G. A. Williamson, 1965, London

EUTROPE   *Abrégé de l'Histoire Romaine*, Latin and French, tr. M. Rat, 1934, Paris

JOSEPHUS   *The wars of the Jews*, tr. R. L'Estrange, 2 vols, 1766, Glasgow; *The Jewish War*, tr. R. Traill, 2 vols, 1847, London; *The Jewish War*, tr. G. A. Williamson, 1970, London; *Complete Works*, tr. W. Whiston-Lassor, 1963, London; *Complete Works*, Greek and English, tr. H. St. Thackeray, R. Marcus, A. Wikgren, L. H. Feldman, 1928–63, 9 vols, New York

JULIAN   *The Works of the Emperor Julian*, Greek and English, tr. W. C. Wright, 3 vols, 1913–23, New York

JUVENAL   *The Sixteen Satires*, tr. P. Green, 1970, London

MACROBIUS   *Les Saturnales*, Latin and French, tr. H. Bornecque and F. Richard, 2 vols, 1937, Paris

MISHNA, tr. H. Danby, 1933, Oxford

NEW ENGLISH BIBLE WITH APOCRYPHA, 1970, Oxford–Cambridge
PHILO   *The Works of Philo Judaeus*, tr. C. D. Yonge, 4 vols, 1854–55, London; *On Flaccus, Greek and English*, tr. H. Box, 1939, London; *The Embassy to Gaius*, Greek and English, tr. E. Mary Smallwood, 1961, Leiden
PHOTIUS   *Biblioteca, Omnia Opera*, vol. III, 1857, Paris
PLINY   *Natural History*, tr. J. Bostock and H. T. Riley, 6 vols, 1855–57, London
QUINTILIAN   The *Institutio Oratoria*, Latin and English, tr. H. E. Butler, 4 vols, 1920–22, London and New York
SEFER HA'AGADA, ed. H. N. Bialik and J. H. Rawnitzki, 4 vols, 1936, Tel Aviv
STRABO   The *Geography*, tr. H. G. Hamilton and W. Falconer, 3 vols, 1848, London
SUETONIUS   *Life of the Caesars*, Latin and English, tr. J. C. Rolphe, 1914, London and New York; *The Twelve Caesars*, tr. R. Graves, 1970, London
SULPITIUS SEVERUS   *The Sacred History*, tr. A. Roberts, 1895, Oxford and New York (in Nicene and post-Nicene Fathers of the Christian Church, vol. XI)
TACITUS   *The Annals* and *The Histories*, tr. A. J. Church and W. J. Brodribb, 1952, Chicago; *The Histories*, tr. K. Wellesley, 1964, London; *The Annals of Imperial Rome*, tr. M. Grant, 1972, London
XIPHILIN   The *History* of Dio Cassius, tr. F. Manning, 1704, London
ZONARAS   *Histoire Romaine*, tr. L. Cousin, 1678, Paris

Secondary Sources

ABEL, F. M.   *Histoire de la Palestine*, 2 vols, 1952, Paris
AVI-YONA, M.   *Yehuda Virushalayim*, Reprint, the 12th Archaeological Convention, Jerusalem, 1957; *Al Homotaich Yerushalayim*, reprint the 25th Archaeological Convention, Jerusalem, 1968; *Karta's Atlas of the Period of the Second Temple*, Jerusalem, 1966
BALSDON, J. P. V. D.   *Roman Women, Their History and Habits*, 1962, London
BARATIER, J. P.   *De Annis Agrippae Junioris, Disquisitio Chronologica*, etc., Ultrajecti, 1740

BARON, S. W.　*A Social and religious history of the Jews*, vols I, II, 1962, New York

BEULE, M. E.　*Etudes et Portraits du siècle d'Auguste: Le Veritable Titus*, Revue des deux Mondes, December 1869, Paris

BONSIRVEN, J.　*Le Judaisme Palestinien*, 2 vols, 1934–5, Paris

CAGNAT, R.　*Comptes Rendus de l'Academie des Inscriptions et Belles-Lettres*, Paris, 1927

COMAY, J.　*Who's Who in the Old Testament*, 1971, London

CROOK, J. A.　'Titus and Berenice', The American Journal of Philology, 1951, Baltimore

DANIEL-ROPS　*Daily Life in Palestine at the time of Christ*, tr. P. O'Brien, London, 1962

DARMSTETER, A.　'Notes Epigraphiques'—Revue des Etudes Juives, vol. I, 1880, Paris

DERENBOURG, J.　*Essai sur l'histoire et la géographie de la Palestine*, 1867, Paris

FARMER, W. R.　*Maccabees, Zealots and Josephus*, 1956, New York

FUKS, A.　*Notes on the Archives of Nicanor*, Journal of Juristic Papyrology, Warsaw, 1951, vol. V

FUKS, A.　*Marcus Julius Alexander*, Zion, Jerusalem, 1948–9, vol. XIII

FUKS, A. AND HALPERN, I.　*Studies on History*, 1961, Jerusalem

GILLIAM, J. F.　'Titus in Julian's *Caesares*', American Journal of Philology, 1967, Baltimore

GOODENOUGH, E. R.　*Jewish symbols in the Greco–Roman World*, 4 vols, 1953–4, New York

GRAETZ, H.　*Popular History of the Jews*, tr. A. B. Rhine, vols I, II, 1930, New York

GRANT, M.　*Herod the Great*, 1971, London

HADAS, M.　*Hellenistic Culture: Fusion and Diffusion*, 1959, London

HAUSRATH, A.　*A History of the New Testament: The time of the Apostles*, 4 vols, tr. L. Huxley, 1895, London

HILL, G. F.　'Olba, Cennatis, Lalassis', The Numismatic Chronicle, 1899, XIX, London

HILL, G. F.　*Catalogue of the Greek coins of Lycaonia, Isauria and Cilicia*, London, 1900

HILL, C. F.　*Catalogue of Greek coins in the British Museum*, Palestine, 1914, London

HOEHNER, H. W.　*Herod Antipas*, Cambridge, 1972

IMHOOF-BLUMER, F. *Porträtköpfe auf antiken Münzen*, 1885, Leipzig

JALABERT, L. AND MOUTERDE, R. *Inscriptions Grèques et Latines de la Syrio*: Emésène, Institut Français d'Archéologie de Beyrouth, 1959, No. 66 (2213–2217)

JONES, A. H. M. *The Herods of Judaea*, Oxford, 1938

KADMAN, L. *The Coins of the Jewish War*, Corpus Nummorum Palaestinensium, vol. III, 1960, Tel Aviv

KADMAN, L. AND KINDLER, A. *Hamatbea Be-Eretz Israel U-Va 'amim*, 1963, Tel Aviv

KENNEDY, G. 'An estimate of Quintilian', American Journal of Philology, 1962, Baltimore

KENYON, K. M. *Jerusalem*, 1967, London

KINDLER, A. *The Coins of Tiberias*, 1961, Tiberias

LE BAS, P. AND WADDINGTON, W. H. *Voyage Archéologique en Grèce et en Asie Mineur*, vol. III, 1847, Paris

LEPAPE, A. *Tiberius Julius Alexandre*, Bulletin de la Société Royale d'Archeologie, Tome 8, No. 29, 1934, Alexandria

LIGHTLEY, J. W. *Jewish Sects and Parties in the Time of Jesus*, 1925, London

LOHSE, E. *Die Texte aus Qumran*, Hebräisch und Deutch, Munich, 1964

MCALINDON, D. 'Claudius and the Senators', American Journal of Philology, 1957, Baltimore

MACURDY, GRACE H. 'Julia Berenice', The American Journal of Philology, 1935, Baltimore

MADDEN, F. W. *History of Jewish Coinage*, 1864, London

MADDEN, F. W. *The Coins of the Jews*, 1881, London

MAGIE, D. *Roman Rule in Asia Minor*, 2 vols, 1950, Princeton, New Jersey

MESHORER, Y. *Jewish Coins of the Second Temple Period*, tr. I. H. Levine, 1967, Tel Aviv

MEYSHAN, J. *The Coins of the Herodian Dynasty*, Essays in Jewish Numismatics, vol. 6, 1968, Jerusalem

MIREAUX, E. *La Reine Bérénice*, Paris, 1951

MOMMSEN, T. *The Provinces of the Roman Empire*, tr. W. P. Dickson, 2 vols, 1909, London

OOST, S. I. 'The Career of M. Antonius Pallas', American Journal of Philology, 1958, Baltimore

PAULY-WISSOWA *Real-encyclopädie*, Stuttgart, 1893

PEROWNE, S.   *The Life and Times of Herod the Great*, London, 1956

PEROWNE, S.   *The Later Herods*, London, 1958

REIFENBERG, A.   *Israel's History in Coins*, London, 1953

REINACH, T.   *Jewish Coins*, 1903

REY-COQUAIS, J. P.   *Inscriptions Grèques et Latines de Syrie*: Ballbek et Bequa, Institut Francais d'Archéolegie de Beyrouth, No. 2784 and footnote, vol. 78, 1967

SCHUERER, E.   *A History of the Jewish People in the Time of Jesus Christ*, 5 vols, tr. J. Macpherson, S. Tucker and P. Christie, Edinburgh, 1885–90

SCHUERER, E.   *Geschichte des Jüdischen Volkes in Zeitalter Jesu Chriti*, 3 vols, 1898 and 1901, Leipzig

SHALLIT, A.   *Hordos Hamelech, Ha'Ish Ufo'olo*, 1960, Jerusalem

SPON, I.   *Voyage d'Italie*, 4 vols, 1678–80, Lyon

STEIN, A.   *Die Präfekten von Aegypten*, Bern, 1950

STEWART, Z.   *Sejanus, Gaetulicus and Seneca*, American Journal of Philology, 1953, Baltimore

SUKENIK, E. L. AND MAYER, L. A.   *The Third Wall of Jerusalem*, London, 1930

TARN, W. W.   *Hellenistic Civilization*, 1952, London

TCHERIKOVER, V.   *Hellenistic Civilization and the Jews*, Philadelphia, 1959

THUBRON, C.   *Mirror to Damascus*, 1967, London

THUBRON, C.   *The Hills of Adonis: A Quest in Lebanon*, 1968, London

THUBRON, C.   *Jerusalem*, 1969, London

VERMES, G.   *The Dead Sea Scrolls*, 1966, London

WADDINGTON, W. H.   *Inscriptions Greques et Latines*, vol. III, 1870, Paris

WAHL, M.   *De Regina Berenice*, 1893, Paris

WESSEX, D. W. T. C.   'Thoughts on Tacitus's Portrayal of Claudius', American Journal of Philology, 1971, Baltimore

WHEELER, G.   *A Journey into Greece*, 1682, London

WILLIAMSON, G. A.   *The World of Josephus*, London, 1964

YADIN, Y.   *The Dead Sea Scrolls*, Jerusalem, 1957, Masada, 1966, London

Index